STUDY GUIDE

Exam Prep Book With 425+ Questions and Explained Answers to Pass the Commercial Driver's License Exam on Your First Attempt

(Full Length Exams for All Classes)

MIKE CHAMBERS
PL EXAM PREPARATION

Second Edition

Second Edition: August 2022

This Paperback Edition First Published in 2022

TABLE OF CONTENTS

BOOK 1: CDL STUDY GUIDE

BOOK 2: CDL PRACTICE TEST

INTRODUCTION

Commercial driving in the United States is an industry that has been booming for decades. No matter what is happening in the world, no matter what things change with the times, and no matter what is trending on social media, the nation needs its cargo transported safely and securely from one place to another.

Carriers and freighters across the nation have been responsible for keeping the world turning, so to speak, especially in light of recent events. When so many lines of production were brought to a screeching halt, truckers and commercial drivers have been the ones to keep themselves on duty, behind the wheel, and taking on the responsibility to adhere to federal and local standards to safely bring each region the goods they needed to survive the unthinkable.

Commercial driving is a profession with a lot of moving parts, a lot of regulations to consider, and a lot of things that you might not think are common sense before you start to get acquainted with the industry. Of course, this is true for most industries, but I am here to tell you that those specialized regulations and those seemingly nebulous procedures are not as hard to understand as you might think.

Each of the things you will need to know to pass your commercial driver's license (CDL) examinations should come to you easily with just the right study aids and guides. Practice tests are incredibly helpful for you to get a feel for the types of questions that could be asked of you. In addition to this, they give you a very helpful frame of reference for the standpoints you should be assuming when you are assessing situations and using your judgement to be the best driver you can be!

With this guide, you will pass your commercial driver's license exam with flying colors and be on the road in no time flat! Congratulations on your new career path and welcome to *"CDL Study Guide: Exam Prep Book With 425+ Questions and Explained Answers to Pass the Commercial Driver's License Exam on Your First Attempt (Full Length Exams for All Classes)"!*

On page 186 of this book, you will find the Bonus Flashcards and the Audio Version that come with the book as a gift.

CHAPTER - 1

YOUR INTRODUCTION TO THE CDL

What Is a CDL?

CDL is short for commercial driver's license. This is the type of certification that is needed in order to drive large vehicles with multiple axles that carry larger loads than typical cars and trucks might. Drivers of these large vehicles have been required to have a CDL since April 1, 1992.

In 1986, the commercial motor vehicle Safety Act was enacted to increase and improve safety on United States roads and highways. It was created so that drivers of commercial motor vehicles would become required to be licensed and experienced enough to operate their machinery safely on American roads.

Since 1986 and 1992, regulations have been put in place, new safety measures have been introduced, and a number of protocols have been developed to keep commercial drivers and other motorists safe on highways and local roads. Part of this has been creating a class system for the CDL that specifies what types of vehicles may be operated under specific types of licensure.

Why Should I Get A CDL?

A CDL opens up your career avenues a bit. If you are interested in driving professionally, being able to operate heavy vehicular machinery can make you far more valuable to companies that are looking for drivers.

It is true that there are a lot of things to know, that there are a lot of regulations to see and understand and that there is a good deal of classes and tests involved over a period of about three to seven weeks to obtain your license. However, many commercial drivers have found themselves recuperating those costs in very little time and have found colleagues and work conditions that are ideal for them.

Driving commercial motor vehicles isn't the right job for everyone, but for many, it's an ideal position. Travel is a given for long-haul drivers. Life on the road has a lot of positives, and the community is lively and thriving.

A commercial driver's license can be used locally as well if you're not too keen on those longer drives across state lines or across the US. There are driving jobs for local pickup and delivery drivers, local routes, and even driving jobs that simply require you to maneuver large machinery around a particular location such as a hub or a warehouse.

Having a CDL makes you eligible for a wide range of jobs over many regions, states, counties, areas, and routes across the whole nation, and even into Canada.

Basic Skills For Commercial Driving

Even though the majority of a commercial driver's hours will likely be spent in transit, driving skills are not the only kind of skills that matter to be successful in this profession. In addition to that, you will also need vehicle maintenance skills, organizational skills, and the ability to operate your vehicle safely regardless of the weather.

Driving skills- One of the most important driving skills to be mastered is backing up your vehicle correctly and it requires hours of practice. If your backing up skills are not fully developed, you may experience difficulty in dropping off a load or delivering cargo. It is best that you make necessary efforts beforehand so you can get familiar with backing your vehicle. As a rule of thumb, always exit the vehicle before backing to prevent any damage while doing so.

People skills- Most of your working time will be spent alone on the road but the right set of people skills will help you interact better with other drivers, shippers, inspection officials, and so on. While it may be hard to work with certain shippers, reacting rudely to them will only worsen the situation. Politeness is crucial in this line of work and should be extended to everyone you work with, including your dispatcher who can be a very valuable resource when you're on a trip. With good people skills, there is a better chance that you will have a successful driving career.

Organizational and cleanliness skills- In this line of business, your truck is more or less your office, and having a clean truck indicates to inspectors that you are concerned about the condition of your living arrangements. It also shows that you take your responsibility to keep all vehicle information and paperwork organized and updated seriously. You can maintain a spotless vehicle by dedicating time for cleaning on a daily and weekly basis; doing so will even help make your driving more enjoyable. Some useful tips on keeping a clean space include using floor mats, having cleaning supplies handy, sweeping out your truck daily or weekly with a small dust broom, using an air purifier, washing the vehicle floor with soap and water, buying a small vacuum machine, etc.

Vehicle maintenance skills- You don't necessarily have to be a truck mechanic to succeed in this industry but mastering your vehicle's basic maintenance will make things much easier for you. With a good set of repair tools in your vehicle, you will be able to make basic repairs when needed and avoid any DOT violations during inspections. Note that any major vehicle repairs should only be carried out by someone with the right skills, experience, and tools for doing so.

What Are the Types of CDL Licenses?

There are different classes of commercial driver's licenses that allow you to drive different types of vehicles. While there are many different makes, models, sizes, shapes, and types of vehicles, you can get a feel for the types of vehicles by looking over those classes and what they allow a driver to operate.

Class A CDL allows an operator to drive any combination of vehicles with a Gross Vehicle Weight Rating (GVWR) of 26,001 or more lbs., provided that the GVWR of the vehicle or vehicles that are being towed weigh(s) more than 10,000 pounds. Examples of this would be cargo trucks (semis), doubles, or fuel trucks.

Class B CDL allows an operator to drive a single vehicle with a GVWR of 26,001 or more pounds or any type of vehicle that is towing a vehicle that is not in excess of 10,000 pounds GVWR. Examples of this would be fire trucks, cement mixer trucks, dump trucks, or garbage trucks.

Class C CDL allows an operator to drive any vehicles (single or combination vehicles) that do not meet the GVWR minimums for Class A or B licenses. However, vehicles for the Class C commercial driver's license requirement should either be designed to fit 16 or more passengers (the driver is included in this number) or should be placarded for hazardous materials. Examples of this would be school buses and passenger buses.

CLP and CDL Requirements

Formerly known as the commercial instruction permit, the commercial learner's permit (CLP) is authorization given by your state of residence which enables you to practice driving in a commercial motor vehicle. This authorization is the first step to getting your class A CDL, and must be gained before you can be granted a license.

Regardless of whether you want to get a CLP or CDL, the basic requirements are the same and are listed below:

Legal Presence

For all lawful U.S. permanent residents and citizens, proof of unrestricted lawful permanent residency or citizenship must be provided at the Department of Motor Vehicles office. Meeting this requirement will save you the stress of proving your legal status later on. However, if you're applying from a foreign jurisdiction, you will need proof of this for every transaction you carry out at the DMV office. You can reach out to your local DMV office for a list of all documents that qualify and can be submitted as proof of your legal presence.

Residency

To be issued a state CLP or CDL, you must be resident in said state. You will need proof of residence in order to transfer, amend, renew, and even apply for your CLP or CDL. If you happen to hold a CDL issued by another jurisdiction and move to another state, you must apply for a CDL of your new jurisdiction within 30 days after you have established residency. Certain states like New York allow for reciprocity in this regard, whereby a new resident can apply to exchange another jurisdiction's CDL for a New York CDL.

Age

To acquire a Class A CDL, applicants must be at least 21 years old. For Class B and C licenses on the other hand, a minimum of 18 years of age is the requirement. If younger than 21, an applicant can only drive a commercial vehicle for intrastate commerce and is restricted from transporting students in a school bus as well as hazardous materials vehicles.

DL, you should have a strong command of the English language. Your ability to speak and read should be to hold conversations with others, provide answers to questions officials ask, take the necessary skills test

to get your CDL, input information on records and reports, and understand highway traffic signals and signs written in the language.

Self-Certification

The regulations of the Federal Motor Carrier Safety Administration (FMCSA) mandate all CLP and CDL holders to certify the type of commercial operations they perform or intend to perform at the Department of Motor Vehicles. Generally, the self-certification driving types are divided into four categories out of which one must be certified before your CLP or CDL can be renewed, amended, or issued to you.

These categories are the non-excepted interstate (NI), excepted interstate (EI), non-excepted intrastate (NA), and excepted intrastate (EA). However, there are states that do not issue licenses to certain categories so it is best to know the certification requirements of your own jurisdiction. For example, California does not grant licenses that are exempt from driver qualification requirements and only non-excepted drivers are licensed to drive commercial vehicles.

Medical Examination

Applicants who self-certify to a non-excepted driving type, (NI or NA) are required by the federal government to undergo a medical examination. This helps in detecting any mental or physical conditions that may hinder you from safely operating a motor vehicle. You can find the requirements for this medical exam in the U.S. Department of Transportation's (USDOT) Federal Motor Carrier Safety Administration Regulations. Note that the exam can only be performed by doctors that are listed on the FMCSA's Registry of Certified Medical Examiners.

Skills Test

Your CDL will be granted only after you have passed the skill test in a vehicle that matches the class, use, and type of the Class being applied for. A skills test may be scheduled by telephone or online but applicants must wait for at least two weeks after their CLP is obtained before taking the test. It is best to schedule the test early as there is usually a timelapse of several weeks after making an appointment before the test date.

Typically, the three types of general skills to be tested are the pre-trip inspection, basic vehicle control, and lastly, the on-road driving test. During the first pre-trip vehicle inspection test, you will prove your ability to know if your vehicle is safe for driving or not. Your examiner will ask you to inspect your vehicle before driving while explaining the things to be inspected and why.

After this test is passed, you will then proceed to the basic vehicle control test where your vehicle control skills will be tested. Your examiner will likely ask you to move the vehicle backward and forward, and then turn it in a specified area. There are different control tests, and your examiner will let you know how exactly each one should be done.

Lastly, the on-road driving test will measure your ability to drive safely in various traffic situations such as intersections, highways, left and right turns, railroad crossings, streets, and so on. Where you are to drive will be shown to you by your examiner.

Alcohol And Drug Test

To operate a motor vehicle, you will need to give consent to a chemical test of saliva, urine, blood, or breath to determine the drug and/or alcohol content in the blood. This helps to ensure that drivers do not drive under the influence and can operate their vehicles safely.

How to Apply for a CDL

- Be at least 21 years old or 18 years old for intrastate driving
- Submit the CDL application for your state and pay the necessary fees
- Check the proof of identity and SSN verification requirements for your state and provide them
- Provide proof of U.S. and state residency
- Submit a Medical Examination Report Form along with the Medical Examiner's Certificate Form
- Pass your vision test
- Pass your knowledge exam
- Get a CLP after passing the exam
- Wait a minimum of two weeks before scheduling a CDL road skills test
- Pass your pre-trip inspection
- Pass road skill and driving exam with your own vehicle
- Pay appropriate fees for your new CDL after passing. Or provide a ten-year record check if you previously had a license in a state or jurisdiction other than where you are applying.

Disqualifiers for the CDL

There are several infractions and situations that could negate your eligibility for a commercial driver's license.

Driving Under the Influence of Alcohol. It is mandatory that a driver who has been found to be driving under the influence of alcohol have their license revoked. This removal constitutes the permanent disqualification from CDL issuance in the future. In some states, this also extends to driving under the influence of alcohol in your own personal vehicle as well, especially if your blood alcohol level is over 0.04%.

Driving Under the Influence of a Controlled Substance. Drivers who have been found to be under the influence of a controlled substance could be subject to a misdemeanor as well as the removal of their CDL. The disqualification for this offense is typically mandated for a minimum of one year after the offense.

Refusal to Test for Drugs or Alcohol. Refusal for testing of these substances can lead to the grounding of a driver, which disallows them from operating a commercial motor vehicle. The license can be held from the driver until a motion to remove the license is granted.

Fleeing the Scene of a Traffic Accident. Traffic accidents happen and they are often unexpected and are sometimes unavoidable. However, drivers are always compelled to remain at the scene to verify that no one has been mortally injured and to verify that no damage has been done. In the case of commercial driving, the drivers must wait for the police and emergency services to arrive on the scene to determine fault and to issue a police report that states their findings. Liability will be determined by that report so the driver and/or company may use them for insurance purposes.

Driving a commercial motor vehicle without Legal Permission. If your license has been suspended, if you have no license at all, or if a condition exists to exempt you from being permitted to operate a commercial motor vehicle, doing so could result in the immediate revocation or disqualification of your CDL. Depending on the state in which this is done, there are differing penalties.

Fatalities as a Result of Driver's Negligence. If the negligent operation of a commercial vehicle results in a fatality, the negligent driver is then disqualified from getting their CDL back. Depending on the findings by officials and the court, the driver could face other charges such as vehicular manslaughter, negligent homicide, or vehicular homicide.

Excessive Speeding. If you are pulled over by a police officer who found you to be speeding more than 15 miles per hour over the posted speed limit, you could be ticketed for or charged with excessive speeding, which is reserved specifically for commercial vehicles. The driver is automatically disqualified from having a CDL in such an event.

Reckless Driving. Reckless driving, when spotted by an officer of the law, is punished swiftly and immediately. The driver is taken into custody by the officer, the vehicle is towed and impounded, and the driver is automatically disqualified from having or regaining a CDL.

Changing Lanes Erratically. This charge is given for changing lanes without signaling, for changing lanes without checking your surroundings to make sure you were safe to do so, for changing lanes several times within a couple of minutes so that you can weave through traffic, if you simply change lanes frequently (even if it's not to weave), or if you pass other motorists in lanes where you are not cleared to do so. This is grounds for disqualification.

Driving a Vehicle With an Unmatching Class of CDL. Operating a CMV with the wrong class of CDL or CLP and/or endorsement for the specific kind of vehicle you're driving is not permitted and can also get you disqualified. Remember that your license was only awarded to you after you had passed the skills test for the kind of vehicle you will be driving. Different CDL classes have different tests, and you might not be qualified to safely operate any other kind of vehicle. To be on the safe side, only drive vehicles that match the class of CDL you were given.

Traveling Too Close to Other Vehicles. Driving closely to other vehicles on the road poses a large threat to their safety. You must keep a safe following distance that will allow you to see the person in front of you clearly and to stop in time should they need to stop suddenly. Traveling too close to other vehicles is grounds for disqualification.

Driving While Distracted by Electronics Such as Cell Phones. Texting while driving or driving while you are distracted by electronic devices poses a large threat to the safety of other motorists on the road. You might drift out of your lane unexpectedly, you might not see that the driver in front of you has stopped or slowed down, or you might miss something that you would otherwise have had ample time and space to react to. Having an accident in this situation could be devastating. If an officer finds you driving in this manner, you will no longer have your CDL.

Driving without Your CDL. As a CMV driver, the law requires you to have a CDL as smooth operations need a good amount of skills. The only way to prove that you're a licensed driver who is qualified to handle such a vehicle is by always having your CDL with you each time you drive a CMV.

Endorsements

Each class of commercial driver's license requires various types of endorsements, which depend on the type of vehicle and the uses of said vehicle. The federal government issues these endorsements through the state licensing authority through which you can obtain your CDL. These endorsements can be obtained from your state's licensing agency by completing the corresponding tests. Some of the tests are written and some are driving tests and they are issued for various purposes, which I'll explain here.

A - This is obtained when you get your Class A CDL and is required for another one of these endorsements.

H - Hazardous Materials Endorsement - This endorsement allows the licensed driver to transport hazardous materials and can be obtained through a written test and a background check that is conducted through the Transportation Security Administration.

N - Tank Vehicle Endorsement - This endorsement allows the licensed driver to operate a tank truck and is obtained by passing a written test.

P - Passenger Transport Endorsement - This endorsement allows the licensed driver to operate passenger vehicles and is obtained with the passing of a written and a driving test.

S - School Bus/Passenger Transport Combo Endorsement - This endorsement allows the licensed driver to operate school buses. In order to obtain this endorsement, you will need to pass a written and a driving test, plus a background check and a sex offender registry check. This endorsement has a prerequisite, which is to have the P endorsement prior to application for the S endorsement.

T - Double/Triples Endorsement - This endorsement allows the licensed driver to operate double or triple semi-trailers and is obtained with the passing of a written test. It is important to note that some states (like Florida, California, and New York) have prohibited the use of triple trailers. Always keep your state's requirements and laws in mind when seeking licensing.

X - Tanker/HAZMAT Combo Endorsement - This endorsement allows the licensed driver to operate a combination of tank vehicles and hazardous materials. In order to obtain this endorsement, you will need to pass a written test.

Restrictions

Just like endorsements, there are restrictions for the CDL that are denoted with a letter and which allow officials to tell, at a glance, what is and what is not allowed by your license. Let's go over those here:

E - No Manual Transmission - Many commercial motor vehicles are automatic so the driver does not need to be certified to operate a manual vehicle.

L - No Full Air Brake - Certain CMVs don't have air brakes (such as buses), so if you don't pass this portion of the examination and you're unable to properly assess these components, you can still obtain your license with this restriction that allows you to operate CMVs so long as they don't have this system.

M - Only Class B and C Vehicles and School Buses - In some special circumstances, you can obtain a Class A CDL with authorization only to operate Class B and C vehicles.

N - Operation of Only Class C - If you or your driver's endorsement is under Class C, yet you or your driver have a Class B CDL, then this classification applies, meaning only the operation of Class C vehicles or school buses is allowed.

O - No Operation of a Class A Vehicle With a Fifth Wheel Connection - Having a fifth wheel connection on your vehicle comes with much extra needed knowledge, so having this restriction means you will not need to operate them.

V - Variance - This restriction is placed on your CDL to let first responders and medical assistance professionals know that there is a medical condition present in the driver that could require special treatment.

Z - No Authorization to Operate a commercial motor vehicle With Full Air Brakes - This restriction is placed on a CDL if the driving test is taken in a vehicle with hydraulic brakes.

Additional Commercial Privilege Rules

Regardless of the state where you're operating your motor vehicle, there are certain federal and state rules that apply to you in terms of licensing and employment. These rules are those referred to as commercial privilege rules. They are:

1. You cannot drive a commercial motor vehicle without having your CDL or CLP. If caught breaking this rule, you may be jailed or fined any amount from $75 to $300.

2. You can only have one license, preferably from your home state. You can be fined or jailed and have your home state license withheld, with any licenses returned.

3. If you're given a hazardous materials endorsement, you must inform and surrender this endorsement to your CDL-issuing state within 24 hours if you renounce your citizenship or are not a lawful permanent resident, have been involuntarily committed to a mental health institution, have a conviction for certain felonies, or are wanted or indicted for some felonies.

4. There is a single computerized system that shares information about all CDL and CLP drivers in all states. Your driving records on this system will be checked to ensure that you do not have more than one CLP and CDL issued to you.

5. Each time you operate a commercial motor vehicle, you must have your seatbelt properly fastened. The safety belt is designed to hold you securely behind the wheel in case of a crash, help you control the vehicle better, and reduce the chances of death or serious injuries. In the absence of a safety belt, a driver is four times more likely to be critically injured if thrown out of the vehicle.

6. When applying for a commercial driving job, you must provide your employer with information on all your previously held driving jobs for the past 10 years.

7. No matter the type of vehicle you were operating, your employer must be notified of any traffic violations within 30 days of your conviction except for parking violations.

8. If your license gets canceled, suspended, revoked, or you get a disqualification, your employer must be informed.

9. Your employer may disallow you from driving a commercial motor vehicle if your CLP or CDL is canceled or revoked, or if you have more than one license.

Special Certificates

Depending on what type of vehicle or load is carried, special certificates may be necessary in addition to a CDL in certain states.

It's worth noting that using a cellphone for non-work activities while driving a school bus or transit vehicle is illegal. The use of a cell phone is only permissible to make emergency calls to police enforcement, a health care practitioner, the fire department, or other emergency services when needed.

You can apply to get the following certificates at the Department of Motor Vehicles field offices:

Ambulance Driver Certificate

This is required for operating a commercially used ambulance during emergencies. A copy of the Medical Examination Report (MER) form and the Medical Examiner's Certificate (MEC) must be submitted to the DMV every two years for those who hold an ambulance driver certificate.

Hazardous Agricultural Materials (HAM) Certificate

This certificate is for drivers that are subject to commercial driver sanctions. With it, persons transporting hazardous trash or placarded loads are exempt from CDL requirements if they meet the following criteria:

- The person must be at least 21 years old.
- The individual works in a farming operation.
- There is no reimbursement for transporting the load.
- A farmer owns or leases the vehicle.
- The individual has completed a CHP-approved HAM program. Despite the fact that a CDL is not required for a person to qualify for a HAM, CMV penalties and punishments will apply.
- Every two years, the person provides a copy of the MER, MEC, or Health Questionnaire form(s) to the DMV.
- A person drives a vehicle that is either an implement of husbandry or requires a noncommercial Class C driver's license and travels no more than 50 miles from one location to the other.

Verification of Transit Training (VTT) Document

This credential requires the completion of specific training requirements by transit bus drivers. Regularly scheduled public transportation is provided by transit bus vehicles, for which a fare is levied. (Note that this does not include general public paratransit vehicles). A VTT is not required for drivers who hold a school bus driver certificate or a school pupil activity bus certificate.

These certificates listed below are intended for only drivers subject to commercial driver sanctions and can be applied for at the CHP if you're based in California.

General Public Paratransit Vehicle (GPPV) Certificate- Anyone who drives must have the following:

- A vehicle that transports no more than 24 people, including the driver, and offers local public transit.
- Students going to or out of a public or private school or school activity who are in or below the 12th grade.

- Vehicles used exclusively for the transportation of disabled people.

School Bus Driver Certificate- Any person who operates a bus for a school district or any party transporting public or private students must have a School Bus Driver Certificate. A school bus driver's CDL must additionally include an "S" endorsement. School bus drivers must submit annual MER and MEC forms to the DMV if they are 65 years old or older.

School Pupil Activity Bus Certificate (SPAB)- Any person who operates a bus for a school district or other entity transporting public or private kids for school-related activities must have this certificate.

Farm Labor Vehicle Certificate- Any person who operates farm labor vehicles and buses. Note that seat belts are mandatory for the driver and all passengers in a farm labor vehicle.

Youth Bus Certificate- Any person who operates a bus, other than a school bus, that transports not more than 16 students and the driver to or from a school, an organized non-school related activity, or their home is required to have this certification.

Tow Truck Driver Certificate- This certification is for drivers in emergency road service companies who offer freeway service patrol operations under an agreement or who contract with a specific public transportation planning authority (traffic commission).

Vehicle for Developmentally Disabled Persons (VDDP)- Any person who drives a vehicle for a corporation, nonprofit organization, or agency whose principal function is to transport people with developmental disabilities for employment must have this certification.

What Are the CDL Tests?

Knowledge Tests

English, Arabic, Chinese, Punjabi, Russian, and Spanish languages are all offered for commercial knowledge tests. All DMV knowledge tests that a CDL applicant or cardholder is required to take must be completed with the use of the automated knowledge testing equipment (AKTE).

Depending on the type of license and endorsements you require, you must pass one or more knowledge tests. The DMV will waive all knowledge and endorsement tests finished or waived on your previous application, as well as HAZMAT if the new application is started within a 12-month period of the previous renewal date or original CDL issue date if you are adding an endorsement but not upgrading to a higher classification.

The following are examples of CDL knowledge tests:

- The general knowledge test, which all applicants must take.
- The passenger transportation test, which all bus driver applicants must pass.
- Drivers of cars using air brakes, including air over hydraulic brakes, are expected to take the air brakes test.
- The test for combination vehicles, which is essential if you want to drive one.
- The hazardous materials test, which is essential if you want to transport hazardous material. A background investigation by the Transportation Security Administration (TSA) is required to obtain this endorsement.

- The tank vehicle test, which is required if you want to transport any liquid or gaseous materials in a tank or tanks with an individual rated capacity above 119 gallons and an aggregate rated capacity of 1,000 gallons or more, which are permanent or temporary attachments to the vehicle or chassis.
- The doubles/triples test, which is required if you intend to haul two or three trailers. Bear in mind that in certain states, the operation of triple trailers is not permitted.
- If you wish to drive a school bus, you must pass the school bus test.
- The firefighter endorsement test is required to operate firefighting apparatus. For CDL holders with a Class A or B license, this is not needed, although it is an option.

If you're taking all of the tests, you'll need about 2 -3 hours. You will not receive a copy of your knowledge and/or endorsement test(s) when you're done. The knowledge test can be taken at any DMV field office, but keep in mind that working hours are subject to change. To schedule an appointment, go to the DMV website (dmv.gov) or call **1-800-777-0133**.

Use of Testing Aids

During the knowledge test, the use of testing aids is prohibited. This includes, but is not limited to, the Commercial Driver Handbook, cheat sheets, and electronic communication devices like cell phones, hand-held computers, watches, and other similar devices.

The knowledge test will be recorded as a failure if any testing aid(s) or a substitute test taker is found in your possession during the knowledge test. The Department of Motor Vehicles may also take action against your driver's license or the driver's license of anybody who assists you during the examination procedure.

The DMV does not authorize the use of testing aids other than the vehicle inspection guide found in this handbook during the vehicle inspection test, which was formerly known as pre-trip. Your commercial skills test will be scored as a failure if an examiner catches you using anything other than the inspection guide.

During the commercial skills test, technological devices such as cell phones, Bluetooth, CB radios, Apple watches, and other similar devices are disallowed. Furthermore, persons waiting in the testing area are not allowed to use hand signals or yell directions. If this happens, the test will be canceled and a commercial skills test failure will be recorded.

If markings are discovered on the vehicle to be used for the test that would assist the applicant in passing the vehicle inspection or basic control skills test, such as writing on the vehicle, tape, paint markings that do not appear to belong there, or markings on the curbs, walls, or trees that would aid the applicant in maneuvering the vehicle for the basic control skills test, the test will be terminated and marked as a failure.

During any commercial skills test, the use of any recording equipment, including a video event recorder also known as a dashcam, is banned. A dashcam is a device that records audio and/or video in a continuous digital loop, but only saves audio and/or video when prompted by an unexpected motion or crash, or when the vehicle is being driven to monitor driver performance.

If the vehicle has a recording device, it must either be turned off or its visual and/or audio recording features deactivated. The applicant must disable the recording device so that no video or audio recordings are made during the road test if the recording device cannot be turned off or disabled, as is usually the case with a commercial motor vehicle.

Skills Tests

You can take the CDL skills tests if you pass the appropriate knowledge test(s). Vehicle inspection, basic control skills, and the road test, formerly known as the drive test, are the three different types of general skills assessments that you must pass. These exams must be taken in the type of vehicle for which you desire to obtain a license. Any vehicle with components that have been marked or labeled is ineligible for the vehicle inspection test. All skill tests must be completed in English and you are prohibited from using an interpreter.

Vehicle Inspection Test. You'll be tested to see if you can recognize whether or not your vehicle is safe to operate. You will be asked to perform a vehicle check and describe what you would inspect and why to the examiner. This test takes about 40 minutes to complete. The remaining tests will be postponed if you do not pass the vehicle inspection test. Retaking the vehicle inspection test on the same application is free of charge.

Basic Control Skills Test. Your ability to control the vehicle will also be put to the test. You'll be required to drive forward, backward, and turn your vehicle within a small location. Traffic lanes, cones, barriers, or other similar markings may be used to demarcate these locations. The examiner will instruct you on how to complete each control test. You will be graded on your ability to complete each exercise correctly. This test takes about 30 minutes to complete. If you fail any of the skills tests, the test is automatically over. Each retest of the basic control skills requires applicants to pay a set retest fee.

Road Test. On a DMV-approved route, you will be evaluated on your ability to safely operate your vehicle in a range of traffic scenarios. Left and right turns, intersections, railroad crossings, curves, up and down gradients, single or multi-lane roads, streets, or highways are all examples of such traffic scenarios. The examiner will direct you to where you should drive. It takes 45–60 minutes to complete this test and if you fail it, you will be charged a retest cost for each subsequent road test.

It is necessary to take a road test:

- For a genuine CDL.
- To get rid of a restriction on your CDL imposed due to vehicle size or equipment.
- To add a "P" or "S" endorsement if desired.
- To renew a CDL expired for more than a 2-year period.

Your Medical Fitness for the CDL

The Department of Transportation takes the safety of motorists very seriously and as such, requires that commercial drivers be of a certain level of physical wellness and fitness to handle the occupation. Most commercial drivers will need to submit themselves for a battery of physical examinations.

Medical examinations required by the Department of Transportation for the commercial driver's license are:

- Health history to be checked and evaluated by a licensed medical professional.
- A vision test to verify the state of the driver's vision and needed prescriptions filled.
- A hearing test to verify that sirens and other audio cues on the road may be heard right away.
- A blood pressure test to certify that the driver will not suffer negative repercussions from time on the road or that they will not suffer an event that could be dangerous.
- Urinalysis to verify that there are no underlying illnesses or usage of substances that could present an issue.
- Physical examination to determine overall health and fitness.

These tests could change depending on the state, the field you're working in, the company you're working for, or the class of license that you're trying to obtain. Your health matters!

The Troops to Trucks Program

The Troops to Trucks program permits qualified military service members who are employed or were employed within the last year, in a military position requiring the driving of a military motor vehicle equal to a CMV on public roads and highways to skip taking the CDL skills test. In addition to any other documentation needed to apply for a CDL, qualified applicants must submit a filled CDL Certification for Military Waiver of CDL Driving Test (DL 963) and a Commanding Officer's Certification of Driving Experience (DL 964) form.

These forms can be found at dmv.ca.gov. Active service members must present their military identity (ID), while veterans must present a Certificate of Release or Discharge from Active Duty (DD Form 214), indicating that their discharge took place within the previous year.

The International Registration Plan (IRP)

IRP (International Registration Plan) - This is an agreement between Canada and the United States which allows for the apportioned payments of registration fees that are based on the distances traveled in varying jurisdictions. All jurisdictions are mandated to register all apportioned vehicles including the calculation, collection and distribution of IRP fees, issuance of cab cards and license plates or appropriate credentials, enforcement of IRP requirements, and auditing of carriers to verify the accuracy of reported fees and distance.

Under this plan, registrants have the responsibility of applying for registration with their home jurisdiction, providing proper registration documentation, paying the right registration fees, displaying credentials, keeping accurate distance records, and making these records available to their jurisdiction for review.

To acquire the IRP license plates, there are certain requirements to be met for "apportionable" vehicles.

For IRP purposes, an apportionable vehicle refers to any power unit that is used or will be used in a minimum of two member jurisdictions for transporting people for hire. This term also applies to power units that are used to transport property and have at least one feature listed below:

1. Has a Gross Vehicle Weight (GVW) over 26,000 pounds or 11,793.401 kilograms alongside two axles.
2. Has a minimum of three axles, regardless of the total weight.

3. Combined with another vehicle to exceed a GVW of 26,000 pounds or 11,793.401 kilograms.

Buses used in transporting chartered groups, vehicles owned by the government, recreational vehicles, as well as vehicles with restricted license plates are not categorized as apportionable vehicles. However, buses for transporting chartered groups and vehicles combined with a GVW of 26,000 pounds or less may still be registered under the IRP, depending on the registrant.

The International Fuel Tax Agreement (IFTA)

IFTA (International Fuel Tax Agreement) - The IFTA is an agreement between the lower 48 states of the United States and the Canadian provinces, to simplify the reporting of fuel use by motor carriers that operate in more than one jurisdiction. This tax is calculated based on how many miles a driver has traveled, how many gallons of fuel were purchased, and some states factor in a weight-mile tax as well. After collection of this tax, the base jurisdiction has the responsibility of remittance to other member jurisdictions, representation of these jurisdictions during tax collection, and performance of audits.

Although similar, "qualified" motor vehicles in IFTA refers to any motor vehicle that is designed, maintained, or used to transport people or property, and has one or more of the following features:

1. Has two axles and a Gross Vehicle Weight of more than 26,000 pounds.
2. Combined with a vehicle to reach a total GVW above 26,000 pounds.
3. Has three axles or more regardless of vehicle weight.

Recreational vehicles are excluded from those categorized as "qualified motor vehicles" by the IFTA. Note that the IFTA licensee and IRP registrant may be the vehicle operator or owner.

What Is the Individual Vehicle Distance Record (IVDR)?

You are mandated to adhere to the record-keeping requirements for driving your vehicle if you are licensed under IFTA and the vehicle is registered under IRP. The Individual Vehicle Distance Record, which is also known as the Driver Trip Report is a universally accepted means of recording necessary information. This document shows the total amount of distance covered by any vehicle that operates interstate under IFTA fuel tax and IRP registration credentials, as well as the amount of fuel purchased for its operations.

While there may be a variance in the original format of the IVDR, the required information always remains the same. To fulfill all requirements for this document, the information below must be included in it.

Distance (Article IV of IRP)

- Start and end date of trip.
- Origin of trip and destination city, state, or province.
- Travel route or routes.
- Start and end (hub) odometer reading.
- Total travel distance.
- Distance covered within jurisdiction.

- Vehicle identification or power unit number.

Fuel (Section P560 of IFTA Procedures Manual)

Acceptable invoices or receipts must include:

- Purchase date.
- Type of fuel.
- Amount of liters or gallons bought.
- Name of buyer.
- Name and address of seller.
- Total sale amount or price per liter or gallon.
- A unique vehicle identifier or unit number.

For each vehicle you drive, you must fill out an IVDR. When logging the vehicle's odometer reading, it is better to do so at the start of the day, when exiting the province or state, and at the conclusion of the day or trip. Apart from logging your trips, you should also document all fuel purchases properly. Ensure that you get a receipt each time you fuel the vehicle and attach this to the completed IVDR document.

All trips that are entered into the record should be filled in descending order, with all provinces or states you passed through included. This rule applies regardless of whether the distance traveled is in one location, or is spread among several. Routes, dates, fuel purchases, odometer readings, and all other information about the trip must be noted at all times. The IRP and IFTA have specific laws on the requirements for distance and fuel record keeping. When you keep accurate records and completely fill out your IVDR document, you can be sure that you and your company are complying with these laws.

As the IVDR is the source document for calculating taxes and fees that are payable to the jurisdictions your vehicle operates in, you have to maintain them for at least four years. Bear in mind that the taxing jurisdictions can also audit your records at their discretion. You could be fined, penalized, and also have your IFTA licenses and IRP registrations revoked or suspended if you are found wanting in keeping complete accurate records. To be on the safe side, have a bag or file for storing all your complete records including the originals.

Tips for Every Trucker to Follow

Ask Lots of Questions. If there is anything you're not certain of, be sure to get your questions answered. You need to know things about your route, your vehicle, your load, your parking spaces, and the areas in which you're traveling. There should be someone in your company who can help you and there are plenty of sources online that can offer answers from those who have had the same experiences that you have had.

Avoid Traffic Where Possible. Traffic can pose a lot of issues for someone who is trying to go a long distance. If you can avoid having to sit in traffic with hundreds of other motorists, then it would behoove you to do so within your route.

Be Aware of Your Trailer Throughout the Trip. Your trailer is something that is in your charge while you're transporting it. You want to be aware of it at all times so you can detect changes in its securement, you want to make sure that it's not moving in a way that it shouldn't be, and you want to be aware of any changes to your trailer as soon as they happen, not hours later.

Change Lanes Only When You Need To. As covered previously in this chapter, the excessive changing of lanes can cause trouble for you and for others on the road. If it's possible for you to stay in one lane of traffic for many miles at a time, it is recommended that you do so to keep your speed, pace, and trajectory even so you don't cause any trouble for yourself or for other motorists.

Be Wary of Cruise Control. A vehicle's cruise control mechanism may help reduce the need to step on the gas pedal or accelerator as much. However, it is advised that you don't use this mechanism in unfavorable conditions such as icy or wet roads, or in places where you have to make many speed adjustments like winding roads and urban areas as doing so can be dangerous.

Don't Swerve to Miss Animals on the Road. An animal in the road here or there is certainly not uncommon for truckers to encounter. When you do encounter them, you must remember that your commercial motor vehicle weighs many thousands of pounds and that cannot easily be moved from side to side within a short distance. Swerving suddenly could throw off your vehicle's balance and you could also hit other motorists. It is best in such situations to simply hold tightly onto the steering wheel to keep the vehicle from losing control on impact and slow down as much as you can in the time before you reach the animal. Follow laws and regulations about roadkill and then carry on with your route.

Drink Plenty of Water and Stay Hydrated. Dehydration can cause a number of very unpleasant side effects and being in a cab for many hours with that air pressure difference, you will want to make sure that you're drinking plenty of water through your routes. If you are worried about having to make frequent stops, just try to drink 8 ounces of water within a 15-minute period. Your body absorbs water at just about that rate, so if you're not drinking 16 ounces within a 15-minute span, you should be fine to hydrate just as much as you need!

During Inclement Weather, Take Your Time. Road conditions can become very precarious for you and other motorists during inclement weather. Pace yourself, keep your eyes on the road in front of you, keep your hands on the steering wheel, and drop your speed if you need to. Focus on getting yourself through the weather and don't feel pressured to travel faster than you are comfortable with.

Get Plenty of Rest. Exhaustion and sleep debt can cause major issues for you on the road. You don't want to end up having hallucinations, being delirious, or having headaches as a result of too little sleep over time. Make sure that you stop and get sleep when you need to and make sure that you are resting up for a week before you hit the road as well. If you are tired from an abnormal sleep schedule when you hit the road, it will be that much harder to get rested during your route.

Eat Healthy and Balanced Meals. When presented with the options of buying your meals or preparing them yourself, doing the latter will help save you a lot of money and also protect your health. With a crockpot or slow cooker, you can conveniently cook your own food whilst controlling the ingredients that are used. At the start of each day, make time for a healthy breakfast portion to keep you full throughout the day. You can then enjoy smaller meals for dinner and lunch. As much as possible, avoid drinking soda as it will not only give you extra weight but will also leave you feeling hungry. If you cannot completely substitute soda for water, try to reduce the number of bottles consumed daily.

Keep an Eye Out for Posted Speed Limits. The speed limits on roads and highways are posted prominently for you to be sure of how fast you are permitted to travel on that road. Those postings will help you to navigate those roads and their curves as safely as possible, so keep an eye out for them and follow them as closely as you can.

Inspect Delivery Spots on Foot. This is commonly ignored by many truck drivers but checking your delivery spots by yourself can save you some hassle along the line. When delivering cargo, especially to a new client, find a safe place to park, leave the rig for about five minutes and look at the area. Although a shipper may often convince you that they receive trucks regularly, an unsuitable docking facility may not only cause problems with a delivery, but your truck can also get stuck and unable to turn. Taking a few extra minutes to step out of your vehicle and scope the area by yourself will help you prepare for any obstacles like a ditch, post, or a low fire hydrant. The majority of truck accidents occur when backing up but having a mental picture will help you guard against hazards.

Always Have Survival Tools Handy. As a truck driver, over 57% of your time will be spent on the road and this means that there can be all kinds of unforeseen circumstances and unwanted situations at any given time. With a set of survival tools in your truck, you will always be prepared to tackle whatever minor issues may come up. A spare tire, blanket, rescue tool, jumper cables, multi-tool knife, fire extinguisher, tire iron and jack, as well as extra food, drinks, and clothing are some important tools you should have with you at all times.

Keep Salt in Your Truck for Icy Conditions. If the road gets icy, you might find yourself stuck in a bit of it. Ice can negate the traction your tires have, so having some salt in your truck can help you to get out of those situations much more quickly than just waiting for the ice to melt on its own.

Leave Plenty of Space Ahead of Your Vehicle. Sometimes it can feel like other motorists think you're only leaving space in front of your vehicle so they can hurry up and fill it, but there are a lot of benefits to making sure you have enough space in front of you on the road. The chief one, of course, is so that if you need to stop, you will have time to do so without hitting the person in front of you.

Look at Your Truck After You've Parked It. Taking a look at your vehicle after it's parked can help you to get a feel for how to improve your skills over time and it can allow you to make changes to your parking if you need to in order to accommodate yourself and other people who would like to park in the same area as your vehicle.

Mind the Path of Your Tires When Parking. Paying attention to the path of your tires is another thing that will give you more certainty and understanding of your vehicle over time. Of course, you can plot the path of your tires, back into a space, then use G.O.AL. (Get Out And Look) to make sure that your predictions were correct!

Plan Ahead. If there is anything you could need on the road, you will want to bring it with you. It is better to have something on your trip and not need it than to need something when you're on the side of the road in the middle of the night without it. If there is anything that you think you will need, go ahead and pack it. Make sure your first aid kits and emergency signaling equipment are replenished, make sure you have the clothing you will need to be comfortable on your route, make sure you have personal hygiene products, and make sure that any other bases are covered.

Get a Pair of Sunglasses. The reflection of sunlight off vehicles, buildings, and snow or blinding glare as a result of low sun is potentially lethal. Wearing sunglasses that have polarized lenses that filter glare can greatly reduce the chances of accidents from such factors. It is best to choose sunglasses with thin frames that help clear peripheral vision, and curved lenses that provide front and side protection.

Put a Flashlight on Dock Lines When Backing at Night. Docks can be poorly lit for night deliveries. In such a case, place a flashlight on the dock lines so you can have a focal point when you're backing. This is a simple little fix that can save you a lot of time and hassle.

Check Weather Reports. Before going on a trip and even while traveling, be up to date on weather conditions. By monitoring the temperature outside, you can be prepared for any change to road conditions. Doing this is a major part of planning your trip properly and will help you to take needed precautions, and also be ready for driving in bad weather.

Take Breaks and Check Your Truck and Load. You should be taking breaks during your travels every few hours or every 150 miles to check on your load, to check on your truck, and to make sure that you have everything you need to proceed comfortably and safely.

Keep Your Lights On. When driving, the clearance lights and headlights should always be properly cleaned and turned on. This is because visibility goes a long way in ensuring your safety. It will be easier and quicker for a fellow motorist to see your equipment and also make necessary adjustments to potential hazards when you drive with the lights on.

Take Your Time and Keep Your Wits About You. Don't rush when you're on the road and make sure that you're paying attention to the things around you. It can be hard to maintain your focus on the road in front of you after so many miles and so many hours, but doing so could be a matter of life and death. If you need to take some time to recenter your mind and get you re-focused, then pull off and do so.

Use a GPS. GPS (Global Positioning System) is an invaluable tool for people who make their living in freight and logistics. GPS can tell you where you are, where you've been, and what's ahead at a glance. Some of them can also tell you if there are obstructions on the road ahead of you. If you end up needing some help on the side of the road or along your route somewhere, you can use the GPS to tell you where the best spots are to pull off, to tell someone where to meet you or to see where you can get help if you need it. They are an excellent tool.

Dress Comfortably. Rather than trying to fit in, wearing clothes that are practical and comfortable will help reduce the stress that comes with each trip. Putting on a pair of comfortable jeans, practical t-shirts, a ball cap or trucker hat, and comfortable driving shoes will ensure that you remain comfortable, especially during long trips.

Use Extra Caution When Driving at Night. Some drivers will opt not to drive at night at all. It can be hard to keep your focus at night when things look much different than they do during the day, when drivers behave a little less predictably, and when you could be tired from a long day of driving. Be aware of these things and try to stay alert when you're driving at night.

Only Buy From Trusted Brands. Just as with every other thing, you may want to save a bit of money wherever possible. However, doing this may end up costing even more in the long run. Although cheaper are better, be careful not to purchase items of poor quality. When shopping for exhausts, batteries, tires, LED and marker lights, or any other item, try to get the best deal from a trusted brand. Off brands with unbelievably low prices should be avoided, especially if you have no previous knowledge of them.

If You Need Help, ASK! No one wants you to go through your whole job by yourself and things are always easier with a helping hand. If you need someone to help you with something or if you just need a little bit more information to get you going, then just ask for it! If there isn't someone right with you who can answer your questions, then consider asking online for some help from other truckers and drivers all over the country!

Much more than simply driving a commercial motor vehicle, you have the responsibility of making sure your vehicle is roadworthy and that your driving does not pose a threat to other motorists. Vehicle safety is a core part of getting your CDL license and it has to be taken seriously as larger vehicles require even more care. In the following chapter, all you need to know about driving safely including how to inspect your vehicle before, during, and after a trip is discussed.

CHAPTER - 2

YOUR VEHICLE SAFETY

Inspecting Your Vehicle

The primary reason for inspecting your vehicle is to ensure the safety of your vehicle, other road users, and even you, the driver. Inspecting your vehicle is something that you should do just before, during, and just after each trip you take in your commercial motor vehicle. Spotting a defect in your vehicle beforehand during an inspection will save you from problems that could cost time and money, or an accident when on the road. Aside from carrying out inspections simply to know if anything is wrong with your vehicle, you are also mandated by federal and state laws to do so. All vehicles are subject to checks by federal or state inspectors and those that are deemed unsafe will be placed out of service until properly fixed.

Before operating any vehicle, look at the last inspection report and if there are any faults, ensure that they have been fixed and the vehicle deemed roadworthy by mechanics. Any item that can affect safety identified in the report must be repaired by the motor carrier and they must certify that such repairs were made or unnecessary. Bear in mind that as the driver, the responsibility of operating a safe vehicle falls on you, and you should only sign the previous report if you are sure all defects have been fixed.

In the following sections, we look at the steps you need to take and the things to be looked out for when inspecting your vehicle.

The 7-Point CDL Pre-Trip Vehicle Inspection

This inspection allows you to take a look at all the parts of your vehicle to verify that they are in good working order and that you're not putting yourself or others in any danger by driving the vehicle.

In addition to conducting this inspection before and after each trip, you should also try to make it a point to inspect your vehicle at least once every 24 hours if the trip you're taking requires you to be on the road for more than just one day. Some trips will take you a few days to complete and it is imperative to ensure that you're driving safely all along that distance.

This inspection allows the driver to take a look at all the most critical points of the vehicle and to verify that each of them is working. It will add some time to your day and you might find yourself wanting to rush through it, but doing these inspections can save lives. Doing these inspections will allow you to catch the possible failures in your equipment before they spring up on you in the middle of a highway, while surrounded by other motorists.

Let's take a look at the seven points of the pre-trip vehicle inspection and how to make sure they're all in good working order before you set out and when you return from each trip you take in your commercial motor vehicle.

Point One: The Vehicle Overview

Review the DVIR from the last trip taken with the commercial motor vehicle.

Make sure the keys are not in the ignition.

Review and determine the overall condition of the commercial motor vehicle.

Check for signs of unusual damage or wear and tear and leaks under the commercial motor vehicle.

If you see anything out of the ordinary or out of working order, write it down and make sure that it is thoroughly addressed before you embark on your next trip

Point Two: Under the Hood

Make sure all the fluid levels are in safe operating ranges.

Make sure that none of the fluids under the hood are leaking.

Check over the alternator and water pump, the compressor belts, and air conditioning system.

Make sure all wiring is securely fastened and free of cracks, frays, or breaks.

With the hood of the commercial motor vehicle open, start the engine and listen.

Make sure there are no unusual sounds such as knocking, whining, creaking, etc.

Close the hood.

Point Three: In the Cab

Ensure the parking brake is on and switch gear to "neutral" for manual vehicles, and "park" for automatic vehicles.

Make sure all the gauges and indicator lamps on the dash are working. Seconds after starting the engine, the oil pressure should rise up to normal. Air pressure should also rise from about 50 to 90 pounds per square inch (psi) in about 3 minutes. Depending on your vehicle's requirements, build air pressure up to governor cut-out which is typically about

120 to 140 psi. Your coolant and engine oil temperature should gradually rise to their usual operating range. The voltmeter and/or ammeter should be inspected as well to make sure they are within the normal range(s).

Test the accelerator, brake pedal, clutch pedal, and steering wheel for looseness or unusual noise or feedback.

Test the turn signals, transmission controls, horn, headlights, dimmer switch, emergency flashers, washers, and wipers to ensure they're working.

Check all your mirrors and position them correctly and clean them if needed. Look out for obstructions like cracks, stickers, dirt, and so on and adjust as necessary.

Check the seat belt and make sure that any needed adjustments are made so it is functioning properly. Look out for rips and frays.

Verify the presence and readiness of all safety and emergency equipment. Your first aid kit and fire extinguisher should all be properly secured and ready to use. Unless your vehicle has circuit breakers, you should have extra electrical fuses alongside three liquid burning flares, six fuses, or three reflective triangles. Check the date on your fire extinguisher and ensure it is properly charged and rated as well as the expiry dates of any medicines in your first aid kit. Optional items like equipment for changing tires, emergency numbers, and chains during wintery conditions should be checked.

Check the indicator lights of your vehicle's anti-lock braking system if equipped. If working properly, the light on the dashboard should flash on and then off. Note that it is likely the ABS has malfunctioned if the light remains on. In trailers, the yellow light on the left rear staying on is a sign that the ABS isn't working properly.

Point Four: Lights and Indicators

Turn off the engine with the parking brake set and hold on to the keys.

Switch on the four-way emergency flashers and low beams and then step out of the vehicle. Check the headlights, the hazards (flashers), the running lights, and the high beams to make sure they're all working properly.

Point Five: Perform a Walk-Around Inspection

To begin, stand in front of the vehicle to see if both four-way flashers are working properly and that the low beam headlights are on.

Press the dimmer switch and inspect the high beam headlights. Switch off the 4-way emergency flashers and headlights.

Turn on the clearance, parking, identification, and side-marker lights. Turn on the right turn signal, and begin the walk-around inspection. As you go around, carefully wipe any glass, reflector, or lights that seem dirty or dusty.

Left Front Side of the Vehicle

At the left front side of the vehicle, check if the door locks and latches work properly. Inspect the tires to ensure there are no bulges, severe cuts, or wear, and that they are sufficiently inflated.

The wheel and rim should be checked for signs of misalignment or bent, broken, or missing lugs, clamps, or studs.

Make use of a wrench to test loose lug nuts and fasten as necessary.

Check for any hub oil leaks and confirm the oil is at a sufficient level.

Inspect the shock absorber, shackles, spring, u-bolts, and spring hangers for any looseness or damage.

Check the condition of the vehicle's hoses and brake disc or drum.

Front of the Vehicle

Inspect the condition of the front axle and steering system for any loose, damaged, missing, or bent parts. Grab the steering wheel to test for looseness.

The windshield should be checked for damage and thoroughly cleaned if dirty. Inspect the wiper arms to ensure there is normal spring tension. Wiper blades should also be firmly attached, and there should be no damage or stiff rubber.

The vehicle's reflectors and lights should be clean, functioning and should always show the right color. Identification, clearance, and parking lights along with the reflectors should display an amber color at the front. As for the front turn signal on the right, the light should be either white or amber on the vehicle's forward-facing signals.

Right Side of the Vehicle

Repeat all checks done on the left front side on this side of the vehicle as well.

If the vehicle is designed such that the cab is over the engine, keep both the primary and secondary safety cab locks engaged.

The fuel tank or tanks should be adequately filled, securely mounted and inspected for any leaks or damages. Ensure that the cap(s) is on and secure along with the fuel crossover line

Right Rear

The vehicle's rims and wheels should be inspected for any missing or damaged parts.

The tires should also be checked to make sure the tire pressure level is adequate and that there is no damage, friction, or obstruction.

All tires fitted on the vehicle should be of a single type and not mixed. For instance, you should not fit a bias tire and radial tire on the same vehicle.

Look for any leaks in the wheel seals or bearing.

Check to see if all the tires are of an even size.

Suspension

Inspect the spring hangers, spring(s), u-bolts, and shackles, and make sure the axle(s) is secure with no lubricant leaks from the powered axle(s).

Check the condition of the shock absorber, air ride components, bushings, and torque rod arms for any damages or necessary adjustments.

If the vehicle is equipped with a retractable axle, examine the lift mechanism thoroughly. In case it is air-powered, look out for any leaks or drips.

Brakes

Adjust the vehicle brakes as needed.

Check the brake discs or drum and hoses for damage or wear from friction.

Reflectors and Lights

The side-marker reflectors and lights should be clean, functional, and display the proper color when in use i.e. red at the rear and amber everywhere else.

Rear

Make sure the vehicle's license plate or plates are present, clean, and properly secured.

There should be damage-free splash guards that are well fastened so they do not come in contact with the ground or the vehicle's tires.

For trucks, verify that your cargo is secure, the end gates work properly, and that they are correctly secured in appropriate stake sockets.

The doors should be properly closed with all necessary lights and/or signs mounted correctly.

Check to see if the reflectors, tail lights, identification, and rear clearance lights are clean and functioning, and show a proper red color at the rear. Look at the right turn signal on the rear and ensure it is working and displaying either a yellow, amber, or red color.

Left Side of the Vehicle

Repeat a check of all items inspected on the right side of the vehicle.

Check the vehicle's battery or batteries if it is outside the engine compartment to see if they're properly secured with the box or boxes firmly mounted to the vehicle.

Verify that the box has a firm cover and that the battery or batteries are prevented from shifting during transit. The battery should be leak and damage-free as well.

Except for maintenance-free batteries, confirm that the fluid is at the right level, cell caps are present and tightly fastened, and the vents in the caps don't contain any foreign material.

Condition of Visible Parts

The engine's rear and transmission should be free of leaks, there should be no cracks or bends in the frame and cross members; and the exhaust system should be secure without leaks or direct contact with wires, air lines, or fuel lines.

All electrical wiring and air lines should be properly secured to prevent wear, friction, or snagging.

If equipped, check for damages to the spare tire rack or carrier and see that the tire and/or wheel is properly mounted.

Lastly, ensure the spare is adequate for your vehicle in terms of correct size and tire pressure level.

Cargo Securement for Trucks

The cargo should be correctly tied, blocked, chained, braced, etc. to the vehicle.

If required, make sure the header board is secure and adequate.

Properly secure the tarp or canvas if required so that there is no billowing or tearing, and the mirrors are not obstructed.

Verify that the curbside compartment doors are working properly and are firmly closed or locked with the necessary security seals on them.

If there are stakes and sideboards equipped, ensure they are strong enough to support the cargo, damage-free, and properly set.

All required signs i.e. reflectors, lamps, and flags should be correctly and safely mounted with all needed permits in the driver's possession if the cargo is oversize.

Point Six: Check Signal and Brake Lights

Get in the vehicle and turn off all the lights. Afterward, switch on your stop lights using your hand brake or ask someone to help with the brake pedal. Turn on the left-turn signal lights.

Step out of the vehicle and check that the stop lights, turn signal light at the left front, and the signal light at the left rear are functioning, clean, and show the correct color. The signal light at the left front should be white or amber on front-facing signals while the one at the rear should be amber, yellow, or red.

Get back into the vehicle and turn off all extra lights that are not necessary for driving.

Confirm that you have all required permits, manifests, papers, etc. that you will need on your trip.

Properly secure any loose items in the cab as these may hit you in case of a crash or hinder you from operating the controls effectively.

Point Seven: Start Engine and Test Brakes

Start the engine back up.

If the vehicle brakes are hydraulic, pump the pedal thrice and then firmly press and hold the pedal for about five seconds. Note that the pedal should be stagnant while doing this- if it moves, there is either a malfunction or a leak somewhere. Make sure that such issues are properly fixed before you drive the vehicle.

Test the vehicle's parking brake or brakes by fasting your seatbelt and setting it. If applicable, release the brake and switch into low gear. To confirm that it holds, pull forward gently against it and repeat these steps with the power unit parking brakes and trailer parking brake set released. The brake should be fixed as soon as possible if it fails to hold the vehicle.

To test the vehicle's service brake stopping response, drive for about 5 mph and firmly push the brake pedal. If the pedal sways to one side or another, it could be a sign that the brake has malfunctioned. A delay in stopping or an unusual feel of the pedal could also indicate trouble.

Additional CDL Inspection Checks for Air Brake Vehicles

Although these seven points are the general steps to inspecting your vehicle before proceeding on a trip, there are certain adjustments to points two (2), five (5), and seven (7) for vehicles equipped with air brake systems. For this kind of vehicle, there are a few extra things you need to inspect whilst checking under the hood and during the walk-around inspection.

Point Two- Under the Hood Checks

If the vehicle has a belt-driven compressor, check the air compressor drive belt to confirm it is in good condition and is tight enough.

Point Five- Carry Out a Walk-Around Inspection

Check the slack adjusters in the vehicle's S-cam brakes- Park the vehicle on level ground and get the wheels chocked so that the vehicle doesn't move. Next, turn the parking brakes off to allow you to move the slack adjusters freely. Grab some gloves and use them to pull firmly on each one within your reach. If any of them moves past about one inch from the point where it is attached to the pushrod, it likely needs to be adjusted. Bear in mind that it can be very difficult to stop vehicles with excess brake slack. As soon as you notice a problem with the adjuster, get the vehicle to a repair facility and don't try to fix it on your own.

Check the vehicle hoses, linings, and brake drums or discs- Take a look at the brake drums/discs and make sure that no cracks covering more than one-half the width of the entire friction surface. The air hoses should also be properly linked to the brake chambers and cuts or wear from friction should be absent. Linings must be made of friction material and should not be soaked in grease or oil. They must also be firmly secured and should not be too thin. All mechanical parts must be accounted for and damage-free.

Point Seven- Air Brake Check

Instead of the hydraulic brake check highlighted in the preceding section, the checks to be done on an air brake vehicle are listed below.

Check low pressure warning signal- When the vehicle has built up enough air pressure, turn off the engine so that the low pressure warning signal remains off. Turn on the electrical power, step on the brake pedal, and step off again so that the pressure inside the air tank is reduced. The warning signal must be displayed before the pressure drops past 60 psi in the air tank or in the tank with the lowest pressure for dual air systems. A faulty warning signal could cause you to lose air pressure without knowing which could result in sudden emergency braking in single-circuit air systems and increased stopping distance in dual air systems.

Check spring brakes- The vehicle's spring brakes should always automatically come on and you can test this by fanning off the air pressure continually. This would involve stepping on the brake pedal and off again to reduce the tank pressure. When air pressure drops to between 20 - 45 psi, the parking brake and tractor protection valve should pop out on a tractor-trailer combination vehicle while the parking brake valve should pop out on other single and combination vehicles types.

Check air pressure buildup rate- It is important to do this because the pressure may drop excessively low while driving if the air pressure takes too long to build up. In dual air systems, air pressure should rise from 85 to 100 psi in 45 seconds when the engine is at its operational rpms. However, vehicles with larger than average air tanks may require more time to build up. As for single air systems manufactured before 1975, it should take about three minutes for the pressure to rise from 50 to 90 psi in an engine with an idle speed between 600 - 900 rpms.

Check air leakage rate- In a vehicle with a fully-charged air system (usually 125 psi), turn the engine off, release the parking brake, and time how long it takes for air pressure to drop. Normally, the loss rate should be lower than two psi in one minute for single vehicles and less than three psi in one minute for combination vehicles. Using the brake pedal, apply a minimum of 90 psi. There is an excessive air loss rate if the air pressure goes higher than three psi in a minute for single vehicles or above four psi for combination vehicles. Before driving, carefully look out for any air leaks and have them repaired.

Check vehicle's air compressor governor cut-in/out pressures- Although it depends on the manufacturer, air compressor pumping should begin around 100 psi and then stop around 125 psi. To check the pressure, start by running the engine at a fast idle. The air compressor should be cut out by the air governor around the vehicle's specified pressure and the air pressure gauge will stop building up. Step on the brake and off again as the engine is idling to lower the pressure in the air tank. The compressor should cut in at the set cut-in pressure and the pressure should start building up. The vehicle's air governor may need some repairs if it doesn't work as described.

Test the parking brake- Carefully bring the vehicle to a stop, put on the parking brake, and then pull against it gently in low gear to see if it will hold.

Test vehicle's service brakes- Wait for the vehicle to reach its normal air pressure before releasing the parking brake. Slowly move the vehicle forward for a distance of about 5 mph and then firmly apply the brakes using the pedal. Watch out for any delay in stopping, unusual feel, or the vehicle swaying to one side.

Inspection during a Trip

During your trip, all your senses need to be at work to notice any signs of problems. You also need to keep a close eye on your vehicle gauges and check essential items like brakes, coupling devices, tires, wheels, rims, reflectors, lights, cargo securement devices, and electrical and brake connections to the trailer at each stop.

Post-Trip Inspection

You should inspect each vehicle you drive carefully after each day, trip, or duty tour. Generally, the post-trip inspection would include filing a vehicle condition report to record any problems or faults encountered. This report helps keep the motor carrier updated concerning the repairs the vehicle needs and when.

Things to Look Out for When Inspecting Your Vehicle

Excessive or insufficient air pressure.

Fabric showing through sidewall or tread or other signs of bad wear.

Separation of tread.

Valve stems that are cracked or cut.

Mismatched tire sizes.

Retreaded, regrooved, or recapped tires on a bus' front wheels.

Cut or damaged tires.

Dual tires contacting vehicle parts or each other.

Joint usage of bias-ply and radial tires.

Damaged rims.

Missing lugs, spacers, clamps, or studs.

Rims or wheels with unsafe welding repairs.

Bent, cracked, or mismatched lock rings.

Rust-coated wheel nuts which may indicate looseness.

Cracked brake drums.

Oily or greasy brake shoes or pads.

Broken, missing, or dangerously thin brake shoes.

Missing cotter keys, bolts, nuts, or other steering system parts.

More than ten degrees of steering wheel play.

Broken, loose, or bent steering system parts.

Leaks in vehicle fluid, pumps, and hoses for power steering systems.

Spring hangers that allow improper placement of the axle.

Broken or missing leaves in leaf springs.

Leaky shock absorbers.

Leaking and/or damaged air suspension systems.

Broken, cracked, loose, or missing frame members.

Missing, damaged, or cracked spring hangers, u-bolts, torque rod/arm, or other axle positioning parts.

Broken or cracked spring hangers.

Shifted or broken leaves in a multi-leaf spring that can hit other vehicle parts or tires.

Leaky exhaust system parts.

Broken, missing, or loose nuts, bolts, clamps, or mounting brackets.

Exhaust system parts rubbing against moving vehicle parts or fuel system parts.

Broken, missing, or loose vertical stacks, mufflers, exhaust pipes, or tailpipes.

Imbalanced or overloaded cargo.

Placarding and proper documentation for cargo containing hazardous materials.

Air Brakes and Their Components

Knowing the components of your vehicle will help you to operate it as safely and efficiently as possible. In this section, we will cover the components of an air brake system and a little bit about each component. To drive a CMV with air brakes, you will need to study this section well. Reading this section carefully, along with Chapter 7 on combination vehicles will come in handy for pulling air brake trailers.

To start with, an air brake is simply a system that makes use of compressed air to make the brakes function. Air brakes consist of three different braking systems namely the service, parking, and emergency brake. The service brake system is engaged in normal driving and is responsible for applying and releasing the brakes. When the vehicle's parking brake control is used, the parking brake system helps to apply and release the parking brakes. As for the emergency brake system, it engages some part of the parking and service brake systems to halt the vehicle in case the brake system fails. Although they are safe and very useful in stopping especially heavy or large vehicles, they must be used correctly and properly maintained.

Air Compressor

Each air brake system needs an air compressor to pump air into the air storage tanks, which are also known as reservoirs. Using gears or a v-belt, the air compressor is connected to the engine of the vehicle. It may also be cooled by air or by the engine cooling system. Likewise, the air compressor may get its oil from a connected source or from the engine oil. If the air compressor on your vehicle has its own oil source, make sure that you check it before and after each trip during your pre and post-trip inspections.

Air Compressor Governor

The air compressor governor is a control for the air compressor that controls when it will pump air into the air storage tanks. Once the air pressure in the tank rises to the "cut out" level or the necessary pressure (about 125 PSI) the governor stops the flow of air. When the pressure has dropped down below the "cut in" level, the governor will re-engage the compressor and bring it back to that cut-out.

Air Storage Tanks

The air storage tanks are the place where the air for your braking system is stored. These are also known as reservoirs. Depending on the size of your vehicle, you might have more or fewer than other vehicles you've seen. Make sure you get acquainted with your vehicle's system and all the tanks it has and needs. These tanks hold enough air to allow the truck to brake several times, even in the event of air compressor failure. If there is an air compressor failure, seek service as quickly as possible.

Air Tank Drains

Compressed air typically has a bit of water and compressor oil in it, which can build up and cause issues for your brakes. The water that gets into the air tank could freeze, which has the potential to cause brake failure. To avoid this, make sure you drain all of your air tanks completely before leaving your truck overnight. Each air tank must be equipped with a drainage valve on the bottom of it. There can be more than one type of drainage valve, however, so make sure you read the manuals for your vehicle and understand how to operate these.

A manually-operated drainage valve is typically activated by using a quarter turn or a pull cable and this should be done at the end of each day of driving.

An automatic drainage valve will drain those tanks on their own, but may have a manual mechanism in case of failure. Note that some air tanks can also be manually drained as well. It is also possible to get an air tank with electric heating devices that prevent and reverse freezing of the automatic drain during freezing weather.

Alcohol Evaporator

This is not a component that all air brake systems have, but it is used to evaporate alcohol that is put into the air system. The purpose of alcohol in the braking system is to help reduce the risk of ice forming in the event of inclement or cold weather. Ice in the air brake system could keep it from working properly.

If there is an alcohol container on your system, check it each day when the weather is cold and fill it to the necessary levels. It should be noted that this does not supplant the need to drain your air tanks daily. You must still purge the water and oil from those tanks in order for them to work properly, so you must either drain them manually or see to it that the automatic drain valves are working.

Safety Valve

This is also known as a safety relief valve. This is a pressure release valve that is placed on the first of your air tanks that is filled by the compressor. This allows you to let off excess pressure before it reaches the rest of the system. This valve is designed to open at 150 PSI, but if this valve does trigger and release air, this is a fault that will need to be addressed by a mechanic who can keep it from happening again.

Brake Pedal

This is a component that most people and all drivers are acquainted with. This is the pedal you push with your foot to engage the brakes and slow the vehicle or stop it. The harder you press down on the pedal, the more quickly you will come to a slow or a stop. Releasing your foot from the brake allows the pressure from the air brakes to release. The air compressor can replace this air pressure, but it will need a little bit of time to do so.

Do your best not to press and release the brake unnecessarily because the air compressor may not be able to keep up with the rate at which pressure is being released and it is possible for your brakes to fail for the lack of that pressure. When the brake pedal is pushed down, a spring and the air pressure going to the brakes are the forces that result in a forceful push against your foot. Having this at the back of your mind can help you feel the level of air pressure the brakes are getting.

Foundation Brakes

The foundation brakes are the brakes that are placed and working right by each wheel of the vehicle. These are the things that you can point out on your pre-trip inspection and which should be inspected each time. Most commonly, you will find the s-cam drum brake. Types and parts of the foundation brake are discussed here:

Brake Linings, Shoes, and Drums - On each end of each axle for your vehicle, you will have brake drums. These drums contain the braking mechanism for each of the wheels, which are bolted onto the brake drums. The brake shoes and linings are pushed against the inside of the drum. Stopping with your vehicle causes friction and the scale of that friction and the wear and tear it causes on the elements of your brakes is up to you and how hard and how long the brakes are used. If there is too much heat, the brakes could fail.

S-cam Brakes - Pushing on the brake pedal allows air into the brake chamber. The pressure from that air extends the pushrod and moves the slack adjuster, which twists the brake camshaft. The s-cam (so named because it is S-shaped) is turned, which forces the brake shoes away from each other and drives them up against the inside of the brake drum. When the brake pedal is released, the s-cam will rotate back into its former position and the brake shoes are moved away from the inside of the drum, which allows the wheels to roll freely once more. The S-cam brakes are the most common type of foundation brakes in vehicles.

Wedge Brakes - This is a different type of brake that is engaged a little bit differently. With wedge brakes, the brake chamber push rod shoves a wedge right between the ends of two brake shoes to force them apart and up against the inside of the brake drum. Some wedge brakes have only a single chamber, while others have two, which allows wedges to push the brakes in opposing directions. It is possible for the wedge brakes to be self-adjusting, but some of them do need to be adjusted manually.

Disc Brakes - Disc brakes that are air-operated are also equipped with a slack adjuster and brake chamber like the s-cam brakes. Instead of that S-shaped mechanism, however, the disc brakes have a component called a "power screw". The power screw is turned with the pressure of the brake chamber on the slack adjuster. The power screw clamps down on the disc or "rotor" between the brake pads on a caliper, which is similar to a large C-clamp.

Of these types, the s-cam brakes are the most common.

Supply Pressure Gauges

If a vehicle has an air brake, then it will have a pressure gauge attached to the air tank. Vehicles with a dual air brake system will either have a gauge for each half of the system or they will have two needles on a single gauge. These gauges tell you how much air pressure is in the air tanks.

Application Pressure Gauge

This is a gauge that is not present on all vehicles. It tells you how much pressure is being applied to the brakes. If you find yourself needing to increase the pressure on the brake pedal just to maintain a speed, this is an indication of the brakes beginning to show their wear and tear. Slow down and drop the vehicle into a lower gear, as this can also be an indication of brakes that are out of adjustment, air leaks, or other mechanical issues that need to be addressed.

Low Air Pressure Warning

It is a legal requirement that your vehicle provides a visible warning signal if the pressure in the air tanks for your air brake system has fallen below 60 psi. On older vehicles, this requirement can also be one-half of the compressor governor cut-out pressure. This signal is usually a red light and may have an accompanying buzzer to draw your immediate attention.

There is also an alarm device called a "wig wag" that may come with this alert. A mechanical arm will drop into your view when the system drops to dangerously low levels and when the pressure level is fixed, it will automatically rise back out of your view. Some are manual and will need to be placed back into the initial position, but they will not stay in place so long as that pressure is too low. If your commercial motor vehicle is a bus, it is common for this alert to trigger at 80 to 85 PSI.

Stop Light Switch

This is the mechanism that allows your brake lights to come on when you hit the brake pedal so that other motorists can tell you're applying your brake and that you're going to be slowing down. When the air brakes are used, this switch switches on the vehicle's brake lights.

Front Brake Limiting Valve

Older vehicles that were manufactured before 1975 usually have this component along with its control inside the cab. Most times, this control is marked "normal" and "slippery", and if put in the latter position, the valve will halve the "normal" air pressure that is applied to the front brakes. These limiting valves were originally designed to reduce the chances of skidding front wheels when driving on slippery surfaces but it's been observed that they lower the vehicle's stopping power. Regardless of the condition, front-wheel braking is very effective and there are tests to prove that there is a slim chance of front-wheel skidding as a result of braking even on ice. For your vehicle to have the standard stopping power, you need to ensure that the front brake limiting valve control is placed in "normal".

On the other hand, there are many vehicles with automatic front wheel limiting valves that cannot be controlled by the driver. These serve to reduce the air going to the front brakes except for when the brakes are applied very hard i.e. an application pressure of 60 psi or more.

Spring Brakes

It is a requirement of most commercial motor vehicles to have a spring brake and a parking brake. These brakes must be held in place by mechanical means, as air pressure tends to leak away and an emergency brake should be ready to work at a moment's notice. The powerful springs are held back with air pressure, but once that air pressure is removed, the springs apply the brakes. All the air in the system can be lost to a leak and this will also cause the brakes to be engaged.

If you're driving a straight truck or tractor, do not wait for them to automatically come on as they will only be fully engaged when the air pressure reduces to the range of 20 to 45 psi. As soon as the low air pressure warning light and buzzer are activated, carefully bring your vehicle to a safe stop. It is better to stop immediately while the brake can still be controlled before things get out of hand. Bear in mind that a spring brake will only be useful if the brakes are properly adjusted. If they aren't, there is a great possibility that the emergency, parking, and service brakes will malfunction too.

Parking Brake Controls

Newer vehicles that contain air brakes also have a yellow, diamond-shaped push-pull control knob that allows you to engage and disengage the parking brake. Older vehicles will have a lever that can be used for this purpose. Regardless of the means of activation, the parking brake should be used whenever the truck is parked.

Caution. Avoid pressing the brake pedal when the spring brakes are engaged. Doing so could damage the brakes with the combined force of the air pressure and the springs. This is something that is taken into account in the development of many brake systems, so there may be protections in place to keep this from happening, but it is best to avoid the situation entirely, as not all systems are designed that way. Creating the habit of avoiding the brake pedal when the spring brakes are engaged is the safest way to go.

Modulating Control Valves. Some vehicles contain a modulating control valve. This is a handle on the dashboard that allows the spring brakes to be applied gradually. This spring-loaded lever allows the driver to get a feel for the braking action and to increase or decrease as is needed. More movement on this lever will cause the brakes to engage more quickly so you can have as much control as possible if your service brakes fail. If you are parking your vehicle with the modulating control valve, move it as far as it will go and then lock it into place with the locking device.

Dual Parking Control Valves. If the main air pressure drops, the spring brakes are engaged. In some vehicles, like buses, there are separate air tanks that can be used to release the spring brakes. This allows you to be able to park the vehicle in an emergency. One of the valves on the dashboard is the type that you push and pull and it is used to engage the spring brakes for parking. The other valve is spring-loaded in the "out" position so that it must be pushed in to release air from that separate tank so the spring brakes are loosened, allowing you to move the vehicle. The release of this button will reapply the spring brakes. The air tank only contains enough pressure to do this a few times, so the driver must plan their moves carefully to make the most of what they have.

The Anti Lock Braking System (ABS)

Anti Lock Braking Systems have been a requirement on all commercial motor vehicles since March 1, 1998. Truck tractors have had this regulation imposed on them since March 1, 1997. Many commercial brakes that were made before these dates are still equipped with these brakes, so be sure to consult your owner's manual to be sure of the system that is in your vehicle. The certification label will tell you the date your vehicle was manufactured.

Anti-lock braking systems are computerized systems that keep the wheels from locking up when the brake is applied hard and fast. Vehicles with ABS often have a yellow warning or malfunction lamp on the instrument panel to inform the driver of an issue.

Trailers also come equipped with yellow anti-lock braking system malfunction lamps on the left side on either the front or rear corner of the trailer. Dollies that were manufactured after March 1, 1998, are also required to have a lamp on the left side for this purpose.

On vehicles that were manufactured more recently, the malfunction lamp for the anti-lock braking system comes on when the vehicle is started up to show the driver that the lamp is there and is working properly. Older vehicles may keep this lamp lit until the vehicle reaches a speed of at least five miles per hour.

If you notice that the lamp is on after you've been driving for a few seconds, or if it comes on again after having done its initial bulb check, then you may have an ABS failure in one or more wheels.

It is important to note that the anti-lock braking system is not an additional feature to the normal brakes on your vehicle. This system does not add to or subtract from your normal ability to brake in everyday driving situations. The ABS engages only when the wheels are about to lock up as a result of sudden braking.

Try to maintain a long braking distance when the anti-lock braking system engages, as the system does not necessarily shorten the distance needed, but it does help you to maintain control of the vehicle during hard braking.

Exhaust

Defects in the exhaust system can be extremely serious because they can lead to poisonous fumes leaking into the cab or the sleeper berth. When you're doing your pre-trip inspection, check the exhaust for anything loose, broken, missing, or leaking. This includes exhaust pipes, mufflers, mounting brackets, bolts or nuts, clamps, and vertical stacks. Make sure to also watch for parts that could be bumping or rubbing up against parts of the fuel system, the tires, or other moving parts of the vehicle.

Inspections on Your Travel Route

When you're on your route, you will want to stop intermittently to inspect your load, inspect your vehicle, and make sure that nothing has happened on the road that will present any problems for you later on.

This inspection won't need to be as thorough as the pre-trip and post-trip inspections that we've covered in this chapter. You will still want to check your tires, your brakes, and do a walk around the vehicle to make sure there isn't anything wrong, but you won't need to open up the hood or check on things that aren't really obvious from a walkaround.

When you inspect your cargo, check for slippage and check for shifting. If there is a lot of shifting, you may want to consider securing your load differently so it doesn't continue to shift while you're on your route.

Power Steering

Power steering is something that all vehicles have, including compact personal vehicles on the road. If you have ever had your car run out of gas or if you have ever had your power steering fluid run out, you know how nearly impossible it is to steer the vehicle without it.

You should make sure that you have enough power steering fluid in your vehicle before and after you go on a trip. You can check this with the dipstick or with the sight glass if your reservoir has one. The level should be well above the refill mark for best results.

Tires

- Tire tread depth on tires that are not at the direct front of the vehicle must not be any less than 2/32 of an inch, the tire must be evenly worn, there must be no cuts or damage to the tread or sidewall of the tire.
- The tread depth on all other tires must be no less than 4/32 of an inch, the tire must be evenly worn, and there must be no cuts or damage to the tread or sidewall of the tire.
- The rims must not be cracked or damaged and must have no evidence of welding repair or damage.
- The axle seal must be free of any leaks and if there is a sightglass, you must check for an adequate level.
- Lug nuts must all be present and in place, there must be no signs of looseness such as rust trails or shiny treads, and there must be no cracked or distorted lug nuts or bolt holes.
- The hub seal must be at an adequate level and not leaking.
- The tire pressure valve stems and caps must be present and not leaking.
- The tire pressure in the front driver's side tire must be anywhere from 90 to 100 psi. (Must be verified by the manufacturer's manual and the state requirements for your vehicle.)
- The tire pressure in the tire must be anywhere from 90 to 100 psi. (Must be verified by the manufacturer's manual and the state requirements for your vehicle.)

Vocabulary & Keywords

ABS (Anti-Lock Braking System) **-** Anti-lock brake systems or ABS are a brake assisting system that must be used in commercial motor vehicles to prevent the wheels from locking up when the brakes are engaged suddenly. When the brakes are engaged, it is possible for the wheels to lock up and skid, which these systems help to avoid.

Air Brake **-** Air brakes use a pressurized air system to bring a commercial motor vehicle to a stop. There is a required Air Brakes Knowledge Test that one must pass in order to demonstrate their skills when using a vehicle equipped with them.

Axle Weight **-** The weight that is exerted on the ground either by one axle or by a set of axles.

Cargo - That which is being carried by the truck and its driver; load, freight.

Container – This is the word used for large, metal shipping containers. They can vary from 20 to 40 feet in length and are typically transported by rail or truck.

Coupling Device Capacity - This is the maximum weight for which coupling devices are rated. These devices must be able to keep vehicles connected, so it is important to make sure that the vehicle can hold onto the weight placed on it.

Dry Bulk - Non-packaged and raw materials that are shipped in large tanks or containers such as grain, metal, or other such things. Some companies specialize only in dry bulk delivery.

Foundation Brakes - The brakes that are engaged when the brake pedal in the footwell of the driver's side is depressed. This is the main braking system that is used to slow and stop the vehicle.

GCVWR (Gross Combined Vehicle Weight Rating) - This is a rating—a specification—provided by the manufacturer which specifies the maximum amount of weight that can be combined and carried by a certain vehicle.

GCW (Gross Combination Weight) -This is the complete weight of a vehicle that includes the load it is carrying, the tractor, and the trailer.

Governor – A device that is used to regulate the top speed at which a commercial motor vehicle can travel. These are used with large fleets to ensure that all of the drivers are staying within safe and legal guidelines that maximize safety and fuel efficiency.

GVW (Gross Vehicle Weight) - The complete weight of the vehicle including the container, cargo, trailer, and tractor.

GVWR (Gross Vehicle Weight Rating) - This is a rating—a specification—provided by the manufacturer which specifies the maximum weight of cargo the vehicle is permitted to carry.

Suspension System - This is the system in the vehicle that is made up of things like the springs, tires, shock absorbers, and linkages that allow the vehicle to link the steering to the wheels so the movements are coordinated and so handling and ride quality are smooth.

Tire Load - The maximum weight approved to be held for each tire on a commercial motor vehicle.

CHAPTER - 3

CONTROLLING YOUR VEHICLE

Accelerating

It is important that you don't roll back when you start to accelerate from a stopped position. You could hit someone that is parked or waiting behind you. If you are driving a commercial motor vehicle with a manual transmission, you will want to partly engage the clutch before you take your right foot off of the brake so that you can keep yourself from rolling back to get started.

If you can feel yourself starting to roll backward, you can put on the parking brake to keep yourself from doing so. Release the parking brake once you have applied enough power from the engine to move the vehicle forward when it is released. Some commercial motor vehicles (like tractor-trailers) are equipped with a trailer brake hand valve that can be applied in order to stop the vehicle from rolling backward.

Acceleration should be done smoothly and gradually so there isn't any jerking going on with the vehicle as it tries to gain speed. Too much roughness during acceleration can cause mechanical damage to the vehicle. If there is a trailer attached to the vehicle, there could be mechanical damage to the coupling from rough acceleration, so it is imperative that acceleration be done smoothly.

Accident Protocol

If you are in an accident and you are not seriously hurt, you must act to prevent further injury or emergencies. Your basic steps to follow are:

1. Protect the area
2. Notify the authorities
3. Care for the injured

Let's break those down so you can see what we mean by each of them.

Protect the Area. The first thing to do after an accident in which you were not seriously injured is to prevent another accident from occurring as a result of the current accident. To do this, you will want to try to get your vehicle to the side

of the road. This will keep the road clear and keep traffic flowing around you. If your vehicle was not involved in the accident and you are stopping to help, park well away from the accident if you can. The area right by the affected people and vehicles will be needed for the emergency vehicles when help arrives.

Put on Your Emergency Lights, Hazards, or Flashers to Signal Distress. Set your reflective triangles out behind the vehicles to warn oncoming motorists to keep clear of the obstruction ahead.

Notify the Authorities. If you have a cell phone or a CB radio, use one of them to call for assistance at your location. If you are able to use the GPS on your phone or nearby road signs, give the emergency operator as much information as you can about where you are located and what the officers and EMTs can expect when they arrive. If you do not have a phone or a CB radio, which should be very unlikely, ask if any of the other motorists present have a phone you may use for that purpose.

Care for the Injured. If there is a qualified person at the scene helping to care for the injured, simply stay clear so they can tend to them easily. If you are the only one there to help, see to the injuries and do your best to help the people who are injured to get to safety and to be as comfortable as possible until help arrives.

If someone is severely injured, do not move them unless they are in immediate, greater danger like fire or passing traffic. If the injured person is bleeding heavily, apply direct pressure to the wound and stop the bleeding. Do your best to keep the injured person warm. If you have an emergency blanket, wrap them in it.

Aggression or Road Rage

Aggression on the road and road rage are not new issues, by any means. However, now that timelines are getting shorter, schedules are getting fuller, and traffic is becoming denser, tensions are running a little higher these days. Be aware that there is no shortage of things to upset a driver on the road and make sure that you are not taking out any of your frustrations when you are in your vehicle, as doing so could have dire consequences.

There is little room for error on such crowded roads and it can make driving even more stressful than it already is. This, of course, does not help with those rising tensions. However, you must be aware that these angering situations exist and that your response to them is the only thing that you can realistically control. You do not need to take the mistakes of other drivers personally and you don't need to spend extra time dwelling on things that didn't go smoothly during certain maneuvers on the road; simply breathe and move forward on your route.

If you're not certain of what aggressive driving is, it is the act of operating a motor vehicle in a manner that is bold, selfish, not smooth, pushy, or unsafe because of anger or aggression that you feel. If you are changing lanes abruptly without notice to spit others on the road, you are driving aggressively and not safely.

If you find yourself operating your commercial motor vehicle with this type of behavior or with the intent to harm or "teach" others, then you are dangerously close to assaulting someone else with your vehicle and you are putting yourself and other motorists in danger as a result.

The way you feel before you set out on your route can have an effect on how you respond to these types of situations. Make sure that if you're not feeling well or if you're under a lot of stress before you hit the road, you do something to help yourself to calm down and center your focus.

If there are types of music that you like to listen to when you're driving to keep you feeling your best and to keep your head clear, then you should absolutely do so! Try to give the route and the drive your full attention so you're in the present moment and stuck on something that happened on the road moments or minutes ago. Try to eliminate distractions and keep your eyes on the road.

Make sure that you're being real with yourself about how long your drive is going to take and try not to let the stress of being behind get to you and to push you into driving unsafely. Driving in that manner will not get you to your destination on time and it could even have the exact opposite effect. With traffic, weather, and accidents being as unpredictable as they are, try to allow for those things to happen and be calm.

It can also help to give other drivers the benefit of the doubt. If they're driving erratically or in a way that is making your job a little bit harder or more stressful, try to imagine why that might be and inform yourself that their behavior has nothing to do with you.

Keep a reasonable following distance on the road; don't follow too closely and keep your hands on the wheel. Those naughty hand gestures might make you feel better for a moment, but having full control of that steering wheel when you're driving is priceless. Those gestures could also anger another driver enough to cause an altercation and it should be your goal to get through every single drive without being confronted by an angry motorist.

If you are confronted by an aggressive driver, then you should do everything in your power to avoid them and stay out of their way without endangering yourself or others. If they are challenging you on the road, do not engage and do your best to fall back and let them know that they should just continue on their drive without thinking of you as an adversary. Try to avoid making eye contact with those aggressive drivers and do not engage with them or react.

If someone is being sufficiently aggressive to worry you for the safety of others, you should report it to the appropriate authorities along with the vehicle description (make, model, color, plate) and the location at which you saw them.

If the aggressive driver you saw behaving erratically before is in an accident that you encounter, park your vehicle at a safe distance from the scene and wait for the police to arrive so you can report the behavior you saw to them. Drivers who behave unsafely and cause accidents should be charged for that so they can deal with their anger in a safer way.

Railroad-Highway Crossings

Railroad-Highway grade crossings are a particular type of intersection at which the roadway crosses train tracks. These crossings are always dangerous, so every time you cross one, you must exercise extreme caution. You should always approach with the assumption that a train is coming. When you see a train coming in the distance, it can be exceedingly difficult to tell how far away it is and how much time you have. If you see a train coming, wait until it has passed and then cross with caution

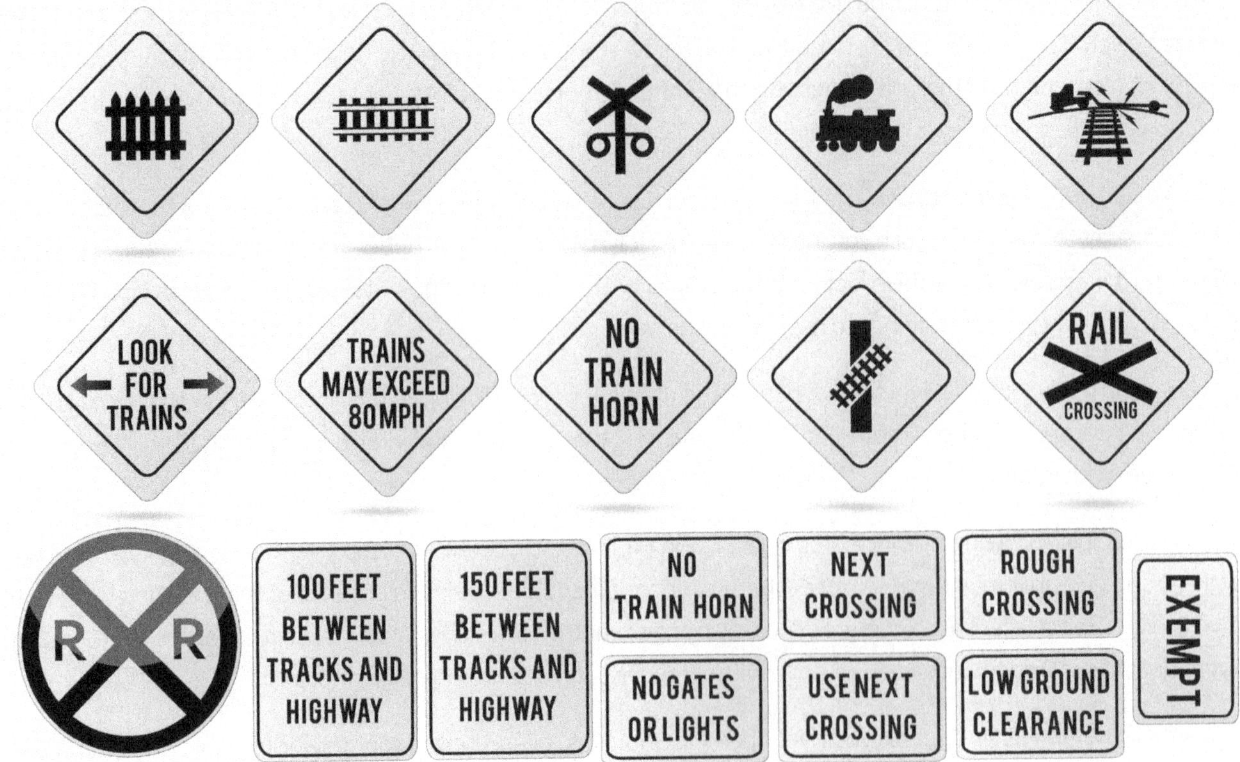

Types of Crossings

Passive crossings- A passive crossing is a crossing without any type of traffic control device. This means that choosing to proceed or stop the vehicle lies completely in your hands. At this type of crossing, you are required to recognize that it is a passive crossing, check for trains on the tracks, and decide whether there is enough clear space for your vehicle to cross safely.

Active crossings- This is a type of crossing with a traffic control device installed to regulate traffic. These devices could be flashing red lights with or without bells, and flashing red lights with gates and bells.

Warning Signs and Devices

Advance warning signs- This round black warning sign on a yellow background is usually placed ahead of a railroad-highway crossing. An advance warning sign informs the driver to slow down, look and listen for any approaching train, and be ready to brake at the tracks if there is one coming. All vehicles carrying HAZMAT and passengers are always required to stop at a crossing.

Pavement markings- A pavement marking conveys the same information as an advance warning sign and they are made up of an "X" with RR and a non-passing marking on two-lane roads. On two-lane roads, there is also a no-passing zone sign which may be a white stop line painted in the pavement just before the tracks. When at the crossing, the front of the bus must remain behind this line.

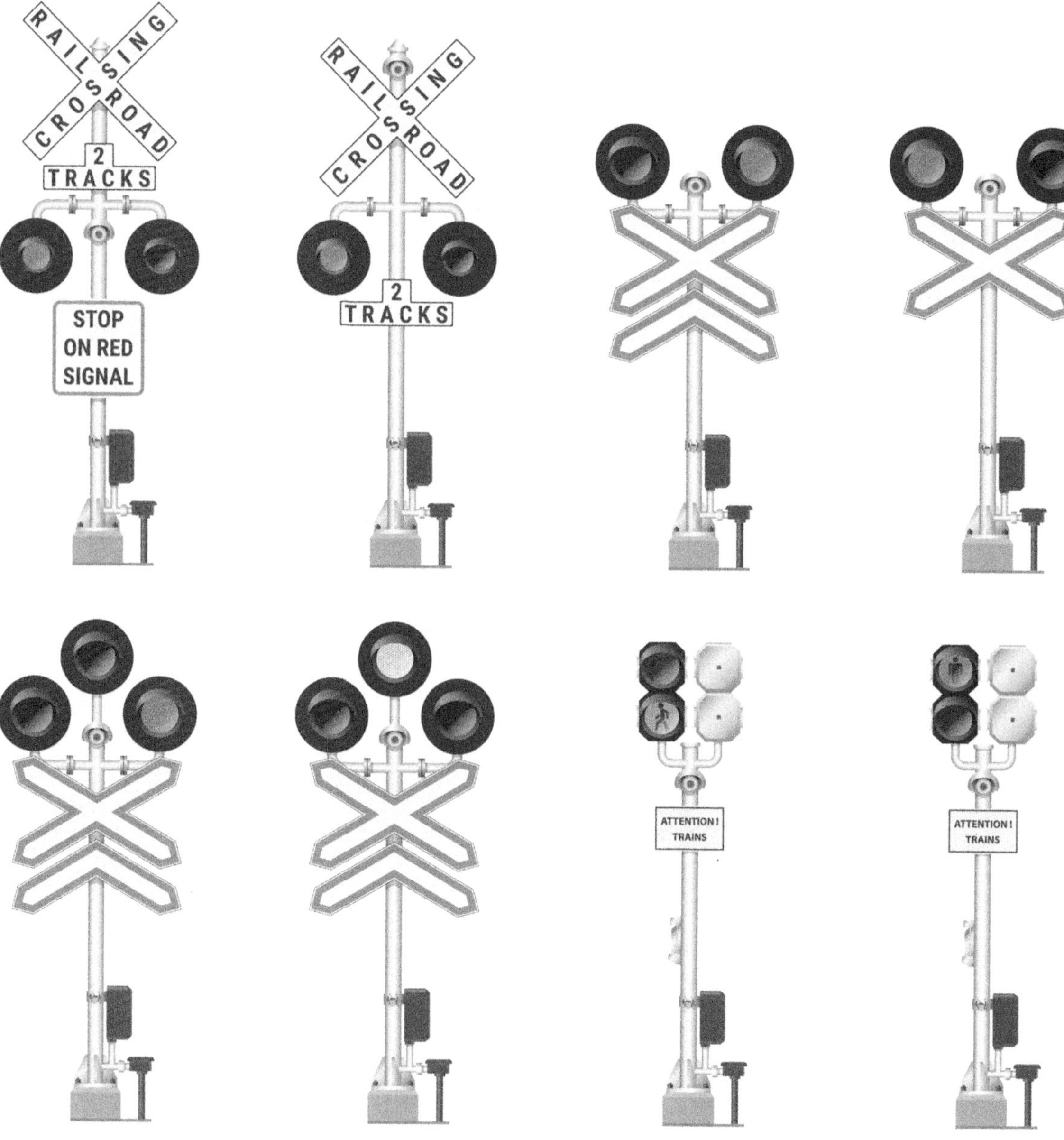

Crossbuck signs- This sign is a marker of the grade crossing and it requires drivers to yield the right of passage to the train. If no white stop line is painted on the pavement, all vehicles must stop no more than 15 feet or above 50 feet from the nearest rail of the closest track if required to stop. When the road crosses above one track, there will be a sign below the crossbuck to indicate the number of tracks.

Flashing red light signals- There are flashing red lights and bells at many railroad-highway grade crossings. You should stop immediately when the lights start flashing as that is an indication that a train is approaching and you are to yield the right of way to it. Be sure that all the tracks are clear before you cross if the number of tracks is above one.

Gates- Gates with flashing red lights and bells are common at a number of railroad-highway crossings. For this warning device, the vehicle should be stopped before the gate is lowered across the road lane when the lights start flashing. You are to remain in that position until the gates are raised once more and the lights are no longer flashing when it is safe to proceed.

Driving Procedures

Avoid racing a train to a crossing. You should never try doing this because it can be very hard to accurately determine the speed of a train as it approaches. Contrary to your predictions, you may be unable to cross in time before the train catches up.

Reduce vehicle speed. The vehicle's speed must be reduced to match your ability to see approaching trains in all directions. The speed must also be maintained at a point that will enable you to stop before the tracks in case there is a need to.

Don't expect to hear trains. Hoping to use a train's horns or sounds as a signal may be harmful as there are certain crossings where they are not permitted to sound their horns. Public crossings like this will usually be identified by a sign so be on the lookout for that. Even if the train horn is sounded, your vehicle's noise may hinder you from hearing until the train has gotten dangerously close to the crossing.

Don't rely on signals alone. Gates, warning signals, or flagmen that warn about a train's approach should not be the sole things you rely on when driving at a crossing as they might not always be there. You will need to be even more alert when approaching crossings without flashing red light signals or gates.

Double tracks need double checks. It is important for you to note that one train on a track may prevent you from seeing one on another track. Before you cross, always look both ways and after one train clears a crossing, be very sure no other one is near.

Yard areas and grade crossings. These can be found in cities and towns and can be just as dangerous as rural grade crossings. When approaching this crossing, you need to be very cautious.

Stopping Safely at Railroad-Highway Crossings

You need to bring your vehicle to a complete stop at grade crossings any time the nature of the cargo requires you to do so under state or federal laws. When stopping, you need to ensure that you do so gradually while looking out for traffic behind you. If there's a pullout lane available, it is advised that you make use of that. Be sure to turn on the vehicle's 4-way emergency flashers when you stop as well.

Crossing Railroad Tracks

When crossing railroad crossings with steep approaches, you need to be cautious because your unit can get hung up on the tracks. As much as possible, avoid traffic conditions that hold you in a position where stopping on the tracks is the only option. You can do this by making sure that your vehicle can make it all the way across before you even start. A typical tractor-trailer unit needs a minimum of 14 seconds to cross a single track, and above 15 seconds to cross a double track. Avoid shifting gears when crossing railroad tracks.

Violations

When driving a commercial motor vehicle across a railroad-highway crossing, there are local, state, or local laws relating to six basic offenses that you need to be cautious of. They are-

- Failure to stop before reaching a crossing if tracks are occupied for drivers who are not always required to stop
- Failure to stop before driving onto the crossing for drivers who are always required to stop
- Failure to successfully negotiate a crossing due to insufficient undercarriage clearance
- Failure to stop without sufficient space to drive through the crossing completely
- Failure to slow down the vehicle and ensure the tracks are clear of approaching trains for drivers who are not always required to stop
- Failure to obey an enforcement official's directions or a traffic control device for all drivers

Note that you can lose your CDL and/or CLP for a minimum of 60 days for your first violation; a minimum of 120 days for the second violation within three years; and a minimum of one year for the third violation within three years.

Driving While Distracted

There is no shortage of things on the road that can thoroughly distract a driver from the road and what they should be doing. Anything that takes your attention (in any measure) away from the road in front of you and from operating your vehicle carefully is considered a distraction. If you are driving a commercial motor vehicle, or any other vehicle for that matter, and your full attention is not on the task of driving the vehicle, you are putting all of the drivers on the road, yourself included, at risk. You are endangering any pedestrians that happen to be around the roads as well.

There are quite a few things you can be doing inside the cab of your vehicle that could keep your attention from being fully on the road. You could be fiddling with the radio or the music that's playing, you could be messing with the climate controls inside the cab to get the air to blow in just the right way, you could be having a soft drink, smoking, trying to pick up something that fell, looking at the screen of your phone or other devices, as well as countless other things that could come up naturally on your travels that you feel like you can just "take care of real quick," before you get back to driving in a focused manner.

You can also be distracted by things that are going on outside the vehicle. If you find that something interesting is happening, that there are signs or billboards to read, that there are cars you'd like to look at, that there are pedestrians doing things that catch your eye, or that you pass an accident and would like to see what happened. There are plenty of things that can happen outside your vehicle that keep your focus off the road in front of you, so don't think that just because you're not texting, that you're not distracted.

Emergencies on the Road

A traffic emergency is something that occurs when two vehicles are about to crash into one another. Vehicle emergencies happen when critical parts of either or both vehicles fail. Following the safety procedures in your state's commercial driver's license manual can help you to prevent emergencies and how to conduct yourself in those emergencies to assure that the least damage possible is done.

Steering to Avoid a Crash. Sometimes, stopping to avoid a traffic collision isn't the best option. You may not have enough space to come to a complete stop, so you may need to steer, not swerve, to the side to avoid a collision in order to avoid the obstruction in your path. The important thing is to maintain vehicle control and to mind the center of gravity for your load so you don't take actions that could flip or topple.

Make sure that you keep both of your hands firmly on the steering wheel when you turn your vehicle away from an obstruction. If you keep both hands on the wheel at all times, you will be much better prepared for just such an emergency.

Quick turns can be risky, but they can be done safely. Some things to remember when you're trying to turn quickly: do not apply the brakes when you are turning. This could cause you to skid out of control. Do not turn any more than what is needed to get you to safety. Overcorrection could land you in a bit of trouble and the more sharply you turn, the greater your chances become for things like skidding and rolling over. You should also be prepared in this scenario to "counter-steer." This means that you will turn the wheel back in the opposite direction of which you were turning once you've passed the obstruction so that you have the chance to course-correct. Emergency steering and counter-steering should be thought of as two parts to one driving maneuver or action.

Now for where you should be steering. If an oncoming driver is drifting or has drifted into your lane, the best course of action is to steer to your right. If the oncoming driver realizes what they have done, the natural response would be for them to correct their path and go back into his or her own lane.

If there is something in your lane as you're coming down the road, then you should assess the lanes around you and pick the best direction to steer. If there are people in the lane to your right, but there is also a lane to your left that is wide open, turn on your turn signal, steer into the left lane, pick up speed to keep up with traffic, then maneuver back into your own lane with your turn signal when the lane is clear. Proper and regular use of your mirrors will help you to know if there is space on either side of you to merge.

If the shoulder is clear while there is an obstruction in the road, that may be your best option. Try to evaluate and make sure that no portions of the roadway would be a better option before diverting to the shoulder. Make sure that you can safely merge back in with traffic when you are ready to do so from the shoulder. Use your mirrors frequently.

If you are blocked on both sides, try to move to the right. Put on your signal and try to merge in safely, but if someone is forced out of their lane by you, it will be onto the side of the road where there is likely a shoulder and a safe place for them to steer into. Doing this while merging left could pose a more serious risk of nudging another motorist into oncoming traffic. Keep your wits about you and choose the safest option you can find. Your judgment is your greatest tool here.

In some situations, leaving the road is the safest option for you. You may need to merge off of the road, onto the side to avoid a collision with another vehicle. Most shoulders are strong enough to hold the weight of a large vehicle and can be a great place for you to come to a stop for a moment, catch your breath, then merge back in with traffic when it is safe and you've shaken that off.

If you do leave the road, try to avoid braking until your speed has dropped to about 20 miles per hour. The ground will be looser than the road and all the weight on your wheels could kick up a lot of ground on its way down, which will make it harder to get back up. If you can, try to keep one set of wheels on the pavement so you can maintain control.

If the shoulder is clear, then stay there until your vehicle has come to a complete stop. Make sure that when you're ready to merge back into traffic, you use your signals. If you must return to the road before you are done coming to a stop, then hold the wheel tightly and turn sharply enough to get back onto the road, and don't try to edge back on gradually. Your tires could grab unexpectedly and could cause you to lose control of the vehicle. Once the two front tires are back on that pavement, counter steer to correct yourself. It should be one fluid steer-counter-steer motion to get you from the shoulder, back into traffic.

If someone pulls out in front of you on the road, your natural response may be to hit the brakes. This response is a good one if there is ample space between you and that vehicle for you to stop and you are using the brakes correctly. Braking in this situation should allow you to continue driving in a straight line without any part of your vehicle swaying or moving out of your control, but allow yourself to turn if it becomes necessary.

You can use the controlled braking method or you can use the stab braking method and we'll go into what both of those are here.

Controlled braking is a method in which you apply the brakes as hard as you can without locking your wheels. Keep very minute and small steering wheel movements while you're doing this. If you need to adjust the steering wheel with larger movements or if the wheels lock on you, release the brake then reapply it as quickly as you can.

Stab braking is a method in which you apply the brakes all the way and then release them when the wheels lock up. Once the wheels start to move freely, apply the brakes once again. It can take up to one full second before the wheels unlock once you release the brakes. If you reapply the brake before the wheels are rolling again, the vehicle will not be able to straighten out.

It is important to note that emergency braking doesn't mean you should just slam your foot all the way down on the brakes all at once because this will just throw you into a skid when the wheels lock up. I say when the wheels lock up because they will lock up if you do that. If the wheels are skidding, there is no possibility of control of the vehicle.

If the emergency on the road is brake failure, here is some information on how to handle that. The first thing to note is that brakes that are kept in good condition and that are serviced properly will rarely simply fail. Most hydraulic brake failures occur for two main reasons: first, the loss of hydraulic pressure. Second, brakes fade on long hills. Let's discuss each of those.

If your brake system has lost hydraulic pressure, you will notice that the brake pedal feels "spongy" or that there is very little resistance when you push the pedal toward the floor. Here are some steps you can take in such an event.

Downshift, also known as putting the vehicle into a lower gear, will slow the vehicle down a bit and help you have better control.

Pump the brakes because doing so could generate enough hydraulic pressure for you to safely stop the vehicle before getting assistance and service.

You can also use the parking brake to slow the vehicle, as it is separate from the hydraulic braking system. When you do this, make sure that you press the release button or pull the release level simultaneously while you use the emergency brake so you can adjust the brake pressure and keep the wheels from locking up.

While you are working to bring the vehicle to a slow or stop, you should look for an escape route. These can be many different things like open fields, runaway ramps, side-streets, etc. Once you find a place to stop, make sure the vehicle doesn't slide backward. Put the vehicle into low gear and apply the parking brake. If you feel it is necessary to do so, roll back into some obstacle that will keep you still while you are parked.

Now for what to do in the event of brake failure on downgrades. If you are traveling slow enough and using your brakes properly, you will almost never have a problem with your brakes on long downgrades. If you are on the downgrade and your brakes fail, however, you will need the help of something outside of the vehicle to bring it to a stop.

Escape ramps or runaway ramps are the best options in such cases and they are meant to help in just such an event. These ramps are typically placed just a couple of miles from the top of a downgrade so that in these cases, the driver has some safe recourse. These ramps are made of soft gravel so that the truck has lots of matter to push around without injuring anyone, namely you. You can also use a nearby hill for this purpose if you can position yourself to drive up the hill, which will kill your forward momentum.

If you don't have an escape ramp or a runaway ramp at your disposal, do your best to make the move to the least hazardous escape route you can, as quickly as you can. The longer you wait, the more speed you will pick up and the harder it will be to bring the vehicle to a complete and safe stop. Unfortunately in these situations, your greatest asset is being able to think fast.

If the emergency on the road is tire failure, your vehicle is in danger and you must act immediately. The first thing to do is to hold firmly onto the steering wheel. If a tire in the front of the vehicle fails, it can jerk the steering wheel out of your hands and the only way to keep control of the vehicle is to keep your grip firmly on the steering wheel with both hands at all times. Keep your foot off the brake despite your natural response to push down on it. Doing so when a tire has failed can cause a greater loss of control, as that wheel no longer has the traction and control it once did. Unless you risk running into something immediately, try to keep your foot off the brake until the vehicle has slowed down, then brake very gently, pull off the road, and come to a complete stop with your hazards on.

Once you've come to a complete stop, put all of your emergency signaling equipment into place and check all of your tires, even if you are certain of the one that has blown. If one of your dual tires fails, you may only know once you get a good look at it.

Fatigue and Night Driving

Driving during the night presents some unique problems of its own that can make the trip more difficult to get through. Because it is dark out, drivers are less likely to see obstructions in the roads and obstacles as easily as they would during the day. Because of this, it takes a bit more time for drivers to be able to respond to those obstacles and this can lead to more accidents on the road.

There are some problems with night driving that lie with the driver. The first of these is vision. Many people get their eyes tested for their CDL under bright conditions and then don't go back again for a new exam, leaving their eyes to struggle, sometimes without the driver even noticing. A driver's vision is essential to their abilities to control their vehicle as you base your acceleration, your braking, and the handling of your steering wheel based on what you see in front of you. If your vision isn't serving you as well as it should be, then you will not be handling those aspects of your driving as smoothly as you ought to be or as you could be.

If you have been prescribed some corrective eyewear for your vision to reach 20/20, you must wear them whenever you are working. Even if you are only driving short distances or if you are driving during the day, you should do everything in your power to bring your vision as close to 20/20 as you can. It is a legal requirement that you wear your corrective lenses, contacts or glasses, while you are driving if they have been prescribed to you by an eye doctor.

It is a good practice to keep an extra pair of your corrective lenses in the cab of your truck so you can put them on whenever you need them. Just in case something happens to the lenses you wear when you set out, you should always have a backup pair on hand.

If you have tinted corrective lenses, you should do your best not to use these during the night. This could cause more difficulty with visibility and could lead to difficulty. You could also get glare on your lenses, which makes it nearly impossible to make sense of your surroundings.

Glare is a big part of visibility difficulties at night. Because there are so many bright lights on the roads, coming toward you from many different angles, it is possible to be momentarily blinded by a bright light. You must keep in mind that if a light keeps you from seeing for two seconds while you're traveling at 55 miles per hour, your car will travel more than half a football field's distance in that time. Do your best to keep your windows clean and your eyes sharp during night hours.

Fatigue is one of the greatest risks to drivers during the nighttime hours. It is physical or mental tiredness that can be brought on by straight of mental or physical nature, monotonous tasks, sickness, stress, and many other things. Sleep can impair your vision and your alertness with the same severity as alcohol or drugs, so you must not take it lightly as a hindrance to your ability to do your job.

Fatigue can cause a driver to make errors in their speed, in their ability to judge distances, and can greatly increase your risk of collision. Fatigue can hinder one's ability to think critically and to think quickly. Some of what we've covered in this section discusses the need for being able to think clearly while on the road and the need to be able to respond to an emergency at a moment's notice. When you are fatigued, your ability to meet these needs is greatly hindered.

The National Highway Traffic Safety Administration estimates that 100,000 police-reported crashes each year are the result of fatigued or drowsy driving. The National Sleep Foundation conducted a poll in which 60% of Americans surveyed admitted to driving while sleepy and more than one-third of them admit that they have fallen asleep at the wheel. Drivers can experience short little bursts of being asleep that last just a couple of seconds, while others fall asleep completely and lose control of the vehicle. Either way, the risk to other motorists and the fatigued driver is increased dramatically.

The risk of getting into a traffic collision because of fatigued driving is not equal amongst all Americans. Crashes are more common during the hours of the day during which people are most sleepy, during the night and in the middle of the afternoon. People naturally become less alert at night, especially once midnight passes. The risk for fatigue and

sleepiness is greatly increased if you have been driving over a long period of time, into the night. Those who drive at night are far more likely to have an unexpected collision.

Young males, those who work late shifts, commercial drivers, particularly long-haul drivers, and people whose sleep disorders have gone untreated are among the groups who are at the highest risk for a fatigue-related traffic collision. Research has shown us that at least 15% of all heavy truck crashes are in some way related to fatigue and sleepiness.

In 1996, The Federal Motor Carrier Safety Administration conducted a study of 80 long-haul truck drivers in the United States and in Canada that found that drivers were averaging less than about five hours of sleep per day. Subsequently, the National Transportation Safety Board reported that driving while drowsy and insufficiently rested was the leading cause of more than half of the crashes that led to the fatality of a truck driver. A study conducted by the National Transportation Safety Board in 1994 concluded that in traffic collisions that involved a commercial truck, an average of three to four people were killed each time.

We know that the studies conducted by the National Sleep Foundation showed that a staggering number of Americans had not only driven while sleepy but had fallen asleep behind the wheel. This is because people can often not tell if they're going to fall asleep, or if they're just feeling a bit run-down. Let's go over some of the signs that you can use to tell you if you're about to have such an incident.

If you are having trouble focusing on the road and you find yourself blinking excessively to keep your eyes open, if you are yawning a lot or rubbing your eyes over and over, if you find your mind wandering and you find that you are daydreaming more than you might otherwise do, if you are having trouble remembering the last few miles of your trip including missing signs or exits, if you are having trouble keeping your head held upright, if you are drifting in your lane, hitting the rumble strips, or following too closely behind another vehicle, or if you are feeling restless or irritable, you might want to pull over and give yourself a bit of rest.

If you are wondering if you could be at risk for driving under the influence of fatigue, you should consider the following:

d. Are you sleep-deprived? Have you gotten six hours of sleep or less in the last 24 hours?
e. Do you suffer from insomnia or are you dealing with poor quality of sleep or sleep debt?
f. Have you been driving long distances without proper breaks for rest?
g. Have you been driving through the mid-afternoon or through the night when you would normally be sleepy or asleep?
h. Have you been taking any medications that are meant to sedate you or which have a drowsy side effect?
i. Have you been working more than 60 hours a week?
j. Have you been working more than one job at a time and does your main job involve shift work?
k. Have you been driving alone on long rural roads that have little in the way of changing scenery?
l. Have you been changing time zones in your travels?

Answering yes to one or more of these questions could mean that you should be pulling over to give yourself a break and allow yourself to recuperate some energy before getting back behind the wheel of your truck.

Now, if you would like to avoid drowsiness on your trips, there are some things you can do before you embark that will allow you to have a little bit more control over your mental and physical fortitude.

a. Get plenty of sleep; eight to nine hours each night is recommended to keep you feeling your best and most alert.
b. Prepare the route carefully before you embark so you are aware of stops along the way, so you know how far you should be traveling between each of them, and make concessions and plans for logistics along the way.
c. Schedule your driving times for the hours during which you are your most alert. For many people this is from nine in the morning to about three in the afternoon, then you can freshen up and drive until about six in the evening.
d. Have a passenger accompany you so they can talk with you and help to keep you alert and focused on the trip.
e. Avoid prescriptions and medications that make you drowsy. If the medication is prescribed, speak with your doctor about non-drowsy alternatives.
f. If you find that you typically suffer from drowsiness in the middle of the day with no warning, speak with a physician to see what you can do to remedy that.
g. In your typical routine, incorporate exercise, as this will give you more energy and stamina that will help you to stay alert.

If you are concerned about fatigue while you're already on the road, there are some other things that you can do to bring your focus back and get your head in the right space.

a. Wear sunglasses during the daylight hours to keep the light and glare to a minimum, allowing your eyes to keep from straining and getting tired too soon during the day.
b. Keep the temperature in your cab at a low-moderate temperature by opening the window or by using the air conditioner.
c. Avoid comfort foods or foods that sit heavy in your stomach, as those can make you feel like you need a nap afterward.
d. Take turns driving with a partner so you can get rest in between the times you spend behind the wheel.
e. Take periodic breaks every couple to a few hours to allow your legs to move, to get some fresh air in your lungs, and to keep your wits refreshed.
f. Stop driving if you feel tired and take a nap.
g. A little bit of caffeine can help you get to your next rest stop if it's not too far off. Avoid using it in large amounts and avoid relying on it to keep you awake. It doesn't stop fatigue, it only makes you feel wired until your body just falls asleep with no warning. The only cure for fatigue is sleep.
h. Avoid drugs that promote wakefulness. They will not take away the fatigue and the alertness you feel will be fleeting.
i. If you find yourself getting drowsy, pull off and get some sleep. There is nothing to be done for it and you will need sleep to bring you back to the energy level needed to proceed.

More about nighttime driving and the risks involved can be found in your state's CDL manual.

Gaining Control and Recovering from a Skid

Skids can happen from a few different causes. We'll break those down here so you can see what they are and how they differ:

Over-Braking- This means that you have been braking too much and the wheels have locked up as a result. The vehicle will skid as a result of this. This can also happen if the road is slippery and the speed retarder is used. If your wheels have locked up, let up off the brakes, allow the wheels to unlock, then gently apply the brake to bring yourself back to a controlled stop.

Over-Steering- If you are turning the wheels too sharply for the vehicle to maneuver on them safely, the vehicle could skid out of control.

Over-Acceleration- If you are too generous with applying the accelerator on wet pavement or even in dry conditions, your wheels could skid and lose their grip on the road.

Driving Way too Fast- Most serious skidding incidents come from the driver taking the speed limit as more of a loose suggestion than a regulation. Particularly in inclement weather or poor road conditions, you should observe and even undershoot those speed limits to maintain control of the vehicle. Drivers cannot over-correct during inclement weather or in poor road conditions and must keep a moderate hold on the brakes, the steering wheel, and the accelerator while driving.

Types of Skids

Drive-Wheel Skids- The most common skid is the one where the rear wheels lose traction as a result of too much braking or acceleration. Skids that happen due to acceleration usually take place on icy or snowy surfaces. Stepping off the accelerator is an easy way to stop such skids. If the surface is very slippery, you will need to push in the vehicle's clutch as the engine can prevent the wheels from rolling and regaining traction.

As for rear-wheel braking skids, they occur when the vehicle's rear drive-wheels get locked. When the wheels get locked, they have less traction in comparison to rolling wheels and the rear wheels will typically slide sideways in an attempt to realign with the front wheels. When this happens, the vehicle will likely slide sideways in a sort of spin-out if you are driving a straight truck or bus. For trailer-towing vehicles, this occurrence can lead to a sudden jackknife, allowing the trailer to push the vehicle sideways.

To correct this kind of skid, the first thing you need to do is step off the brake. Doing this will allow the rear wheels to start rolling again and prevent them from sliding. Next, you need to counter-steer. This is important because the vehicle tends to continue turning as it returns on course. If you don't quickly steer the vehicle the other way, it may end up skidding in the opposite direction. Correcting a drive-wheel braking skid successfully requires a lot of practice and you can use a "skid pad" or a driving range that can comfortably fit your vehicle.

Front-Wheel skids- The majority of front-wheel skids happen when a vehicle is going too fast for certain conditions. Other times, it could be due to an imbalanced cargo that places too little weight on the front axle, or an absence of tread on the vehicle's front tires. Regardless of how much you turn the steering wheel, the front end of the vehicle will likely remain in a straight line when this kind of skid happens. If the vehicle is on a very slippery surface when it happens, it will be very difficult to steer it around a turn or curve.

Unlike drive-wheel skids, the only way to stop this kind of skid is to allow the vehicle to decelerate. Braking and/or steering so hard will do little to help the situation. To stop skidding, simply slow down the vehicle as soon as you can.

Hazards

Spotting hazards on the road is imperative for the safety of a driver on the road. There are so many things that can constitute a hazard on the road and knowing how to spot them and how to deal with them can save you a lot of trouble. The sooner you can spot hazards on the road, the sooner you will be able to respond to them safely and continue on your route unhindered.

Here are some of the things that can present hazards on your route. Knowing to look for some of these seemingly innocuous things can help you to be aware of the dangers they pose and to respond to them properly in good time.

- Confused drivers.
- Drivers whose vision is in some way obstructed as with glare or large vehicles around them.
- Delivery trucks that are temporarily parked outside of designated zones to load and/or unload.
- Parked vehicles that have people getting into or out of them, or that are parked in places or positions that are irregular.
- Pedestrians and bicyclists.
- Distracted drivers.
- Children who are running around outside and who could run into the road unexpectedly.
- People who are talking to one another and thus not paying attention to their surroundings.
- Road workers who are changing the flow of traffic or who disrupt the flow of traffic with their equipment or by being on the road while drivers are trying to pass.
- Ice cream trucks that could be servicing young children and could be drawing children to run out into the road.
- Vehicles that are broken down or stopped on the road, posing an obstruction to the flow of traffic.
- Accidents that are obstructing traffic or which are in the middle of being cleared.
- Shoppers in shopping centers or districts who may not be moving at a quick pace or keeping traffic in mind as they move about the area.
- Slow drivers who operate well under the posted speed limit.
- Drivers who are signaling a turn and taking too long to make that turn fully.
- Drivers who are in a rush to get where they are going and who are thus not driving as safely or carefully.
- Drivers who are impaired by drugs, alcohol, or fatigue.

Knowing to look for some of these things could help you to keep a cool head when they arise and it can give you a much better prediction for the dangers in seemingly everyday and harmless situations.

HAZMAT Protocol

Hazardous materials are products that pose a risk to health, safety, and property during transportation. This term is usually abbreviated into HAZMAT, which you may have seen on trucks, signs by the side of the road, and on buildings that deal with that kind of thing. These materials cover a wide range of materials such as explosives, gases, flammable substances, and other materials. Because these things can pose so many risks to so many things all at once, the government takes their regulation and the regulation of their transportation very seriously.

You may be unable to find a particular substance in the posted government regulations about hazardous materials, as there are more and more as companies develop and innovate. The characteristics of the material are what will dictate the type of placard, care, and transportation it needs.

The governmental regulations that are in place require that vehicles that are transporting specific amounts of these materials and certain types of them to display placards that clearly denote the risks that they pose. These placards are square-on-point diamond-shaped placards that are to be prominently displayed on the outside of the vehicle's trailer.

The regulations for transporting these types of goods are ever-changing, so you will want to make sure that you have checked on the latest regulations and publications from your local government to make sure you have the most up-to-date and relevant information that you will need to pass your examinations!

Hot Weather Safety

Driving during very hot weather can pose some risks to the machinery you are using. There are some things that you will want to make sure you're checking frequently in such conditions. We will cover those shortly. In addition to the things you are about to read concerning the safety of your vehicle in these conditions, it is very important that you properly cool and hydrate yourself. Make sure that you are not exposed to temperatures that make you sweat for more than about 30 minutes at a time. Make sure that you are drinking plenty of water to keep up with the sweating, and make sure to replenish with plenty of electrolytes as well.

Dehydration can cause many of the same issues and pose many of the same risks as fatigue, so it is imperative to your safety and the safety of the motorists around you that you get all the water and electrolytes that you need so you don't feel run-down or worse while you're on the road.

Things you will want to check when you are driving your commercial motor vehicle through extremely hot temperatures are as follows:

1. Check to make sure the tire, its mounting, its pressure, and the treads are looking good with no signs of expanding or damage. If the tire is too hot to touch, keep the vehicle stopped until it cools down. Driving on such a tire could pose a blow-out risk or they could simply catch fire.
2. Check your engine oil to make sure there is enough. In hot weather, you do not want any additional heat in your engine that doesn't absolutely need to be there. Check and top off frequently.
3. Make sure that you have enough coolant in your engine to help kill some of the heat. This is something you should make sure you are stocked on before you hit the road. If you find the engine is overheating when you are on your trip and you need to add more, you will need to shut off the engine, wait for it to cool, use gloves to turn the radiator cap to the first stop to alleviate pressure, add more coolant, then return the cap to its closed position.
4. Check the tightness and the integrity of your engine belts to make sure no breakage or sagging has occurred.
5. Check hoses for any signs of breakage or leakage.
6. Watch for spots in the road where tar has seeped up to the surface of the road, as this can be very slippery under your tires.

Managing Your Space

To drive as safely as you possibly can, you will need to make sure that the space around your vehicle is well-managed and that you have all the room you will need to think and to take action should something occur during travel.

Of all the space you will need around your vehicle, the space at the front of it is the most important because this is the space that you will need to use to stop and slow down should something obstruct your path in the lane ahead of you. Do your best to keep this area as clear as you can and manage it well.

A good rule to bear in mind is that you should need at least one second for every ten feet of vehicle length when you are traveling at speeds lower than 40 miles per hour. At speeds that are greater than 40 miles per hour, you should add one second to that total. For example, if you are driving a vehicle that is 40 feet long, you should leave about four seconds of stopping space ahead of your vehicle. If you are traveling over 40 miles per hour, then you will need five seconds of stopping time.

If you would like to get a feel for how much space you have ahead of your vehicle, wait for the vehicle in front of you to pass a shadow on the road or some item that is right by the side of the road. Then count by saying "One thousand and one, one thousand and two," to see how long it takes for you to pass the same spot. You can adjust as you need to and you might find that you have to redo this a few times when other motorists decide to merge into your space. If the road is slippery, you will want to greatly increase the space in front of your vehicle if you can do so.

As for the space at the back of your vehicle, you will find that other motorists will be inclined to tailgate you when you are working up to speed, especially when you're going up a hill. If you are carrying a heavy load, you will want to stay in the rightmost lane if you can and just steadily pick up speed as you can. If you are being tailgated, then you should avoid changing your position quickly. If you need to slow down or if you need to turn, make sure you signal well in advance so they can back up off your bumper and allow you to maneuver safely. If you are able to do so, increase your following distance to give you more room for the tailgater to get around you. Don't speed up, as it is safer to be tailgated at a low speed than it is to be tailgated at a high speed. Don't try to turn on your brake lights or flash your brake lights to spook the other driver. Stick to the tips above and drive safely.

Try to keep your vehicle centered in the lane so that you have as much space as possible on either side of your vehicle. You will find that you take up most of the lane, but you will want to have that extra space between your vehicle and the others on the road for safety and to minimize any interference.

Mountain Routes

When you are driving on a mountain route, gravity is going to be one of the biggest factors that you will need to consider. Whenever you are on a hill or a steep incline, you will need to consider gravity. It will slow you down considerably when you're working your way up the slope and it will increase your speed on your way down it. Both of these things require your attention and proper handling of the vehicle to maintain and control.

When you're on your way down the slope, you will want to make sure that you are not riding the brakes so much that they "fade." This means that you will have to work harder on the brake pedal to make sure that you are braking enough to keep your speed reasonable. If you continue to use the brakes hard, they will continue to fade until the vehicle can stop. In these situations, it is best to pull over to bring yourself to a complete stop if you can do so to allow the pressure to build back up.

You will want to select and maintain a safe speed when you're driving on a mountain. You don't want to choose a speed that is too fast for the total weight of the vehicle and its cargo, the length of the grade, the steepness of the grade, the road conditions, and for the weather.

If you can see a posted speed limit in the area, be sure that you do not exceed it. The braking effect of the engine is its best when it is near the governed rpms and the transmission is in the lower gears. Make sure that you don't go so fast that you need to tire out and fade your brakes before you would otherwise need them if you observed the posted speed limit.

Choosing the right gear before you start down the hill will help you to keep your speed and motion even. You will not be able to downshift once your speed has already built up from the momentum on the downgrade. If you have an automatic transmission and you try to force it into a lower gear at high speeds, you could do damage to your transmission and could lose any effect from the brakes having been applied in a higher gear.

It is important to remember that the use of brakes when you're on a long and steep downgrade is only a supplement to the braking effect of the engine. Once you've gotten your vehicle into low gear, you will need to use the following techniques for braking:

- Push on the brakes just hard enough to feel a definite but not sharp drop in speed.
- When you have gotten the vehicle slowed down to about 5 miles per hour under the posted speed limit, you can release the brakes.
- When your speed once again reaches that posted speed limit, repeat the previous steps.

Remember that the escape ramps and runaway ramps are there for you if you should lose control of your vehicle and its speed. Use them if you need them!

Reversing

Reversing with a large vehicle can be quite tricky as it is impossible for you to see everything that is happening behind your vehicle. Therefore, it is best to park in a way that allows you to pull forward when leaving whenever you can to reduce the need for reversing. However, if you do need to reverse at any point, here are some simple safety rules you can follow-

Start in the Right Position. To begin, put your vehicle in the best position that allows for safe reversing. Note that this position will mostly depend on the kind of reversing you want to do.

Look at Your Path. Before you start reversing, inspect your line of travel carefully. Step out of your vehicle and walk around, checking the vehicle's clearance overhead, to the sides, in, and near the path to be taken by the vehicle.

As a general rule, drivers are advised against backing maneuvers as they can get dangerous quite quickly. They should be avoided as much as possible and you should only plan to park your vehicle in areas you can pull out through. In the event that you have no other option or you are backing towards a loading dock, here are some tips that will help you to back your truck and trailer safely:

Look at the Steering Wheel. When reversing your tractor-trailer, keep in mind that you can use your steering wheel for assistance. This is one of the most helpful tips that every driver should learn during their training. The trick is that the steering wheel's top or the area toward your windshield signifies the truck, and the trailer is by your lap right at the bottom.

When you turn the steering wheel to the right while reversing, the top goes right and the bottom goes left. This indicates that your trailer will turn left. The bottom of your steering wheel will swing to the right if you turn it to the left. This indicates that your trailer will swing towards the right.

Get Out and Look (G.O.A.L). Many drivers tend to overlook this tip because they think observing it makes them look like they can't drive. Any time the need arises, never feel afraid or ashamed to step out of your truck and take a closer look at what you're doing. Taking this extra step when backing in an attempt to avoid hitting something is nothing to be shy of and even if somebody else has a negative thought about you doing so, you'd do well to ignore them. Each time you drive your truck, never worry about what some other driver has to say.

Do a Lot of Practice. With sufficient practice, you will be able to get a feel of how your trailer operates and also responds to your driving. As time goes on, you too will be able to back up your truck with little or no hassles. When learning how to back, it would help you to remember that no two drivers are the same and that the technique that works for other drivers may not necessarily work for you as well. When you practice enough, it will be much easier for you to discover the exact backing maneuver that works for you.

Switch Off All Distractions. Getting rid of as many distractions as possible will help you to properly focus on backing your trailer and not hitting anything. Turning off your Citizen's Band, vehicle stereo, as well as your cell phone for the minutes you need to back is always advisable.

Only Get Help From an Experienced Truck Driver. If you do seek assistance from another person to help you look behind the vehicle, also known as a spotter, make sure they're a trucker. If you can have someone behind your vehicle to help direct you, that is ideal. Having someone stand behind your vehicle allows them to see the things that you can't and to signal to you how you should proceed to avoid them. Before you start reversing your vehicle, agree on a set of hand signals that both of you can understand. Someone who has zero knowledge of driving a tractor-trailer doesn't know how to back up a trailer and may end up causing more damage than good. If someone offers to help but the person isn't a truck driver, politely decline.

Drive Slowly. Take your time, look in your mirrors, and step out of the truck to evaluate your progress. It's far preferable to take your time backing up than to speed up and collide with another tractor-trailer. Any time you have to reverse, do it as slowly as possible with the vehicle on its lowest reverse gear. This way, it is easier to correct any steering errors and also brake quickly if needed.

Use Both Side Mirrors. As you reverse, check the mirrors on both sides of the vehicle from time to time. If you're still uncertain about the path, step out of the vehicle and recheck. When using your mirrors, however, avoid fixating on one mirror but try to shift your gaze back and forth between the two mirrors.

Reverse and Steer Towards the Driver's Side. As you reverse, steer toward the driver's side to enable you to see better. It is dangerous to steer toward the right side because visibility might not be as clear. Reversing and turning towards the driver's side allows you to make use of the side window to watch your vehicle's rear end. Even if it requires driving around the block to put the vehicle in the right position, always use driver-side reversing as you are assured of added safety.

Reversing a Trailer

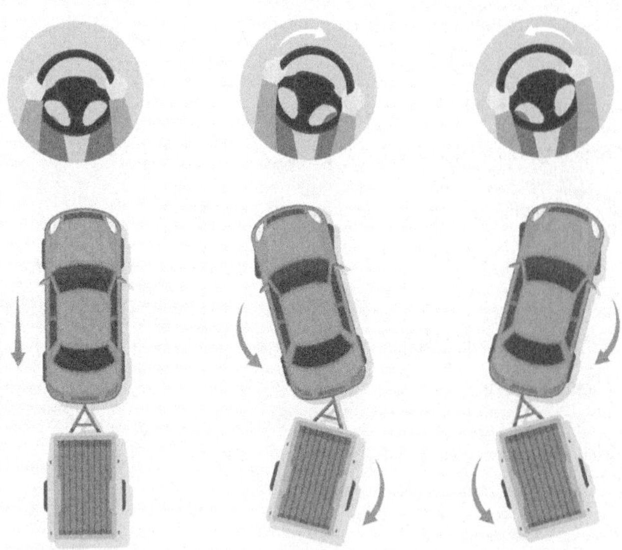

If you're reversing a straight truck, bus or car, remember that the steering wheel should be turned in the direction you want the vehicle to go. On the other hand, you need to turn the steering wheel in the opposite direction when reversing a trailer. As soon as the trailer starts turning, turn the wheel the other way to follow the trailer.

Try to position the vehicle in a way that allows you to reverse in a straight line. If you unavoidably have to reverse on a curved path, steer towards the driver's side so that you can see. Reverse slowly so that you can make any needed corrections in time before going off course.

If reversing a trailer, there are 2 extra safety rules you will need to keep in mind. They are-

Correct drift immediately. Correct the vehicle's position by steering in the direction of the drift immediately after the trailer starts getting off track.

Pull forward. When reversing, make pull-ups as needed to re-position the vehicle.

Types of Reversing

Backing up or reversing a trailer can be quite hard to do, even for experienced truck drivers. There will definitely be days where it may seem like backing just isn't working for you but with sufficient practice, your backing skills don't have to make or break your career as a truck driver. While you may never completely master doing it, practicing will help increase your confidence, thereby helping you to get more comfortable with backing your truck.

Depending on your location, you may be asked to perform one or more types of backing during your CDL test. The only difference will be the use of cones instead of vehicles. Below are the five major kinds of truck backing, and how you can perform them successfully:

Straight line backing- This is the easiest maneuver to grasp and is required for all other backing techniques. All that is required is for you to drive straight ahead and backward without touching any cones. When tension is high, though, anything can happen, and people occasionally fail this section of the test.

HOW TO DO A STRAIGHT LINE BACKING:

- To ensure that the truck has enough maneuvering distance to finish the exercise properly, pull forward and place the steer tires on the boundary start.
- Idle forward in third gear while keeping the equipment between the two lines.
- Reverse the truck and let go of the clutch, allowing the equipment to back up on its own.
- Keep an eye on your mirrors to make sure the trailer's rail stays parallel to the lines as you back the vehicle.
- If any modifications are required, steer towards the source of the problem by keeping an eye on the back of the trailer. So, if the trailer is drifting to the left, turn to the left and wait about 5 seconds before returning to the center, allowing the truck to get back underneath the trailer.
- On the right, it's the same thing. If the trailer is retreating to the right, steer to the right for about 5 seconds before returning to the center.
- Once the tractor and trailer have cleared the rear cone/line, press the clutch and come to a complete stop.

Alley dock backing- This takes place at loading docks when the driver has to back in from between two vehicles or off the street. It involves backing up while turning into a location that is 90 degrees to the tractor.

HOW TO DO AN ALLEY DOCK BACKING:

- The first step is to double-check that you have enough room to reverse the trailer in. The width of a conventional trailer is about eight and a half feet.
- One suggestion instructors typically give is to draw forward a little further and then cut a lesser amount over a longer distance.
- Just until you can see the landing pad foot in your left rear mirror, maneuver or cut the back of the trailer to the right, just until the point when you can view the landing pad foot in the vehicle's left rear mirror.
- Lean out the left window and take a look back.
- Adjust slightly as the trailer returns, then follow it into the gap.
- As your trailer approaches the two parked trucks, step out and take a look around, paying close attention to your blind side spot at the back.

- Back up some more into the space, steering towards your right where you can gauge the distance better.
- Lastly, take extra caution when performing this procedure to avoid hitting the driver's side mirror on the truck parked beside you.

Parallel Parking: Just like parallel parking a regular car, this means backing into a space along a curb or dock, and it is more difficult to learn while driving a tractor-trailer. This is because the truck must fit perfectly into a measured area and must also remain within specific borders along with its trailer.

HOW TO DO A PARALLEL PARKING:

- The parking space measures about 12 feet in width and 15 feet in length, which is longer than the truck and trailer, and also means that you have sufficient space to carry out the procedure.
- Continue past the parking spot until the trailer's rear is parallel to the front cone.
- Turn the wheel as far as it will go clockwise (right). Take your foot off the brake and roll back while counting to three with the vehicle in reverse.
- Start steering back (counter-clockwise/left) until the tractor and trailer are in line.
- Back up until the back of the trailer crosses the parking space's boundary, then turn counter-clockwise (left). The trailer will automatically turn into the box.
- Steer the wheel clockwise (right) until the trailer is 85 percent within the box as soon as the rear passenger axle is in the box.
- To get back in alignment with the trailer, turn counter-clockwise (left) while pulling ahead.
- Set the brakes, exit the vehicle, and inspect the alignment.

Offset Backing: This maneuver involves pulling forward, and then backwards into a lane on your left side or right side. The examiner will tell you where exactly you need to back into but note that there will be boundaries you're not allowed to cross. Be sure to practice as much as you can especially if you are a new driver as it can be tricky to keep the vehicle within those boundaries.

HOW TO DO AN OFFSET BACKING:

- The track typically measures about 180 feet long and 24 feet broad for this activity. Two lanes, each 12 feet wide by 40 feet deep, run through the course.
- You will need to pull straight forward from one alley to the course boundary, and back into the second alley.
- Pull forward from the left alley to the far end cone. You have two free pull-ups and two opportunities to get out and look, or "G.O.A.L." before any points are deducted.
- Put the vehicle in reverse when you reach the forward cone boundary, but before you start rolling, turn it hard counter-clockwise (left) as far as possible.
- Remove your foot from the clutch and brake, and then let the vehicle roll backward. Wait three seconds while it is doing so before turning hard right until the tractor and trailer are properly aligned. On the course, they will be in a diagonal line.
- You should be able to see the cones in the middle row in your left mirror after the tractor and trailer are lined up.
- Reverse until the trailer's rear crosses the extended imaginary center line. Start turning into the alley at this point.

- Turn the wheel three times clockwise (right). Correct turn by steering counterclockwise (Left) when the trailer is 90 degrees inside the alley. The truck and trailer will be able to re-align as a result of this.
- Reverse straight into the alley until the tractor's snout passes through the front set of cones.
- Apply the brakes and sound the horns

When you are reversing your vehicle, you must be absolutely certain of anything that is behind you. Look out the window at the side of your vehicle and judge the path of your tires. Like every other aspect of driving your commercial motor vehicle, make sure you are paying attention and exercising good judgment and caution!

Shifting Gears

Shifting gears in your vehicle is important. If you are unable to get into the right gear, you will have a much harder time assuming and keeping control of your vehicle. There are manual and automatic transmissions, as well as retarders which reduce the need for brakes.

Manual Transmissions

HOW TO UPSHIFT

If your vehicle transmission is manual, you will want to use the basic method for shifting up. Most heavy vehicles with an unsynchronized manual transmission will require double clutching to change gears. Double clutching is not required on a synchronized manual transmission.

- Release the accelerator, push in the clutch and shift into neutral at the same time.
- Release the clutch.
- Let the engine and the gears slow down to the rpm required for the next gear up. This is something that will take you a bit of progress.
- Push in the clutch and press the accelerator at the same time.
- Release the clutch and press in the accelerator at the same time.

Double clutching and shifting gears are things that will take a bit of practice to master. If you keep your vehicle in neutral for too long, you might find it harder to shift the vehicle into the next gear. It's important not to force it in such a case. Simply return it to neutral, release the clutch, increase the engine speed, and try again.

You can know when it's time to shift up using two means:

- The speed of the engine (rpm)
- The speed on the road (mph)

Whichever method you use, you will need to use the sound of the engine and you will need practice to get the hang of it.

HOW TO DOWNSHIFT

Here are the steps for the basic procedure to use when shifting down:

- Release the accelerator, push in the clutch, and shift to neutral all at once.
- Release the clutch.
- Press down on the accelerator, increase engine and gear speed to the rpm required for a lower gear.
- Push in the clutch and shift to a lower gear at the same time.
- Release the clutch and press the accelerator at the same time.

Being able to downshift does require prior knowledge of when to shift and how to do so, so make sure you are well practiced! You will want to downshift when you are starting down a hill or when you are entering a curve.

Multi-Speed Rear Axles and Auxiliary Transmissions

Multi-speed rear axles and auxiliary transmissions are present on a large number of vehicles to provide them with extra gears. There is typically a selector knob or switch on the gearshift lever of the main transmission. There are many different shift patterns, so make sure you learn the right one for your vehicle so you know how to use it when you need it.

Automatic Transmissions

Certain vehicles are equipped with automatic transmissions which allow you to choose a low range to get better engine braking as you go down grades. The lower ranges stop the transmission from shifting higher than the chosen gear unless you have already exceeded the governor rpm.

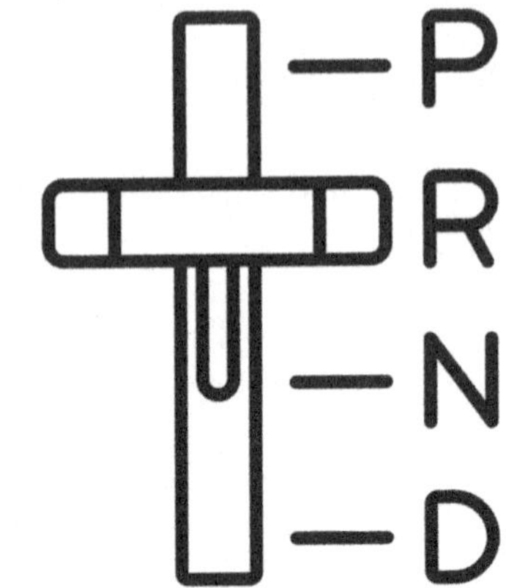

Retarders

Retarders are devices that can be turned on and off to reduce your need to apply the vehicle's brakes. With them, you have another way of slowing down your vehicle and also reducing brake wear. The 4 main types are the engine, electric, exhaust, and hydraulic. Certain vehicles allow you to adjust the retarding power as needed. When switched on, they apply braking power to the vehicle's drive wheels when you completely step off the accelerator pedal. Retarders can be quite noisy so if your vehicle is equipped with one, ensure you only use them where permitted.

It is important to note that retarders may cause skidding if your wheels have poor traction. Therefore, when driving on a snowy, wet, or icy surface, always turn off the retarder.

Speed Control

Controlling the speed of your vehicle, whether you're on a steep incline or not, is a huge part of ensuring the safety of yourself and the other motorists around you. You must make sure that you observe the posted speed limits, that you think with the weight of your vehicle, including your load, and that you keep firm control of your vehicle within those limits.

Don't allow yourself to give in to the pressures of other drivers, and don't allow the long hours on the road to keep you from observing and obeying the posted speed limits.

Steering

When you are driving, you must keep both of your hands on the steering wheel. If you hit something in the road unexpectedly, if something comes into your path, or if you suddenly need to regain control of the vehicle, you will need both of your hands on the wheel. Keeping both of your hands on the wheel will allow you to respond within a moment's notice.

If you have other things in your hand or if you have to change your position to resume steering the vehicle to regain control, then you will lose precious seconds of control that will keep you from being able to get out of the situation as safely as possible.

Using Your Mirrors to Help You Out of a Bind

Using your mirrors when you are in a bind can help you to see as much as possible and can help you to get a better perspective on what you need to do to get out of it. Using your mirrors is something that should become automatic for you, no matter where you are on the road or otherwise. You must keep your eye on the areas that are around your vehicle and you must watch for other motorists, obstructions, and other things that will allow you to maintain the best control possible on your vehicle.

If you are watching your mirrors when you are driving on the highway, you will be able to know at a moment's notice who is in the lanes on either side of you. This will allow you to merge quickly if you need to or at least to know what the best possible path would be in just such an event. Watching your mirrors while you're driving is a great practice to keep.

When driving, you need to be able to see what is happening behind you and at the sides. Be sure to check your mirrors at regular intervals, and even use them more regularly in special situations. Check your mirrors quickly as you drive and try to understand the environment around you before moving. As you drive, keep your eyes on your mirrors as well as the road ahead of you. Avoid focusing too long on your mirrors as you may end up traveling for a distance without knowing what is happening in front of you.

The majority of large vehicles come with curved mirrors which allow you to see a wider area compared to flat mirrors. While this feature is usually very helpful when driving, you need to remember that objects appear smaller and farther away than they really are in convex mirrors.

Before starting any trip, you need to check that your mirrors are properly adjusted and this can only be accurate when the trailer is in a straight position. Check each mirror and adjust it carefully so that each of them shows some of the vehicle's parts. Adjusting the mirror this way will serve as a reference point you can use to judge the position of other images.

As you drive, check your mirrors regularly to keep an eye on traffic, as well as your vehicle. When looking out for traffic, check the mirrors to look out for vehicles behind you and on either side. In case of an emergency, you may need to confirm if it is safe for you to quickly switch lanes. Your mirrors will help you to see overtaking vehicles in such situations. However, there are areas known as "blind spots" that will be hidden from your mirrors. Using the mirrors regularly allows you to see the exact position of other vehicles around you, including when they move into your blind spots.

Your vehicles' mirrors will also come in handy for checking your tires. It is a good way to notice a tire fire quickly; and if carrying open cargo, your mirrors will also help you spot loose chains, ropes, straps, or flapping tarps quickly. During special situations like tight maneuvers, turns, lane changes, and merges, you will have to check your mirrors even more regularly to ensure you drive safely.

As you change lanes, check to be sure that no vehicle is about to drive past you or beside you. For lane changes, you should always use your mirrors after signaling to check that there is no one in your blind spot; before changing lanes to make sure there is enough space; right after starting to change lanes to be very sure of a clear path, and after changing lanes. At any turn, use your mirrors to see that your vehicle's rear end is clear and will not hit anything. Mirrors should also be used when merging to ensure your vehicle can conveniently and safely move into the gap in traffic. When in situations where you're driving in close quarters, use your mirrors often to be sure the vehicle has sufficient clearance.

What Is a Vehicle Blind Spot and How Can You Handle It?

Driving with blind spots can and often does result in accidents, which can be a very unpleasant situation. Fortunately, the presence of blind spots does not rule out the possibility of maintaining road safety.

A blind spot is defined as an area around the vehicle that the driver is unable to see. This means that neither the outer rearview mirror (ORVM) nor the inner rearview mirror (IRVM) can show these locations. The driver's inability to see these areas makes it quite hard to know if there are other vehicles, pedestrians, or other obstacles in these blind spots. Here are some pointers to help you deal with blind spots and safeguard your life, while also looking out for other road users' safety.

The first and most important aspect of managing a vehicle's blind spot while driving is determining the exact location of its blind spots. This can be done by quickly scanning the outer rearview mirror to determine what you cannot see. It will be easier for you to exercise necessary caution when you have this knowledge.

Before driving, double-check that the outer and inner rearview mirrors are properly adjusted and that you have the widest field of view. It's a good idea to look out the windows to see whether there's a vehicle, a person, or anything else in your blind spot. This is particularly useful before you change lanes or directions. To be a safe driver, you must first recognize that every vehicle, including your own, has a blind spot. You should always consider this while driving; ideally, this translates to ensuring there is sufficient space when overtaking another vehicle and similar safe driving practices.

Visibility

Visibility is a huge part of driving safely. You must make certain that you can be seen and that you can see as far as possible. commercial motor vehicles are required to have many reflectors, lights, lamps, signals, and reflective tapes that allow other drivers to see you in the nighttime hours or in the event of inclement weather.

Seeing other drivers when you are in your commercial motor vehicle can be very difficult as well. Make sure that you are checking around your vehicle while you're in transit for people that may have slipped in around you without you noticing.

Try to keep your windows, mirrors, and windshield clear so you can see the most of the world and traffic around your vehicle. The more you can see, the more you can know about what is coming or what could be coming. The more you can see, the more you can safely avoid! You have to look far enough ahead because switching or stopping can take up a lot of distance. When you're aware of all that is happening at all sides of the vehicle, you'll be sure that you have enough room to maneuver safely.

The majority of commercial motor vehicle drivers choose to look a minimum of 12 to 15 seconds ahead which means looking ahead of the distance to be covered in that amount of time. Typically, this should be about one block when driving at a slower speed. At highway speed, the distance should be about a quarter of a mile. It is best to look that far ahead because you may need to switch lanes or brake too quickly if you don't. However, having to look 12 to 15 seconds ahead does not mean that all your attention should be on objects that are closer to your vehicle. For the best driving practices, try to shift your attention back and forth, observing both near and far areas as you drive.

Looking out for traffic is also a good way to maintain proper visibility when driving. Watch out for turning vehicles, vehicles that are driving onto the highway, or those that are coming into your lane. Observing such things far enough ahead allows you to switch lanes and adjust the vehicle's speed as necessary before encountering any problems. If approaching a traffic light that has been green for some time, note that the light will likely change before your vehicle gets there. In such situations, start stepping on your brake pedal and be ready to stop the vehicle.

The condition of the road you're on will also affect your driving and you should be observant of any curves or hills along your route. Generally, you should be on the lookout for anything that may require you to change lanes or slow down. In doing this, traffic signs and signals can be very helpful as they can alert you to road conditions that may need you to change speed beforehand.

Winter Driving

Driving during the winter months and in cold weather, you will want to make sure that you are checking things on your vehicle that could present problems thanks to the cold. Here is a list of the things that you should keep your eye on during those months to make sure that you are keeping your vehicle in the best possible condition to complete your routes and deliveries.

When you are driving in the winter, you will need to check the following items carefully:

Antifreeze Amount and Coolant Level- Check to make sure the vehicle's cooling system is full and that there is enough antifreeze to prevent freezing. A special coolant tester can be used to inspect this.

Heating and Defrosting Equipment- The defrosters have to be functional as they are essential for safe driving. Not only should you ensure that the vehicle's heater is working, but you should also know how to operate it. Check how to use other heaters like fuel tanks, mirror, or battery box heaters beforehand if you think you might need them.

Wipers and Washers- The windshield wiper blades have to be in good working condition and should ideally press hard enough against the window to wipe it clean. If not, the wipers may be unable to sweep snow off correctly. Ensure that the washer works and that sufficient washing fluid is in the reservoir. To keep the washer liquid from freezing, use the windshield washer antifreeze. If your wipers fail or your visibility is hindered while driving, it is best to look for a safe spot to park and then correct the problem.

Tires- You need to be sure that there is enough tread on your tires to provide traction to push the rig through snow and on wet surfaces. It is especially important to have sufficient tread during winter conditions. There must be a minimum of 4/32 inch tread depth in all major grooves of your front tires, and a minimum of 2/32 inch depth on all other tires. You can make use of a gauge to check if the tread on your tires is safe for driving.

Tire Chains- Having tire chains handy may sound unnecessary but some conditions are impossible to drive in without them, even to get to a safe spot. To avoid any dire situations, always have extra crosslinks and the right amount of tire chains in your vehicle. Ensure that they fit the drive tires, and inspect for broken, worn, or bent hooks, side chains, and cross-links. It is advised that you learn how to use the chains before there is an actual need for them.

Lights and Reflectors- Your lights and reflectors need to be properly cleaned as they are even more important in bad weather conditions. Keep an eye on them as you drive in such conditions to be sure that they remain clean and are working correctly.

Steps, Handholds, and Deck Plates- To reduce the possibility of the car slipping, you need to get rid of all snow and ice that may be present on these surfaces.

Windows and Mirrors- Before starting each trip, ensure that there is no snow, ice, or other obstructions on the vehicle's mirrors, windows, and windshields. If needed, you can use a defroster, scraper, or snow brush.

Radiator Shutters and Winter Front- Ice should be removed from the radiator shutters and the winter front should not be too tightly closed. The vehicle's engine may end up overheating and stopping if the winter front is shut too tightly, or the radiator shutters freeze shut.

Exhaust System- Leaking exhaust systems could be especially dangerous when there is poor ventilation with the windows rolled up. A loose connection could lead to a leakage of carbon monoxide in your vehicle that can cause you to feel sleepy, or even kill you if the amount is large enough. Be sure to inspect your vehicle's exhaust system before each trip for signs of leakage and loose parts.

Driving in Fog

Fog can happen at any time while driving and it can be very dangerous if it does while you're on the highway. This is because it occurs suddenly in most situations and can cause rapid deterioration of visibility. For you to maneuver your vehicle successfully in such conditions, you need to watch out for fog and be ready to reduce the vehicle's speed. It can be dangerous to maintain the vehicle's original speed, assuming that the fog will thin out after entering it. If you're driving and weather conditions suddenly worsen, the best advice is to stop driving immediately. Instead, pull off into a truck stop or rest area and wait until visibility improves.

In case you have no other options but to keep driving, below are some things you should do to make the journey less tasking:

- Pay attention to and obey all fog-related warning signs.
- Bring your vehicle to a slow speed before driving into a foggy area.
- Switch on your fog lights and low-beam headlights even during the daytime to improve visibility. Watch out for other motorists who may forget to switch their vehicles' lights on.
- Turn on the vehicle's 4-way emergency flashers to help vehicles approaching from behind notice you better.
- Look out for vehicles parked on the side of the road as headlights or taillights up ahead may not necessarily indicate how the road goes in front of you.
- Use the roadside highway reflectors as guides to determine how the road may curve up ahead.

- As visibility will be significantly reduced, listen for signs for incoming traffic you can't see.
- Avoid overtaking other vehicles.
- Unless there is an absolute need for it, do not stop your vehicle along the roadside.

Driving on Slippery Surfaces

If you happen to find yourself on a slippery road, the trick is to drive as smoothly and slowly as possible. However, you should not be driving at all if it is excessively slippery, and should stop at the first safe spot you can find.

When starting out at first, drive gently and slowly so that you can get a proper feel of the road. You will also need to check for any ice that may be on the road, especially when driving on overpasses and bridges. You can determine if ice has formed on a road by looking out for a spray from other vehicles. The absence of one is a clear sign of ice formation on the road. Aside from this, ice on the vehicle's wiper blades and mirrors indicates that there will likely be ice on the road as well.

All turning and braking should be as gentle as possible to match the present conditions and you should not step on the brake pedal harder than is needed. The use of speed retarders or engine brakes should also be avoided as they can lead to skidding of the driving wheels on slippery surfaces.

Another thing you will need to do is to adjust your speed accordingly. Unless it is very necessary, you should hold back from overtaking slower vehicles. Drive slowly and ensure that you look ahead far enough to maintain a steady speed. Slowing down and then speeding up should be avoided as much as possible in such conditions. To be on the safe side, approach curves slowly and don't apply the brakes while you're in a curve. Bear in mind that the road will get even more slippery as the temperature rises to a melting point and you will have to slow down more.

As much as possible in such conditions, avoid driving alongside other vehicles and maintain a longer following distance instead. If there is a traffic jam ahead, stop the vehicle until it clears up or slows down. Although it might require more effort, try to predict stops early enough and bring the vehicle to a gradual slowdown. By doing this, you eliminate the need to slam down on the brakes suddenly, which could be very dangerous given the situation. Be on the lookout for sand and salt trucks, as well as snowplows, and give them enough allowance.

If you're driving in deep standing water or heavy rain, your brakes will definitely get wet which can lead to weak, grabbing, or unevenly applied brakes. When this happens, it can cause wheel lockups, absence of braking power, pulling to one side, and jackknife if a trailer is being pulled. The best way to avoid any issues resulting from wet brakes is to avoid driving through flowing water or deep puddles whenever possible. In case there's no way around doing so, do these 5 things to control your vehicle better:

- Slow down the vehicle and put the transmission in low gear.

- Put on the brakes gently to press linings against brake drums/discs and prevent water, silt, mud, and sand from getting in.
- Increase the engine rpm and cross the water with light pressure on the brakes.
- Keep light pressure on brakes for a short distance to allow them to heat up and dry out after crossing the water.
- When it is safe, carry out a test stop. Look behind to ensure that no vehicle is following and then apply the brakes to be sure that they work correctly. If they don't, you can dry them out further by keeping light pressure on them as described above. Be cautious when doing this so that you don't apply excess pressure on the accelerator and brake as it can lead to overheating of the brake linings and drums.

Vocabulary & Keywords

Air Brakes - Air brakes use a pressurized air system to bring a commercial motor vehicle to a stop. There is a required Air Brakes Knowledge Test that one must pass to demonstrate their skills when using a vehicle equipped with them.

Brake Fade - The reduction in stopping power that can come from the repeated or sustained use of the brakes, particularly on an incline.

Cargo Tank - A vehicle that is certified to carry certain types of hazardous materials.

Carrier - This term is used to refer to the individual or the company who is responsible for the transport of a load from one location to another.

Consignee - This is the term for the entity or party that is responsible for the financial burden of the shipment, typically the recipient.

Double Clutch - The action of depressing the clutch twice while changing gears in a manual transmission vehicle that has no synchronizer.

Escape Ramp - These are often placed on steep grades. They are wide, dirt areas onto which a truck may pull if they have lost power in their brakes. It slopes upward to allow the truck to come to a stop safely.

FMCSA (Federal Motor Carrier Safety Administration) - This administration is the one that provides regulations for the US commercial trucking industry.

Freight Container - A reusable container for freight that has a volume of at least 64 cubic feet. Primarily intended for the containment of units of freight in transit.

Gross Mass/ Gross Weight - This is the total weight of a package or freight including the container and its contents.

Hazard- A feature or obstacle that is potentially risky or dangerous, and must be avoided by the driver.

HAZMAT (Hazardous Materials) - This is the label given to materials that pose a threat to health, safety, property, or the environment. These materials require special care and a specific understanding of how to care for and transport them safely.

Limited Quantity - The maximum allowable amount for a specified substance, material, cargo, or inventory.

Load - That which is being carried by the truck and its driver; cargo, freight.

PSI (Pounds Per Square Inch) - The unit of measurement used for calculating how much air is in the tires or the brake system.

RPM (Revolutions Per Minute) - This measures how many times the crankshaft of the vehicle is making full turns per minute. This tells you the "engine speed."

Runaway Ramp - These are often placed on steep grades. They are wide, dirt areas onto which a truck may pull if they have lost power in their brakes. It slopes upward to allow the truck to come to a stop safely.

Sleep Debt - Sleep debt or sleep deficit is the cumulative effect of not getting enough sleep. A large sleep debt may lead to mental or physical fatigue.

CHAPTER - 4

COMMUNICATION ON THE ROAD

The Importance of Communication on the Road

Communicating with the other drivers on the road around you is very important. You must know that if the other drivers on the road around you cannot see you or cannot tell what you're about to do, the risk for accidents increases significantly. Imagine if people merged into other lanes of traffic without signaling, changing speeds, or even looking to see if there was someone there! Allowing other drivers to see you and to discern your intentions in your maneuvers is a form of communication that can save lives!

Communicating Your Presence

The droning of the road on long trips could stop other motorists from noticing that you are there, so communicating your presence could go a long way to help others to know that you are there. If you're about to pass someone, don't assume that they can see you. Flash your lights or tap your horn lightly if you think that someone might not see you or if the visibility conditions are poor. If it is hard to see, then you will want to make sure that you are using your headlights and your signals to show others that you are there.

If you need to pull over by the side of the road to stop for any reason, make sure that you use your hazard signals. This will give other drivers the chance to see you before they come close enough to cause another, worse emergency.

Communicating Your Intentions

Other drivers on the road don't have a means of knowing what you are going to do before you do it. For them to know that, you will need to tell them. Signaling will allow you to tell the other motorists what it is that you intend to do and there are some general rules for signaling that you should know. One of the best to know is that if you would like to warn the drivers behind you that you need to come to a stop, you can ease onto the brakes slowly to activate your brake lights, then ease slowly onto the brake to slow as you need to.

You must use the signals that you have on your vehicle to let people know that you are intending to move in one direction or another. You must use your speed to let people know whether you are intending to slow down or to continue speeding up.

One of the things that you must do your best to avoid is directing traffic. Many drivers will hold up a hand and wave to tell other motorists if they should proceed or

pass. This is something you should avoid because if there is an accident as a result of these gestures, you could be found to be at fault for the damage and the accident.

What Is CB Radio Code or Lingo?

CB radios have a long and illustrious history in trucking. Before the advent of email and mobile phones, the CB radio was a wonderful way to communicate with friends all over the world. One of the things that distinguish CB Radio users from others is that they have their own lingo which is also known as trucker lingo. To communicate with your friends or even strangers effectively, you must understand the CB radio code as well as the CB terminology. For instance, different number codes mean different things in the world of CB lingo.

These radios are a valuable asset, especially for truckers, since they transmit information to other truckers while on the road. It also allows them to communicate with their home base. You also need to remember that the CB radio might be beneficial in an emergency case when a cell phone or the Internet is unavailable. The CB will continue to work even then, and you will be able to communicate with the base.

Truckers, in particular, need to be well-versed in CB codes and terminology so that others can understand them. The CB radio code is a concise form of communication when driving your vehicle. Below is a quick list of CB 10 codes, along with their meanings so that you, too, can know how and when they are used.

10-1: Poor reception/ Receiving poorly (I can't hear you).

10-2: Proper Reception/Receiving well (I can hear you).

10-3: Stop transmitting (Stop speaking).

10-4: Affirmative/ I concur/Okay/ Message Received.

10-5: Relay message (Pass it on).

10-6 : Busy/Hold on a second/Stand by.

10-7: Out of Service/ Leaving air (You're going out of range or no longer using radio).

10-8: In-service (You've just signed on or entered range).

10-9: Reiterate the message (Pardon?).

10-10: The transmission has been completed/ Standing by.

10-11: Speaking too quickly (Take a breath and try again).

10-12: Visitors are present.

10-13: Advise on weather/road conditions.

10-16: Make a pickup at... (hitching a load).

10-17: Urgent Business (Pay attention to what I'm about to say).

10-18: Is there anything you can do for us?

10-19: There isn't anything for you/Return to base (No).

10-20: What's your location?/ My location is...

10-21: Make a phone call.

10-22: Report in-person to...

10-23: Be on the lookout/ Stand by (pay attention).

10-24: I finished the last assignment.

10-25: Can you contact...?

10-26: Disregard the last statement/Cancel last message/Ignore.

10-27: I'm driving to channel...

10–28: Identify your station.

10-29: Contact time is up.

10-30: Does not comply with FCC regulations.

10-32: I'll do a radio check on you.

10-33: Traffic emergency/Emergency traffic at this station.

10-34: There's an issue at this station/Help needed.

10-35: Private information.

10-36: This is the correct time...

10-38: An ambulance is needed at...

10-39: Your message has been received.

10-41: Please switch to channel...

10-42: There's a traffic accident at...

10-43: There is a traffic jam at...

10-44: I'd like to leave you a message.

10-45: All units(within range), please report.

10-50: Break channel.

10-62: Cannot copy, use a phone.

10-65: I'm waiting for your next message/assignment.

10-67: All units comply.

10-70: Fire at...

10-73: Speed Trap at...

10-75: You're interfering with the airwaves.

10-77: Negative Contact.

10-84: This is my phone number...

10-85: My home address is ...

10-91: Speak closer to the microphone.

10-92: Your transmitter is out of sync.

10-93: Search for my frequency on this channel.

10-94: Please provide me with a long count.

10-95: Send a dead carrier for five seconds.

10-99: The task has been finished, and all units secured.

10-100: Need to use the restroom.

10-200: Police are needed at ...

CB Radio Slangs

- *Affirmative*- Yes.
- *All locked up*- The weigh station is now closed.
- *Anteater*- The Kenworth T-600, which was one of the earliest trucks with an aerodynamic design and was named after its slanted hood. Aardvark is another name for it.
- *Alligator*- A piece of roadside tire, generally a recap from an exploded tire, that resembles an alligator on the road. These alligators are dangerous and should be avoided as much as possible. They can "bite you" if you run over them, bouncing back up and damaging hoses or belts, fuel crossover lines, or the body of your tractor. They can also bounce up and collide with another car, resulting in a collision. Alligator bait is several small tire pieces, and a baby alligator is a small piece of tire. It's also known as a "gator."
- *Back door*- Something is at your back.
- *Back it down*- Drive slowly.

- *Backed out of it*- No longer able to maintain speed and requiring a downshift. When a truck is climbing a steep slope and the driver has to ease up on the accelerator for any reason, they will lose any momentum they had and will have to downshift.
- *Back row*- In a truck stop, the last rows of parking.
- *Bambi*- A deer, whether it's dead or living.
- *Base station/unit*- A strong CB radio installed in a fixed location.
- *Bear*- A law enforcement officer of any rank, but most commonly a state trooper or highway patrol.
- *Bear bait*- A speeding vehicle, usually a four-wheeler, that can be used to shield other speeding vehicles following it.
- *Bear bite*- A speeding ticket.
- *Bear den/cave*- The headquarters or station of a law enforcement agency.
- *Bear in the air*- A law enforcement aircraft that can be used to keep an eye on the traffic and speeds below.
- *Bear in the bushes*- Law enforcement (at whichever level) is hiding someplace, most likely with a traffic radar gun.
- *Billy big rigger*- Another word for a "super trucker" who brags about themself or their flashy, fast truck.
- *Bingo cards*- These cards had stamps from each state in which a motor carrier operated; they are no longer in use, having been replaced by the Single State Registration System (SSRS).
- *Bedbugger*- Can be used to refer to a household moving business or the individual household mover.
- *Big R*- A truck for the highway.
- *Big road*- It usually refers to the interstate, although it can also refer to any major roadway.
- *Big truck*- This term refers to a tractor-trailer or 18-wheeler.
- *Bird dog*- A radar detector.
- *Big word*- When referring to weigh stations, the term "closed" is used. In bright lighting, there is usually a large sign in front of the weigh station stating whether it is open or closed. You can't determine what the word means from afar, but you can typically tell whether it's a big or tiny word. As a result, you'll know the weigh station is closed when you hear "the big word is out."
- *Black eye*- There's a headlight out.
- *Bobtail*- Driving the tractor without the trailer.
- *Boogie*- The transmission's top gear.
- *Boulevard*- The interstate highway system.
- *Brake check*- A traffic jam is ahead of you, which will require urgent slowing or stopping.
- *Break*- If the radio station is busy, say "break-19" to obtain access to the channel and start talking.
- *Breaking up*- You have a weak or fading signal.
- *Brush your teeth and comb your hair*- Using a radar gun to shoot vehicles.
- *Bubba*- What you nickname another driver, usually in jest.
- *Bull dog*- A Mack truck, to be precise.
- *Bull frog*- This is an ABF vehicle.
- *Bull hauler*- A livestock transporter.
- *Bumper sticker*- A car that is following too closely. Sometimes referred to as a "hitchhiker."
- *Bundled out*- Heavily loaded, or at maximum capacity.
- *Buster brown*- A UPS driver or a UPS truck.
- *Cabbage*- A steep slope grade in Oregon.

- *Cabover*- Cab-Over-the-Engine (COE) tractors are referred to as COE tractors.
- *Cash register*- A tollbooth.
- *Checking ground pressure*- The weigh station is open for business, and vehicles are being driven across the scales.
- *Chicken coop*- A weigh station which is sometimes known as a "coop."
- *Chicken lights*- The additional lights on a trucker's truck and trailer.
- *Chicken hauler/truck*- A massive, extravagant vehicle; a big, traditional tractor with many lights and chrome. A person who transports live chickens is also known as a chicken hauler.
- *Comedian*- The stretch of space between opposing traffic lanes known as the median.
- *Container*- Intermodal transportation or refers to an overseas container.
- *Come-a-part engine*- The vehicle engine is a Cummins.
- *Come back*- An offer to converse with the other driver. When you can not hear the last transmission, you might use this.
- *Come on*- Telling another driver that you can hear him calling and that they should go ahead and speak.
- *Comic book*- The vehicle log book.
- *Convoy*- A convoy of trucks on their way somewhere.
- *Copy*- Transmission has been acknowledged, consented to, or understood.
- *Cornflake*- A Consolidated Freightways truck is referred to by this term.
- *County Mountie*- A sheriff's deputy who is part of the county police force.
- *Covered wagon*- A flatbed trailer with sidewalls and a tarp used.
- *Crotch rocket*- Not a Harley-Davidson, but a motorcycle engineered for speed.
- *Deadhead*- Towing a trailer that isn't loaded.
- *Destruction*- Building of roads.
- *Diesel car*- A tractor that is semi-automated.
- *Diesel cop*- Commercial vehicle enforcement officer from the Department of Transportation.
- *Donkey*- Behind you.
- *Do what?*- I didn't hear or understand what you were saying.
- *Double nickel*- 55 mph.
- *Doubles*- This term refers to a pair of double trailers.
- *Drawing lines*- Filling out your log book.
- *Driver*- How drivers address other drivers on the CB, especially if their CB handle is unknown.
- *Driving award*- A speeding ticket.
- *Downstroke*- On a slope, driving downwards, downhill.
- *Dragon wagon*- A tow truck.
- *Dragonfly*- A truck that has no power, specifically while traveling uphill.
- *Dry box*- A freight trailer that is not refrigerated. Also known as a dry van.
- *18-wheeler*- Any tractor-trailer.
- *85th Street*- Interstate 85, which is a major highway.
- *Evil Knievel*- A security officer on a motorcycle.
- *Eyeball*- To look at something.
- *Feeding the bears*- Paying a citation or a ticket.
- *Fingerprint*- Unloading a trailer by oneself.

- *Flip-flop*- A U-turn or a return trip.
- *FM*- A radio with AM and FM frequencies.
- *42*- Yes or Okay.
- *Four-letter word*- Open, used to refer to weigh stations being open or closed.
- *Four-wheeler*- Any passenger vehicle, including cars and pickup trucks.
- *Freight shaker*- A Freightliner truck.
- *Front door*- In front of you.
- *Full-grown bear*- State trooper, or the highway patrol.
- *Garbage hauler*- Produce carriers or a produce load.
- *Gear jammer*- A driver who frequently accelerates and decelerates.
- *General mess of crap*- A GMC pickup truck.
- *Georgia overdrive*- On a downhill, putting the transmission into neutral to drive very fast. Doing this is not advised.
- *Go-go juice*- Diesel fuel.
- *Good neighbor*- A common expression used to express gratitude to another driver.
- *Got my nightgown on*- I'm in my sleeper, and I'm ready to doze off.
- *Go to company*- When you instruct another driver in your firm to use the company's allocated CB channel. This allows drivers to discuss company business or personal topics without dominating channel 19.
- *Go to the Harley*- Switch to channel 1 on your CB.
- *Got your ears on?*- Are you paying attention?
- *Gouge in it*- Go quickly, pump the throttle, step on it, etc.
- *Granny lane*- On a multi-lane highway or the interstate, this is the right, slower lane.
- *Greasy*- Icy or slippery.
- *Greasy side up*- A vehicle that is flipped over.
- *Green stamps*- Money.
- *Grossed out*- The gross vehicle weight is set to its maximum capacity, which is usually 80,000 pounds.
- *Ground pressure*- The weight of the vehicle.
- *Gumball machine*- The lights on a patrol car's roof.
- *Hammer down*- Step on it fast.
- *Hammer lane*- The passing lane on the left side of traffic
- *Hand, Han*- What a driver may refer to another driver as. It comes from the term "farmhand" and implies "assistant" or "coworker."
- *Handle (CB handle)*- The Federal Communications Commission (FCC) supports the usage of CB handles. CB handles are nicknames that are used instead of a real name to identify the speaker. A driver's handle is usually chosen by him, one that he believes expresses his personality or describes his driving style.
- *Happy happy*- New Year's greetings.
- *Having "shutter trouble"*- Having a hard time staying up.
- *Ho Chi Minh Trail*- Refers to California Highway 152, which is notorious for its high accident rate.
- *Holler*- Contact me on the radio.
- *Home 20*- The address of a driver's residence.
- *How 'bout*- "How 'bout you, eastbound?" can be said when attempting to contact other vehicles.

- *Hood*- A standard tractor, rather than a cab-over.
- *Hundred dollar lane, high dollar lane*- Trucks will be restricted from driving in the far left lane in certain densely populated locations, with violators facing steep fines. This word refers to the lane that is prohibited.
- *Jackpot*- Refers to the lights on a patrol car, just like "gumball machine".
- *Key down*- When you speak over someone who is trying to send a message. A more powerful, larger radio can easily block out a smaller one.
- *Key up*- Pushing the CB microphone's transmit button.
- *In my back pocket*- A location you've visited before or behind you.
- *In the big hole*- The transmission's highest gear.
- *K-whopper*- A Kenworth tractor, abbreviated as KW.
- *Kojak with a Kodak*- A radar gun being used by law enforcement.
- *Land line*- A landline phone, not a cell phone.
- *Large car*- A traditional tractor with a large sleeper, a lot of chrome and lights, etc.
- *Left Coast*- The West Coast.
- *Local information*- When a driver wants directions in an unfamiliar place, he asks for local information.
- *Local-yokel*- A police officer in a county, city, or small town.
- *Lollipop*- On the sides of the route, there are little reflectors or marker posts called lollipops.
- *Lumper*- Casual labor that loads and unloads your trailer for a fee, which is usually paid in cash.
- *Mama-bear*- A female law enforcement officer is referred to by this term.
- *Mash your motor*- Drive fast.
- *Meat wagon*- An ambulance vehicle.
- *Merry merry*- Christmas greetings.
- *Motion lotion*- Diesel fuel.
- *Moving on*- I'm on my way down the road.
- *Mud duck*- There is a feeble radio signal.
- *Negatory*- Negative or no.
- *95th Street*- Interstate 95 which is a major highway in the United States.
- *On the side*- On standby.
- *Parking lot*- A vehicle transporter that is frequently used when the trailer is empty.
- *Pay the water bill*- Taking a stop to use the restroom.
- *Pigtail*- The tractor's electrical connection to the trailer.
- *Plain wrapper*- A law enforcement vehicle that isn't marked and usually has a color added to it as a description.
- *Plenty of protection*- Normally, this indicates that there are a lot of police in the area, but it can suggest that drivers should go ahead and accelerate because there are fast four-wheelers ahead blocking or covering for them.
- *Pogo stick*- A metal, flexible support mounted on the tractor catwalk that usually holds up the trailer's connections.
- *Power up*- Accelerate.
- *Preeshaydit*- Thank you very much; I really appreciate it.
- *Pumpkin*- A Schneider truck, due to its orange color.
- *Radio*- A Citizens Band radio.

- *Radio check*- How's it going with my radio? Is it transmitting and getting out there?
- *Rambo*- Someone who speaks passionately on the radio, especially while no one else is aware of their whereabouts.
- *Ratchet jaw*- Someone who talks a lot on the radio while simultaneously keying-up the entire time and not allowing anyone else to speak.
- *Reading the mail*- Not saying anything; simply listening to the radio.
- *Reefer*- Usually refers to a refrigerated van trailer. However it can also refer to a single reefer unit.
- *Rest-a-ree-a*- Another term for a rest stop.
- *Road pizza*- Any roadkill on the side of the road.
- *Rockin' chair*- A truck that is sandwiched between two other trucks.
- *Roger*- Yes, it's true.
- *Roger beep*- When a person has un-keyed the microphone and ended their transmission, an audible beep occurs. Only a small fraction of radios have this feature, and it is not encouraged.
- *Roller skate*- Any little car.
- *Rooster cruiser*- A large vehicle; a gigantic, traditional tractor with plenty of lights and chrome.
- *Runnin' you across*- The weigh station is open, and vehicles are being weighed, most likely very quickly.
- *Salt shaker*- In the winter, this refers to the road maintenance vehicles that spray salt or sand on the highways.
- *Sandbagging*- Listening to the radio without talking; also known as "reading the mail."
- *Sandbox*- An escape ramp that uses sand to stop automobiles on an escape ramp.
- *Schneider eggs*- Construction zone orange cones.
- *Seat cover*- Used to refer to four-wheeler drivers and passengers
- *Sesame Street*- Channel 19 on the Citizens Band radio.
- *Shaky*- Generally refers to California, sometimes Los Angeles, and San Francisco occasionally.
- *Shiny side up*- Your vehicle hasn't overturned after a rollover or accident. "Keep the shiny side up" means to have a safe journey.
- *Shooting you in the back*- Being shot with a radar gun as your vehicle passes by a law enforcement vehicle.
- *Short short*- A short period of time.
- *Shutdown*- Being put out of service by the DOT due to some violation.
- *Skateboard*- A flatbed, or flatbed trailer.
- *Skins*- Tires.
- *Smokin' scooter*- A law enforcement official riding on a motorcycle.
- *Smokin' the brakes*- Smoking trailer breaks from overuse down a mountain grade.
- *Smokey/Smokey bear*- A law enforcement official who is usually highway patrol.
- *Split*- A junction where the road separates into various directions.
- *Spy in the sky*- A law enforcement aircraft.
- *Stagecoach*- A tour bus.
- *Stand on it*- Accelerate.
- *Swinging*- I'm hauling a load of swinging meat.
- *Taking pictures*- Law enforcement operating a radar gun.
- *10-4*- Okay, your message has been received. Some drivers simply say "ten."
- *Thermos bottle*- This is a tanker trailer.

- *Through the woods*- Getting off the interstate and onto secondary routes.
- *Throwin' iron*- Putting snow tire chains on.
- *Too many eggs in the basket*- A term used to describe gross weight, or load that is overweight.
- *Toothpicks*- A truckload of wood.
- *Travel agent*- The dispatcher, or broker in some cases.
- *Triple digits*- Over 100 miles per hour.
- *VW*- A tractor manufactured by Volvo-White.
- *Wagon*- Some drivers call their trailers wagon.
- *Walked on you*- Keying up at the same time, causing your transmission to be drowned out.
- *Wally world*- A Wal-Mart truck, or a Wal-Mart store or distribution center.
- *West Coast turnarounds*- The idea behind uppers, such as speed or benzedrine pills, is that a driver can travel from the East Coast to the West Coast and back without sleeping. It goes without saying that using these is against the law.
- *Wiggle wagons*- A group of two or three trailers.
- *Yard*- A company terminal, etc.
- *Yardstick*- A mile marker that can be found on the highway.

Communication Rules for Transporting Hazardous Materials

When it comes to transporting hazardous materials, there are some words and phrases with special meanings that may be different from what you are familiar with. Some of them may be on your CDL test and learning their definitions would be beneficial.

A ***material's hazard class*** shows the risks that are associated with it, and there are nine different classes. They are:

Class 1- Explosives such as dynamites, ammunition, explosive devices, display fireworks, etc.

Class 2- Flammable gases, non-flammable gases, and poisonous/toxic gases such as propane, helium, compressed fluorine, etc.

Class 3- Flammable liquids and combustible liquids such as gasoline, fuel oil, etc.

Class 4- Flammable solids, spontaneously combustible materials, and dangerous-when-wet materials such as wetted ammonium Picrate, white phosphorus, sodium, etc.

Class 5- Oxidizers and organic peroxides such as ammonium nitrate, methyl ethyl ketone peroxide, etc.

Class 6- Poison (inhalation hazard) and infectious substances such as potassium cyanide, anthrax virus, etc.

Class 7- Radioactive materials such as uranium.

Class 8- Corrosives such as battery fluid.

Class 9- Miscellaneous hazardous materials such as polychlorinated biphenyls (PCB).

Other Regulated Material- Domestic materials such as food flavorings and medicines are also classed.

A ***shipping paper*** contains a description of the hazardous materials that are being transported. Manifests, shipping orders, and bills of lading are all examples of shipping papers.

If there is a spill or leak or an accident, you may get injured and be unable to share details of the materials being transported. You can assist police and firefighters to reduce or prevent damage or injury at the accident scene if they know the HAZMAT you are carrying. Their swiftness in locating the shipping papers could go a long way in protecting your life and those of other people around. Therefore, all HAZMAT shippers are required to correctly describe their load and also include an emergency response number on the shipping papers.

Carriers and drivers are also required to identify shipping papers quickly or place them above other shipping papers along with the needed emergency response information. Lastly, all HAZMAT shipping papers are to be kept on the driver's seat when you're out of the vehicle, in a pouch on your door, or in clear view and within easy reach while driving with the seat belt fastened.

Package Labels

Most HAZMAT packages have hazard warning labels shaped like diamonds placed on them by shippers to inform others of the hazard. In case this diamond-shaped label can't fit on the package, it may be put on a tag that is firmly attached to the package. For example, compressed gas cylinders cannot hold labels and will therefore have decals or tags instead.

List of Regulated Products

Placards - These are signs which identify the cargo's hazard class that are put on bulk packages and on the outside of a vehicle to warn others of hazardous materials. If a vehicle is placarded, there must be a minimum of four identical placards on both sides, rear, and front of the vehicle. All the placards should be readable from all four directions, and they must be diamond-shaped, square-on-point, and a minimum of 9.84 inches.

As for cargo tanks and other bulk packaging, their contents' ID number is displayed in placards, orange panels, or white square-on-point displays which are the same size as a placard. These ID numbers are four-digit codes that are used by first responders in identifying HAZMAT. One ID number may be used to identify more than one chemical with the letters "UN" or "NA" preceding the ID number. The United States Department of Transportation's Emergency Response Guidebook (ERG) provides a list of the chemicals along with their respective ID numbers.

When identifying hazardous materials, there are three main lists that carriers, drivers, and shippers make use of. These are the Hazardous Materials Table, List of Hazardous Substances and Reportable Quantities, and the List of Marine Pollutants. Before you transport any material, the best practice is to go through each of these lists to find its name. Note that while you may find some materials on all three lists, others may be found on just one.

Hazardous Materials Table - The Hazardous Materials Table usually has six columns containing information on the shipping mode affected by the entry and other details about the shipping description; the material's shipping name, ID number, required labels, hazard class, and packaging group. Below are these columns, along with the details each of them contains:

Column 1

There are six different symbols that may be found in this column of the table and they all have different meanings.

(+) Displays the correct hazard class, shipping name, and packing group to be used even if the material does not match the definition of the hazard class.

(A) Means that the hazardous material described in column two is subject to Hazardous Materials Regulations only when it is intended or offered for air transport unless it is a hazardous waste or substance.

(W) Means that the hazardous material described in column two is subject to hazardous materials regulations only when it is intended or offered for water transport unless it is a marine pollutant, hazardous waste, or substance.

(D) Means the proper shipping name is suitable for describing materials to be transported domestically, but may not be suitable for international transportation.

(I) Identifies a proper shipping name used in describing materials for international transportation. Another shipping name may be used for domestic transportation only.

(G) Means that the hazardous material described in column two is a generic shipping name that must be followed by a technical name on the shipping paper. A technical name is a specific chemical that makes the product being shipped hazardous.

Column 2

This column contains an alphabetical list of the correct shipping names and details of regulated materials. Proper shipping names are shown in regular type on the shipping paper and not in italics.

Column 3

This column shows the material's hazard class or will contain the "Forbidden" entry. Be wary of materials classed as "Forbidden" as they should never be transported. All placard shipments are based on the hazard class and quantity of the hazardous material. Knowing the amount being shipped, the material's hazard class and the amount of all hazardous materials of all classes on the vehicle will help you decide the kind of placards to use.

Column 4

The ID numbers for each proper shipping name are listed in this column and are preceded by the letters "UN", "ID", or "NA". "NA" deals with proper shipping names that are used only to and from Canada, and within the United States. "ID" deals with proper shipping names that are recognized by the International Civil Aviation Organization (IACO) technical instructions for air transport. The ID number must be seen as part of the shipping description on the shipping paper and it must also show on the package, including cargo tanks and other bulk packaging.

Column 5

In this column, the packing group assigned to a specific material is shown in Roman numerals.

Column 6

This column shows the correct hazard warning label/labels all shippers must put on hazardous material packages. Some products may require more than one label if there are multiple hazards present.

Column 7

Here, the additional or special provisions regarding this material are listed. If information is entered into this column, you have to consult the CFR for the specifics. In this column, numbers one - six mean the hazardous material being transported is a poison inhalation hazard which has special regulations for placards, marking, and shipping papers.

Column 8

This column has three parts which show the section numbers that cover packaging requirements for each hazardous material.

List of Hazardous Substances and Reportable Quantities- The Department of Transportation and the Environmental Protection Agency wants to be informed about spills of hazardous substances. These substances are named in this list and each has a reportable quantity or "RQ". When transporting these materials in a reportable quantity or greater in a single package, shippers must display the letters "RQ" on the package and the shipping paper as well. They may appear before or after the basic shipping description. If a spill occurs while you're transporting any of these materials in RQ, remember that you or your employer are mandated to report.

Below are these hazardous substances alongside their reportable quantities in pounds and kilograms:

Phenyl mercaptan	100 (45.4)
Phenylmercury acetate	100 (45.4)
Phenylthiourea	100 (45.4)
Phorate	10 (4.54)
Phosgene	10 (4.54)
Phosphine	100 (45.4)
Phosphoric acid	5,000 (2270)
Phosphoric acid, diethyl 4-nitrophenyl ester	100 (45.4)
Phosphoric acid, lead (+2) Salt (2:30 salt	10 (4.54)

Note that if the words "INHALATION HAZARD" are written on the shipping paper or the package itself, you are required to display "POISON INHALATION HAZARD" or "POISON GAS" placards as appropriate. These placards must be used in addition to other placards required by the substance's hazard class. Even if you're carrying small amounts, be sure that the hazard class and "POISON INHALATION HAZARD" placards are displayed.

List of Marine Pollutants- This contains names of chemicals that are harmful to marine life. When it comes to highway transportation, the list only applies to chemicals in a container that can fit in 119 gallons or more without any label or placard as specified by the Hazardous Materials Regulations.

If you're shipping any bulk packages of a marine pollutant, the package must display the "MARINE POLLUTANT" marking, which is an image of a white triangle containing a fish and an "X" through the fish. This marking is not a placard

and should be shown on the outside of the vehicle. There also has to be a notation made on the product's shipping papers near its description: MARINE POLLUTANT.

Shipping Paper

There are certain items a shipping paper for hazardous materials must include. They are:

- Page numbers if there is more than one page, with the first page telling the total page numbers. E.g. "Page 1 of 3."
- Proper shipping description for each hazardous material.
- Shipper's certification saying the shipment was prepared in line with the Hazardous Materials Regulations, signed by the shipper.

Item Description

If you're shipping both non-hazardous and hazardous materials, note that on the shipping paper, the hazardous material must be:

- Entered first.
- Highlighted in contrasting color.

Or

- Identified by an "X" in front of the shipping description (ID number, shipping name, hazard class, and packing group) in a column titled "HM". If you need to identify a reportable quantity, you may use "RQ" instead of "X".

Note that the basic description for hazardous materials is usually ordered: ID number - proper shipping name - hazard class – packing group, if any. The packing group may have the letters "PG" before them and are displayed in Roman numerals. Unless it is specifically authorized in the Hazardous Materials Regulations, you are not to abbreviate a product's ID number, shipping name, and hazard class or division.

The description must also show the product's unit of measure and total quantity; type and number of packages e.g. 5 drums; the letters "RQ" if it is a reportable quantity; name of hazardous substance if absent in shipping name and of reportable quantity; and the hazardous material's technical name for materials showing letter "G" in the first column.

Unless exempted, the product's shipping papers must also contain an emergency response phone number. This number is the shipper's responsibility and is important because it can be used by emergency responders in case of a fire or spill to get useful information. The listed telephone number has to belong to the person offering the hazardous material for transportation if the offerer/shipper is the emergency response information (ERI) provider. If not, it should be the number of an organization or agency that can and is responsible for providing the necessary information in detail.

For each hazardous material being shipped, shippers also have the responsibility of providing emergency response information to motor carriers. This information must be able to be used away from the shipping vehicle and should provide all needed information on safely handling incidents regarding the material. At the least, the following information must contain the following details:

- Risks of explosion or fire.
- Immediate health hazards.
- Product's basic description and technical name.
- Immediate precautions in case of incidents of accidents.
- Immediate fire-handling methods.
- Preliminary first aid applications.
- Initial methods for handling leaks or spills.

All this information may be found in the shipping paper or another document showing the hazardous material's basic description and technical name. It could also be found in a guidance book like the Emergency Response Guidebook (ERG) which should ideally be kept in each HAZMAT-carrying vehicle by motor carriers. As a driver, you are to provide this information during an investigation or incident to any responding local, state or federal authority.

While you may not abbreviate the ID number, shipping name and hazard class, you may do so with the unit of measurement and packaging type, e.g. 9 ctns., UN1263, Paint, 3, PG II, 500 pounds. The shipper is also required to put "WASTE" before the material's proper shipping name on the shipping paper, e.g. UN1090, Waste Acetone, 3, PG II. Note that only hazardous materials may be described by an ID number or hazard class, and this does not apply to non-hazardous materials.

A copy or electronic image of all shipping papers for two years (three years for hazardous waste) must be kept by shippers after the first carrier accepts the material. If the shipper is only serving as a carrier and is not the shipment's originator, the carrier is mandated to keep this information for a period of 1 year. For the complete regulatory requirements for transporting hazardous materials, you can refer to the CFR, Title 49, Parts 171-180.

Shipper's Certification

When a shipper packages HAZMAT, they need to certify that said package was prepared according to Hazardous Materials Regulations. This signed certification should appear on the original shipping paper and the only exceptions are when the package is provided by the carrier or the shipper is a private carrier transporting their own product. You may accept the certification about proper packaging unless it does not comply with regulations, or is clearly unsafe. When you accept any HAZMAT shipment, ensure that you follow your employer's rules as some carriers have extra rules about shipping such materials.

Package Markings and Labels

The required markings are usually printed directly on the product's package, or on an attached tag or label. One important marking is the specific name of the hazardous material which is the same as that which is on the shipping paper. Note that the requirements for marking each package vary in terms of size and the material being shipped. When it is required, the name and address of the shipper or consignee, the HAZMAT's shipping name and identification number, as well as all required labels are to be displayed on the package.

If you're shipping any hazardous material, it is always a good idea to compare what is written on the shipping paper to the package's markings and labels. You should ensure that the correct basic description is shown by the shipper on the paper and that the package has all the proper labels. In case the material in question is one you're not familiar with, you can ask the shipper to get in touch with your office

Depending on the nature of the material, the shipper will put RQ, BIOHAZARD, INHALATION-HAZARD, HOT, or MARINE POLLUTANT on the package if the rules require them to. As for packages containing liquid substances, there will be package orientation markings with arrows showing the correct upright position. During transportation, these arrows must always point upwards and the attached labels must display the product's hazard class. If a single package requires more than one label, they must be placed close together, and near the product's proper shipping name.

Hazardous Waste Manifest

When you transport hazardous wastes, you need to sign and also have a Uniform Hazardous Waste Manifest. This manifest must contain information about the name and EPA registration number of the carriers and shippers, as well as the package's destination. This manifest must be prepared, dated, and signed by hand by shippers, and must be treated as a shipping paper when the waste is being transported. The shipment should only be given to a disposal or treatment facility or to another registered carrier. The manifest must be hand-signed by each carrier transporting the shipment and you should keep your own copy after delivery. Each copy of the manifest should have all the necessary dates and signatures, including those of the person receiving the waste.

Placarding

Before driving, you have to attach all the right placards to your vehicle as you can only move an improperly placarded vehicle during emergencies where life or property is at risk. All the placards you use must be seen on both sides and ends of the vehicle and each one must be easily visible from the direction it faces. They must be placed so that the numbers or words are on the same level and can be read from left to right. Placards must also be placed a minimum of 3 inches away from other markings if any, and free of devices or attachments like tarpaulins, doors, and ladders. The placard must be fixed on a background of contrasting color and remain clean and undamaged to enable proper visibility of the format, message, and format. Bear in mind that you are not allowed to use "Drive Safely" and other slogans.

In order to know the placards to use, you will need to know the materials' hazard class, the amount of hazardous material being shipped, and the total weight of all HAZMAT classes in your vehicle.

Placard Tables

In HAZMAT transportation, there are two placard tables used in categorizing materials namely Table 1 and Table 2. The difference between these two categories is that all materials in Table 1 must be placarded, regardless of the amount being shipped. On the other hand, the hazard classes in Table 2 only need placarding if the total amount shipped is up to or above 1,001 pounds, including the package. The only exception to this is if the shipment is in bulk packaging. To determine this amount, add the amounts on all shipping papers of the products in Table 2 that you have on board. Below are the 2 HAZMAT shipping placard tables:

Placard Table 1

If vehicle contains any amount of:	*Placard as:*
1.1 Mass Explosives	Explosives 1.1
1.2 Project Hazards	Explosives 1.2
1.3 Mass Fire Hazards	Explosives 1.3
2.3 Poisonous/Toxic Gases	Poison Gas
4.3 Dangerous When Wet	Dangerous When Wet
5.2 (Organic Peroxide, Type B, liquid or solid, Temperature controlled)	Organic Peroxide
6.1 (Inhalation hazard zone A & B only)	Poison/toxic inhalation
7 (Radioactive Yellow III label only)	Radioactive

Placard Table 2

Category of Material

(Hazard class or division number and additional description, as appropriate)	*Placard Name*
1.4 Minor Explosion	Explosives 1.4
1.5 Very Insensitive	Explosives 1.5
1.6 Extremely Insensitive	Explosives 1.6
2.1 Flammable Gases	Flammable Gas
2.2 Non-Flammable Gases	Non-Flammable Gas
3 Flammable Liquids	Flammable
Combustible Liquid	Combustible*
4.1 Flammable Solids	Flammable Solid
4.2 Spontaneously Combustible	Spontaneously Combustible
5.1 Oxidizers	Oxidizer
5.2 (other than organic peroxide, Type B, liquid or solid, Temperature Controlled)	Organic Peroxide

6.1 (other than inhalation hazard zone A or B)	Poison
6.2 Infectious Substances	(None)
8 Corrosives	Corrosive
9 Miscellaneous HAZMAT	Class 9""
ORM-D	(None)

*FLAMMABLE may be used in place of a COMBUSTIBLE on a cargo or portable tank.

"" For domestic transportation, a Class 9 Placard is not required.

Instead of separate placards, you may make use of DANGEROUS placards for each hazard class in Table 2 in two basic situations. The first is when you have up to or more than 1,001 pounds of two or more Table 2 hazard classes, requiring different placards. You may also do so when you have not loaded up to or above 2,205 pounds of any Table 2 hazard class material at any one place.

Note that using the DANGEROUS placard is not a requirement and you can always placard for the materials. If "INHALATION HAZARD" is written on the package or shipping paper, you have to display "POISON INHALATION" or "POISON GAS" in addition to other placards required by the material's hazard class. These materials are not subject to the 1,000-pound exception.

For products that are dangerous when wet, the "DANGEROUS WHEN WET" placard must be displayed in addition to any others required by the product's hazard class. These materials are not included in the 1,000-pound placarding exception.

All placards that are used in identifying a material's primary or secondary hazard class should have the hazard class number shown on the lower corner of the placard. However, subsidiary hazard placards without a hazard class number that are permanently affixed may be used as long as they remain within color specifications. As long as the placard indicates the hazard of the material that is transported, it may be displayed for hazardous materials even if it is not required.

CHAPTER - 5

CARGO SAFETY

Cargo Inspections

In order to get your commercial driver's license, you must know how to safely load and secure cargo on your vehicle. Knowing these basic rules will be a requirement for passing the CDL written examination.

Incorrectly loading cargo or insufficiently securing your cargo can be a danger to yourself, to other motorists, and it can also make controlling your vehicle more difficult and less efficient. Cargo that is improperly secured on a vehicle could be cast off into the road where other motorists are driving. This can endanger lives and can cause a number of problems that could incur fines or charges. You never know when you're going to need to brake hard in your vehicle, so you must be sure that your cargo is secured to withstand just such an event.

In addition to these issues, you can cause issues for yourself and your vehicle if your vehicle is overloaded. An overabundance of weight on your vehicle's axles can cause troubles with maneuverability, with vehicle efficiency, and it can also pose many safety complications. Overloading your vehicle or loading it improperly can severely affect how you need to steer in order to safely maneuver your vehicle through traffic. It is best to properly load your cargo so you don't need to deal with these complications.

As the driver and operator of your vehicle, you are responsible for the cargo on it. You are responsible for inspecting the cargo to ensure it's properly loaded and that there is nothing dangerous about it, you are responsible for recognizing overloads or improperly balanced weight in the back of the truck, you must know for certain that the load does not obstruct your emergency equipment, and you must know that the cargo is loaded in such a way that your view is never obstructed by it during travel.

If you are carrying hazardous cargo, you must also make sure that you have the appropriate placards displayed, that you have all the necessary endorsements and requirements to safely transport that cargo, and that you are carrying that load as safely as possible.

Inspecting Your Cargo. When you're performing your pre-trip inspection, you should add some time to inspect your cargo if you have any. You should be checking to make sure that it's balanced and secured properly.

Once you set out on the road, give yourself time to stop about 50 miles into your journey to check the cargo once again for shifting. If there has been a lot of shifting, make sure to reset your load in a safer formation with more securing devices, as needed.

As often as you can throughout a trip, check your cargo to ensure the securing devices are holding and that the load is properly supported. It is recommended that you inspect your load after you have driven for three hours or 150 miles, whichever comes last, and at each break you take during driving.

Make sure that you are aware of any federal or local regulations or requirements for commercial motor vehicle weight, cargo securement, vehicle coverings, and where you are allowed to drive your vehicle. Knowing these things before you set out will help you to be the best driver possible.

When you are trying to secure your cargo, you need to make sure that you're using the proper methods and tools to do so. There are a few different methods you can use to secure a load before taking off and you should know what they are so you can adequately secure your load and minimize risk and difficulty.

Weight and Balance in Your Cargo

Being responsible for the cargo on your vehicle means that you must know the weight ratings for your vehicle and that you must be aware of any local and federal regulations on the subject and adhere to them. Ensure that you don't overload your vehicle for the number of wheels and axles you have and that you don't load your cargo in such a way that will make it harder for you to maneuver through traffic.

In addition to making it harder to steer the vehicle, adding too much weight to it can make it harder to accelerate, brake, and move about freely. The brakes may also be unable to keep up with a load if it is more weight than the system is rated to handle. If the weather is inclement or the roads are slippery, these risks increase greatly and it becomes very unsafe to operate your overloaded vehicle.

Balance is key so the wheels and suspension are bearing equal weight because you could overload one or more axles and cause them to malfunction. In addition to this, if the front axle of your vehicle is not properly weighed down from the load you're carrying, it could be too light to allow the vehicle to steer properly.

Some things that you should bear in mind as guidelines for your cargo:

Don't Allow the Load to be Top Heavy. Cargo that is stacked up too high is a much greater fall risk. With the turns that you take on the roads and with the steep inclines you will likely need to navigate from time to time, you will want to make sure that the stacks of cargo are centered low enough that this is not a risk.

Keep the Weight Evenly Distributed. You don't want all of the weight to be on one side of the vehicle or the other and you don't want to place the cargo in such a way that it will be given the freedom to slide around and move a bunch. It is best to center the load in the vehicle with the use of proper securing devices so that you can ensure a nice, even ride.

How to Secure Your Cargo

There are several methods you can use to secure your cargo and many devices that will help you to ensure that your load goes through minimal shifting throughout your trip. We'll go over some of them here to give you an idea of what you will need to do and look for. For official training on securing loads, seek out professional training courses, as the practical exercises associated with this will ultimately give you the best means of understanding and mastering it.

Bracing and Blocking. Blocking is something that is done in the front and back and/or the sides of a load to keep it from sliding during transport. Blocking is designed to fit securely around the load to prevent movement. Bracing is additionally used for this very same purpose. Bracing extends from the top of the load, down to the floor, and/or to the walls, whatever will give the load the most securement and protection.

Tying Down Cargo. Cargo tiedown is typically used on flatbed vehicles that have no barriers to keep the cargo from shifting off the sides. As you may have already deduced, when the vehicle has no walls around the cargo, the securement of the load must be top-notch, to say the least. You will be competing with wind resistance, the pull from the speed on the roadways, and any other ambient movement that could be expected from the load you're carrying. In addition to the obvious risk, this could pose to the motorists around your vehicle, the shifting of the load can greatly affect your ability to handle and maneuver the vehicle.

Tiedowns for your vehicle must be the appropriate type and size for your load and your vehicle, to make sure of that before you embark. Federal regulations require the aggregate working load limit of any securement system used to secure an article or group of articles against movement must be at least one-half times the weight of the article or group of articles. Proper tiedown equipment must be used including ropes, straps, chains, and tensioning devices such as ratchets, clinching components, and winches. Tiedowns must be properly secured to the vehicle using hooks, rings, rails, and/or bolts.

Header Boards. Front-end header boards are also known as "headache racks," and are used to protect the driver from shifting cargo in the event of an emergency stop or a crash. The front-end structure must be in prime condition to protect the driver. The header board must be able to stop the forward motion of any cargo that is being carried. The same is true for the bulkhead, which is an added safety measure for just such an event.

Covering Your Cargo. Covering the cargo in your vehicle is typically done to protect other motorists from spilled or cast-off cargo, or to protect the cargo from the weather. This method is typically used on a vehicle that has side panels, but not top covering. Even if the driver has taken this measure, the driver should check their mirrors from time to time throughout travel to ensure that the cover isn't flapping or looking like it's going to give way. Flapping might seem innocuous at first, but the force against that covering is strong and it could lead to very large tears. Make sure that the covering is not, at any time, blocking your view in your mirrors or the view of another driver.

Sealed Loads and Containerized Cargo. Freight is typically containerized before being carried part way by rail or by ship. If containerized freight is being hauled on a truck, it is typically either on one end of the trip or the other to get it to another one of these means of travel. Some containers have tiedown devices that go along with them or locks that secure them directly to a specialized frame that is meant for them. Others must be loaded onto a flatbed and properly secured just as any other cargo would be.

These containerized loads are sealed and there is no possibility of inspecting them, but you should make sure that you're not exceeding any gross weight and axle weight limits before you embark.

When Your Cargo Needs Special Attention

Dry Bulk. Dry bulk tanks require special care because their center of gravity is high and the load can easily shift. Extreme caution is encouraged when you're going around curves and making sharp turns, so take them slowly and carefully. Time is always a factor in delivering goods, but in 100% of cases, safety takes precedence.

Hanging Meat. This type of load is precisely what it sounds like. Sides of beef, large cuts of pork, and other large cuts of meat must be suspended during transport. These, of course, make for a very unstable load, as they swing and have a very high center of gravity. When you encounter sharp turns, ramps, hills, or slopes with this kind of cargo, exercise as much caution as possible and take your time.

Livestock. As you might expect, transporting livestock can come with its own set of complications, as you are transporting animals that are sometimes very large and heavy that will move around throughout travel. Handling can be very difficult with this kind of load, but you can use false bulkheads to keep the livestock more or less corralled in the back of the vehicle. Even when the livestock is bunched, special care is needed because this kind of load can lean when going around curves and turns and the shifting center of gravity can increase the rollover risk.

Oversized Loads. This term is used for items and loads that extend beyond the limits of the flatbed on which it's being carried. This type of cargo requires its own type of permit and you may also need special equipment to notify other drivers of the overage. In some cases, these loads breach the limits of traffic lanes and extreme caution and awareness must be exercised while traveling. These types of loads often require "wide load" banners, flashing lights, poles, reflectors, flags, etc. Check the local regulations as well to find out if your load needs a police escort or a pilot vehicle to get you safely to the destination.

Vocabulary and Keywords

Bulkhead - The bulkhead is a strong wall or barrier (sometimes a full compartment) used as a block between the load and the cab. It can also be like a baffle, a barrier placed inside the trailer to keep the load from shifting and disturbing the balance and control of the vehicle.

Containerized - Cargo that has been packed and secured inside of a container.

Headache Rack – A barrier attached to the tractor that protects the driver from a shifting load in the trailer.

Pilot Vehicle - An escort vehicle that is meant to drive ahead of large loads or convoys of vehicles to assist them to get where they need to be and to notify other motorists and officials of the group or load that follows.

CHAPTER - 6

PASSENGER SAFETY

If you drive a passenger vehicle that is built to carry more than ten people including you, you must have a CDL with a "P" endorsement. Passenger transportation vehicles include buses, farm labor vehicles, or general public paratransit vehicles when said vehicle is built, used, or maintained for carrying more than 10 passengers including the driver, either for profit, hire, or by a nonprofit group or organization. If your driving test is taken in a van that is built, used or maintained for carrying a maximum of 15 persons in total, you will be limited to driving a 15-passenger small-size bus or less.
A CLP holder who has a "P" endorsement and/or an "S" endorsement is not allowed to operate a commercial motor vehicle with passengers, apart from other trainees, federal/state auditors and inspectors, the accompanying CDL holder, and test examiners.

Vehicle Inspection

When you're getting ready to embark on a route with passengers, you will need to inspect your vehicle to make sure that it is as safe as it can be. You will need to check the following areas:

- Access doors and panels for functionality.
- Coupling devices, if any.
- Emergency equipment.
- Emergency exit handles.
- Emergency exits.
- Emergency signaling equipment.
- Floor coverings.
- Handholds and railings.
- Horn.
- Lights and reflectors.
- Parking brake.
- Rearview mirrors and side-mounted mirrors.

- Seats (for safety).
- Service brakes, including any air hose couplings if present.
- Signaling devices, including internal signaling devices.
- Steering mechanism.
- Tires (make sure that your front wheels have not been recapped or regrooved).
- Wheels and rims.
- Windshield wipers.

Access Doors and Panels

When inspecting the bus' exterior, close any open access panels for engine, baggage, restroom service, etc., and emergency exits before you drive the vehicle.

Bus Interior

Sometimes, buses that are left unattended get damaged by people. Therefore, you should check the bus' interior before driving to be sure that the vehicle is safe for riders. For one, the stairwells and aisles must be clear at all times. Apart from these parts, the floor covering, emergency exit handles, handholds and railings, and signaling devices must be in safe and proper working conditions. All seats must also be safe and securely attached to the bus.

Check emergency exits for correct markings, ease of operation, and make sure that all required devices or buzzers are functioning properly. You should never operate a vehicle with the emergency window or door open. On the vehicle's emergency door, there must be a clearly visible "Emergency Exit" sign. If present, the red emergency door light must work and should be turned on at night or any other time the exterior lights are in use.

If you're driving a farm labor vehicle, all sharp-edged or cutting tools must be safely kept in a covered container in the passenger compartment. Any other equipment, materials, or tools that are transported in this compartment must be secured to the vehicle's body. At all times, all passengers including you, the driver must wear seatbelts.

Roof Hatches

Some emergency roof hatches may be left partly open to allow for the free flow of fresh air. However, they should not be left open regularly, and you will need to mind the vehicle's high clearance when you do so.

Loading and Trip Start

When you are loading passengers into your vehicle, you must follow these steps to ensure safety:

- Passengers should wait in a designated location for the bus, facing the bus as it approaches.
- Passengers should board the bus only when signaled by the driver to do so.

- Keep an eye on all your mirrors during loading to ensure you can see anything that could come up.
- Wait until the passengers have found their seats before moving the vehicle.
- Check all the mirrors to ensure there aren't any straggling passengers or obstructing motorists.

Hazardous Materials

You need to be watchful of baggage or cargo containing HAZMAT as the majority of them are prohibited from being shipped on a bus. The Federal Hazardous Class Definitions Table indicates which materials are hazardous. They are mostly those that are risky to safety, property, and health when being transported. All HAZMAT containers are to be marked with material name, ID number, and hazard label by shippers. Note that you should avoid transporting any hazardous materials unless you are very sure the rules permit you to.

Forbidden Hazardous Materials

Buses are allowed to carry drugs, emergency hospital supplies, and small-arms ammunition classified as ORM-D. For other hazardous materials that cannot be transported by any other means, you can carry small amounts. There are 5 major types of HAZMAT that buses are not allowed to carry. They are-

- Above 100 pounds of solid Class poison.
- Irritating material, tear gas, liquid Class 6 poison, or Division 2.3 poison gas.
- Explosives in the same space occupied by people, excluding small-arms ammunition.
- Labeled radioactive materials in the same space occupied by people.
- Above 500 pounds total of permitted HAZMAT, and a maximum of 100 pounds of any one hazard class.

Sometimes, bus riders may board your vehicle with an unlabeled HAZMAT in their possession. Be careful not to allow riders to bring common hazards like gasoline or car batteries on a trip. On the other hand, medicine that is medically prescribed and in a container for personal use is permitted if found in the possession of a passenger.

Except for school buses, wheelchairs that are carried on buses must have brakes or any other means of holding still while lowered or raised on the wheelchair platform. All batteries must be firmly attached to the wheelchair and spill-resistant. Note that flammable fuels are not permitted for use with wheelchairs.

Standee Line

Riders should not stand in front of the rear of the driver's seat. For buses that are built to allow passenger standing, there must be a two-inch line drawn on the floor, or any other means to inform riders where they shouldn't stand. This line is referred to as the standee line and all standing riders must remain behind it.

At Your Destination

When you arrive at an intermediate stop or destination, you are to announce the specific location, reason why you stopped, next departure time, and the number of the bus. As riders step off your bus, gently remind them of their carry-ons so they don't forget them on the bus. If the level of the aisle is lower than that of the bus seats, remind them to mind the step-down. It is always best to remind them of this before you bring the vehicle to a complete stop. If driving a

charter bus, do not allow riders on board until it is time for departure to prevent vandalism, or even worse, theft of the vehicle.

Animals

Except for certified guides, signals, or service dogs accompanying physically challenged passengers, transporting animals is forbidden.

On the Road

When you are ready to embark with your passengers, you must do so by:

- Closing the door.
- Engaging the transmission.
- Releasing the parking brake.
- Disengaging any signal lights that told motorists you were stopped.
- Engaging the left turn signal.
- Checking the mirrors once again.
- Allowing any traffic to disperse before you merge back in.
- Merging safely and continuing on your route.

Passenger Supervision

A lot of intercity and charter carriers have specific rules concerning passenger safety and comfort. At the beginning of the trip, carefully list out any drinking or smoking rules, as well as those relating to the use of electronic devices. By taking the time to explain these rules at the start of the trip, there is a lower probability of having any issues concerning them. As you drive, you are to keep an eye on your bus' interior, sides, rear, and the road ahead. Bear in mind that it may be necessary to remind riders about these rules, or to keep all body parts inside the vehicle.

At Stops

Stumbling is possible among riders when boarding or alighting from the bus, and when it starts or stops. For this reason, you are to caution them to watch their steps when disembarking from the bus. Remember that you need to keep all starts and stops as smooth as possible to prevent rider injury.

There may be times when a disruptive or drunk rider boards your vehicle. When this happens, you have the responsibility of ensuring their safety, including that of other riders. Such riders must only be discharged at a safe spot and not somewhere unsafe. This safe spot may be a well-lit area or the next stop. A number of carriers have guidelines and rules for dealing with disruptive riders, and you should be aware of those that apply to you.

Common Accidents

The majority of bus accidents usually take place at intersections so you need to be extra careful when approaching one even if there is a stop sign or signal to control other traffic. Sometimes, mass transit and school buses hit passing vehicles or scrape mirrors when driving out of a bus stop. To be on the safe side, be aware of your bus' needed clearance and look out for tree limbs or poles at bus stops. Knowing the size of the gap your vehicle needs to speed up and merge with traffic will also help reduce the chances of an accident. Before pulling out of a stop, be sure that the needed gap has opened up, and don't assume that other motorists will slow down to give you room when you start or indicate to pull out.

Too much speeding, especially on slippery roads can lead to death and destruction of buses. There is a safe "design speed" for every banked curve. During good weather, this speed is ideal for cars but may be too fast for many buses. If the bus has good traction, it may roll over but if not, it may slide off the curve. When approaching curves, it is important to reduce your vehicle speed. You are driving too fast if the bus leans toward the outside in a banked curve.

Railroad-Highway Crossing/Stops

When stopping at a railroad crossing, you should stop your vehicle about 15 to 50 feet before the crossing. Listen carefully and also look in both directions to check for approaching trains, opening your forward door may help you see or hear a coming train better. After a train has passed, be sure that no other one is coming in the other direction before you cross. For buses with a manual transmission, you should never switch gears while crossing tracks.

Although you're not required to stop, you must slow down and check for other vehicles at streetcar crossings, green traffic signals, crossings marked as "abandoned" or "exempt", where a flagman or peace officer is directing traffic, and at tracks that run by and on the roadway in a residence or business district.

Drawbridges

You should stop at drawbridges without a traffic control officer or signal light. Stop the vehicle a minimum of 50 feet before the draw of the bridge and look to be sure that the draw is completely closed before you cross. You do not have to stop but you should slow down when there is a traffic light with a green light or a traffic officer controlling traffic whenever the bridge opens.

Inspections Post-Trip

When you complete a trip with passengers, it is important to check through the vehicle for some things to make sure that everything is as it should be. When you conduct your post-trip inspection, you should be looking for:

- Articles left on the bus by passengers.
- Sleeping passengers who may have missed their stops.
- Open windows and doors that will need to be secured before the end of the day.
- Any mechanical or operational system errors or issues that need servicing.
- Vandalism or damage.
- Any problems that stand out that will need immediate attention or resolution.

Brake-Door Interlocks

Mass transit vehicles in cities may have an interlock system between the brake and accelerator. This applies the brakes and holds the throttle in an idle position if the rear door has been opened. This only releases when that rear door or emergency door has been closed and latched. It is not recommended that this system be used in the place of the emergency brake or the parking brake.

Prohibited Practices

Unless it is completely necessary, you should not fuel your bus while you have riders on board. You also should not refuel with riders on board in a closed building. All your focus needs to be on the road so you should avoid conversations with passengers, or any other distracting activity while doing so. You should not push or tow a faulty bus with riders aboard unless it is dangerous to get off at that point. If this is the case, the bus should only be moved to the closest safe spot for passengers to alight. All employers have guidelines on pushing or towing disabled buses so follow your employer's rules regarding that.

Tips for Operating a Passenger Vehicle Safely

Keep out of Blind Spots- There are blind spots on all four sides of large trucks and buses. If you can't see the driver of another vehicle in the side mirror, assume they can't see you either. Driving in a blind spot is never a good idea and you need to stay visible by slowing down or moving ahead. You will also need to merge with caution.

Overtake Safely- In the vehicle mirror, double-check that you can see the driver. After signaling appropriately, move into the left lane and accelerate too quickly and safely pass the truck or bus. Avoid staying in the blind spot for too long. Before you pull in front of the truck or bus, make sure it's visible in your rearview mirror and allow it plenty of room. Never pass trucks or buses on downgrades where they are likely to accelerate, and never pass from the right lane. Stay to the right and hit the brakes when passing a bus or truck; allow them extra room to merge in with traffic, or change lanes.

Avoid Cutting it too Close- Cutting off a commercial bus or truck is very risky. You'll most likely end up in a blind spot if you move in quickly. Even if you're visible, due to the time it takes to stop, the vehicle may not be able to slow down quickly enough to avoid a collision. Cutting in too close in front of another vehicle is always risky, but "cutting off" a commercial bus or truck is even more dangerous. You're likely to be in a blind zone if you move in swiftly from either side, and the driver may not spot you in time. Even if you're visible, the vehicle may not be able to slow down fast enough to prevent an accident due to the time needed to stop.

Keep a Safe Distance Between You and Other Trucks- When you're tailgating a truck or bus, you put yourself in a blind spot. As trucks are so high off the ground, it's possible that your car will slide or get shoved under a truck during a crash.

Anticipate Wide Turns- Buses and trucks require more turning space and they swing wide or may begin a turn from the middle lane. Never try to squeeze past a turning car or get between it and the curb as doing so could be very risky. At an intersection, you also should never "block the box" or stop in front of the line in order to allow buses and trucks to turn safely.

Exercise Patience- Trucks and buses require additional time to accelerate and may be equipped with technology such as speed limiters. Distractions and collisions can be caused by honking, driving aggressively, or weaving through traffic.

Use Your Seatbelt- One of the simplest and most vital things you can do to save lives is to wear a safety belt and also encourage its usage amongst your passengers. Ensure that children are always buckled up, in car seats, or in the rear seat.

Remain Focused- If you need to do anything other than drive, get off the road and come to a complete stop. Driving while distracted is just as dangerous as driving while intoxicated.

Get Some Rest if Tired- Take frequent breaks, have another driver relieve you, or exit the vehicle to find a safe place for rest

Don't Drive Under the Influence- Remember that there is no amount of alcohol that is safe for drinking before operating a vehicle. Alcohol, drugs, and the likes interfere with a person's sense of judgment and reaction time. Over-the-counter drugs, as well as prescription medicines, may also result in sleepiness, dizziness, and/or slow reaction time. If you have to use a medication bearing such a warning, avoid operating any vehicle.

CHAPTER - 7

COMBINATION VEHICLES

What is a Combination Vehicle?

Combination vehicles are typically longer, heavier, and require a higher level of skill than other commercial motor vehicles. Those who drive these combination vehicles must know a good deal more about them and must be prepared for any eventuality than those who drive simpler vehicles. This section will cover some of the more key points about them, how they work, and how to operate them safely.

Driving Safely

Rollover Risks

Truck rollovers account for more than half of drivers' deaths in accidents. Piling up more cargo in a truck moves the vehicle's "center of gravity" higher above the road, making it easier for the truck to roll over. Rigs that are fully loaded are ten times more likely to turn over during an accident compared to empty rigs. To prevent rollover, ensure that the loaded cargo is as close to the ground as possible, and slow down at turns. It is even more important to keep a low cargo height in combination vehicles than it is in straight trucks. The cargo should be centered and should be spread out to reduce the chances of a rollover. When the load is piled at one side, making the trailer lean, the vehicle is more likely to roll over. Reducing vehicle speed off-ramps, on-ramps, and around corners will help prevent rollovers as they happen as a result of quick turns. Try to avoid making sudden lane changes, especially when the cargo is fully loaded.

Steer Gently

For trucks with trailers, there is something known as the "crack-the-whip" effect which can be very dangerous. During quick lane changes, this effect can overturn the trailer. When pulling trailers, you need to steer as gently and smoothly as possible. Making sudden movements with your steering wheel can lead to your trailer tipping over if care isn't taken. Be sure to leave enough space between your vehicle and the one in front of it- a minimum of one second for every ten feet of vehicle length, plus another second if the speed is above 40 mph. Once again, bear in mind that sudden lane changes can be dangerous so it is always best to look far enough down the road you're on to avoid any surprises. For night driving, you should keep the vehicle at a slow speed so that you can see any obstacles with the headlights before it is too late to stop gently or switch lanes. Before approaching a turn, bring the vehicle to a slow and safe speed.

Brake Early

You must control the vehicle's speed at all times whether it is empty or fully loaded. Note that large combination vehicles need more time to stop when empty than when they're fully loaded. With light loads, their strong brakes and stiff suspension springs give little traction, making it very easy for the wheels to lock up. When this happens, the trailer can swing out and hit other vehicles or quickly jackknife. Tractors without semi-trailers, known as "bobtail tractors", also require extra care as it can be difficult to bring them to a smooth stop. They usually take a longer time to stop compared to a tractor-semitrailer at maximum gross weight.

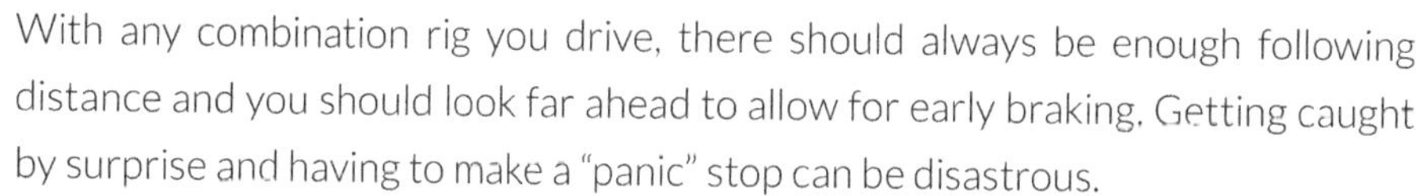

With any combination rig you drive, there should always be enough following distance and you should look far ahead to allow for early braking. Getting caught by surprise and having to make a "panic" stop can be disastrous.

Railroad-Highway Crossings

These crossings can also cause problems especially when the trailer being pulled has a low clearance underneath. Two kinds of trailers that can be stuck on raised crossings are:

- Trailers with low slung units such as car carriers, lowboy, or moving vans.
- Single-axle tractors pulling a long trailer with landing gear set to fit a tandem-axle tractor.

If you happen to get stuck on a railroad-highway crossing, step out of the vehicle and keep away from the tracks. You can look for signal housing or signposts at the crossing to get information on the emergency notifications. You can put a call through to 911 or any other emergency number. When you do so, share the crossing's location using all landmarks you can identify, especially the DOT number if it is posted.

Prevent Trailer Skids

A trailer has a high probability of swinging around when the wheels lock up and this is more common when the trailer is empty or is carrying a light load. This kind of jackknife is often referred to as a trailer jackknife. To stop a trailer skid, you first need to recognize skidding. The best and fastest way to know if your vehicle is starting to skid is by seeing it in time with your mirrors. Each time you have cause to slam down on the brakes, you should look at the mirrors to check whether the trailer remains where it should. If the trailer swings outside your lane, it will be harder to avoid a jackknife.

After seeing the skid, step off the brakes so that the vehicle can regain its traction. If the vehicle is equipped with a trailer hand brake, avoid using it in an attempt to straighten the rig. Doing this is wrong because the use of the brakes on the trailer wheels led to the skid in the first place. As soon as the wheels can grip the road again, the trailer will follow the tractor and align with it.

Turn Wide

When going around a corner, a vehicle's rear wheels follow a path different from the front wheels and this is known as "cheating" or off-tracking. It is normal for longer vehicles to off-track more. The powered unit's rear wheels will be off-track to some extent and the rear wheels will be off-track even more. If the vehicle has more than one trailer, the rear wheels on the last trailer will off-track the most. What you need to do in such situations is to steer the vehicle's front end wide enough around a corner to prevent it from running over the pedestrians, curb, etc. However, you will have to keep the vehicle's rear close to the curb to prevent other motorists from passing you on the right. If it is impossible to complete your turn without driving into another traffic lane, turn wide as you turn the vehicle. It is better to do this rather than swinging wide to the left before you start turning because other drivers will be unable to overtake on the right side.

Combination Vehicle Air Brakes

In combination vehicles, there are braking system parts for controlling the trailer brakes aside from the general air brake parts highlighted in Chapter 3 of this guide. They are:

Trailer Hand Valve

Also known as the Johnson bar or trolley valve, this is responsile for working the trailer brakes. Note that it should only be used in testing trailer brakes and not while driving as it can lead to the trailer skidding. The foot brake supplies air to all the vehicle's brakes, including the trailer(s). Using the foot brake greatly reduces the danger of a jackknife or skid.

The hand valve should also not be used for parking as all the air might leak, leading to an unlocking of the brakes in trailers without spring brakes. Each time you park, make use of the parking brakes. For trailers without spring brakes, you can prevent the trailer from moving with the use of wheel chocks.

Tractor Protection Valve

This vehicle part keeps air in the truck or tractor brake system in case the trailer develops a bad leak or breaks away. This valve is controlled by the cab's trailer air supply control valve which allows you to open the tractor protection valve and also shut it. If there is low air pressure in the range of 20 – 45 psi, the valve will close automatically. When it closes, it keeps air from escaping from the tractor, and also releases air through the trailer emergency line. This engages the trailer emergency brakes, with possible control loss.

Trailer Air Supply Control

On newer vehicles, this is a red knob with 8 sides that can be used to control the tractor protection valve. To supply air into the trailer, you push it in and pull it out when you want to shut off the air and engage the trailer emergency brakes. When air pressure drops within the range of 20 – 45 psi, the valve will pop out. As for older vehicles, the emergency valves or tractor protection valve controls may require manual operation and instead of a knob, there may be a lever instead, the "normal" position is for pulling a trailer while the "emergency" position is for shutting off the air and putting on the emergency brakes.

Trailer Air Lines

There are two air lines in every combination vehicle and they are the emergency and service lines that run between each vehicle whether trailer to dolly, tractor to trailer, dolly to the second trailer, and so on. Also known as the signal or control line, the service air line carries air and is controlled by the trailer hand brake or foot brake. The pressure in this line can be adjusted depending on how hard you press the hand valve or foot brake. Service lines are connected to relay valves which enable the trailer brakes to be applied faster than would be possible without them.

The emergency line is also known as the supply line and has two main purposes. The first is to supply air to the trailer air tanks and the second is to control the emergency brakes in combination vehicles. When there is a loss of air pressure in the emergency line, the trailer emergency brakes are engaged. This loss of pressure could be a result of a trailer detaching and this tearing the emergency air hose apart. It could also be due to breakage of a metal tubing, hose, or any other part which leads to the air escaping. When pressure is lost in the emergency line, the tractor protection valve will shut and the air supply knob will pop out. Oftentimes, emergency lines are coded with red so that they do not get mistaken for the blue service line.

Hose Couplers

Hose couplers or glad hands are coupling devices that are used in linking the emergency and service air lines from the tractor or truck to the trailer. These couplers are equipped with a rubber seal to prevent air from escaping. Before making any connection, clean them along with their rubber seals carefully. When you're connecting them, the two seals should be pressed together with the couplers at a 90-degree angle to each other. Turning the glad hand attached to the hose will join the couplers and lock them.

When you couple, you should be sure that you are coupling the correct glad hands together. Sometimes, colors are used by vehicle manufacturers to help you avoid mistakes. Red is used in marking the emergency lines while blue is used for service lines. Other times, metal tags may be attached to these lines with "service" and "emergency" written on them.

If the air lines are crossed, supply air will go to the service line instead of charging the trailer air tanks as it should. As a result of this, there will be no air to release the trailer's spring brakes. If you're driving and the spring brakes don't release when you press the trailer air supply control, take a look at the air line connections.

Older trailers are not equipped with spring brakes and if the air in their air tank has leaked away, there won't be emergency brakes, causing the wheels to move freely. Crossing the air lines will make it possible for you to drive away but you won't have trailer brakes which can be very dangerous. Before you start driving, always test the brakes by pulling the tractor protection valve control, or hand valve. To be sure that they work, all you need to do is pull against them gently in low gear.

There are some vehicles with dummy or "dead end" couplers that you may attach hoses to when they're not in use. Using them will keep dirt and water from entering the air lines and coupler. Note that the dummy couplers should only be used when the air lines are not connected to a trailer. Without dummy couplers, glad hands can get locked together sometimes, depending on the kind of couplings. Keeping your vehicle's air supply clean is very important.

Trailer Air Tanks

Every trailer and converter dolly has a minimum of one air tank which is filled by the emergency line connected to the tractor. These air tanks provide the required air pressure needed to operate trailer brakes. Relay valves help to send air pressure from the air tanks to the brakes.

The pressure in the service line indicates the amount of pressure to be sent by the relay valves to the trailer brakes. The trailer hand brake, if equipped and the brake pedal are responsible for controlling the pressure in the service line. Maintaining these parts is very important because the brakes may malfunction if water and oil build up in them. There is a drain valve on each tank which should be drained on a daily basis. Tanks with automatic drains will keep most moisture out but you still need to have a look at the drains to confirm.

Shut-off Valves

These are used in the supply and service air lines at the back of trailers used in towing other trailers. When you're not towing another trailer, the shut-off valves close the air lines off. Ensure that all the valves are open except for those at the back of the last trailer, which have to be closed.

Trailer Service, Parking, and Emergency Brakes

Just like truck tractors and trucks, newer trailer models are equipped with spring brakes. However, trailer and converter dollies that were manufactured before 1975 are not required to have them. Instead of the spring brakes, they have emergency brakes that receive air supply from the air tank. Whenever there is a loss of air pressure in the emergency line, the emergency brakes are engaged. These older models have no parking brake as well. The emergency brakes come on any time the trailer is disconnected or the air supply knob is pulled out. A serious leak in the emergency line will lead to the tractor protection valve closing and the trailer emergency brakes will be engaged. However, the brakes will only hold if there is air pressure in the air tank. After some time, all the air will leak away and there will be no brakes. To avoid this and ensure safety, make use of wheel chocks when parking trailers that do not have spring brakes.

Sometimes, you may not take note of a serious leak in the service line until you try putting on your brakes. Afterward, the air loss will quickly reduce the pressure in the air tank and if it gets low enough, the trailer emergency brakes will be engaged.

Coupling and Uncoupling

Coupling and uncoupling is a very specific procedure that is essential to the safe operation of coupled vehicles. The general steps for coupling and uncoupling will be listed in this section, but you must note that practicing with these steps on a real vehicle will be the best way for you to get acquainted with the procedure to be able to drive a vehicle that you have coupled yourself.

If You Are Coupling Tractor-Semitrailers

Part One- Inspect the Fifth Wheel:

- Check for damaged or missing parts.
- Check that the mounting tractor is secure and that there are no cracks in the frame.
- Check that the fifth wheel is properly lubricated.
- Check if the fifth wheel is in the proper position for coupling to occur.
- The wheel tiled down toward the rear of the tractor.
- The jaws are open.
- The safety unlocking handle is in the automatic lock position.
- The sliding fifth wheel is in the locked position (if you have one).

Part Two- Inspect the Area and Chock Wheels:

- Keep the area around the vehicle completely clear.
- Make sure the trailer wheels are chocked and the spring brakes are on.
- Check that any cargo is secured against any movement that will occur during coupling.

Part Three- Position the Tractor:

Put the tractor directly in front of the trailer, but never back under the trailer at an angle because you could push the trailer at an angle and break the landing gear.

Check the position via the outside mirrors by looking down both sides of the trailer.

Part Four- Back Up to it Slowly:

Back up your vehicle until the fifth wheel just touches the trailer.

Do not hit the trailer.

Part Five- Secure the Tractor:

Engage the parking brake.

Throw the transmission into neutral.

Part Six- Verify the Trailer Height:

Make sure that the trailer is low enough that it is raised slightly when the tractor is backed under it. Make changes to the height of the trailer as needed.

Ensure that the kingpin and the fifth wheel are aligned.

Part Seven- Connect Air Lines to the Trailer:

Check the glad hand seals and then connect the tractor emergency air line to the emergency glad hand on the trailer.

Check the glad hand seals and then connect the tractor service air-line to the service gladhand on the trailer.

Ensure that the air lines are supported in a spot where they won't be crushed or caught during the backing process.

Part Eight- Supply Air to the Trailer:

Push in the "air supply" knob that is located inside the cab or move the tractor protection valve control from the "emergency" to the "normal" position to supply air to the trailer brake system.

Allow the air pressure to normalize.

Check for crossed air lines in the brake system.

Shut off the engine so you can hear the brakes.

Apply and release the brakes on the trailer and listen to the sound of them. You should hear the air.

Check the pressure gauge for the air brake system for signs of major air loss.

When you are certain that the brakes are working, start the engine once again.

Verify that the air pressure is up to normal.

Part Nine- Lock Trailer Brakes:

Push in the "air supply" knob that is located inside the cab or move the tractor protection valve control from the "emergency" to the "normal" position to supply air to the trailer brake system.

Part Ten- Back Under the Trailer:

Shift into the lowest reverse gear.

Back up slowly, under the trailer to avoid hitting the kingpin with too much force.

Part Eleven- Check the Connection for Security:

Raise the trailer landing gear so it is slightly off the ground.

Pull the tractor forward gently while the brakes on the tractor are still locked, to verify that the trailer is locked onto the tractor.

Part Twelve- Secure the Vehicle:

Put the transmission into neutral.

Put on the parking brakes.

Shut off the engine once again and take the key with you just in case someone else tries to move the truck while you are under it.

Part Thirteen- Inspect the Coupling:

Bring a flashlight with you if it is necessary.

Make sure that there is no space in between the upper and the lower fifth wheel. If you see that there is space between them, this is an issue that will need to be remedied immediately.

Get under the trailer and check the back of the fifth wheel to make sure that the jaws have closed securely around the shank of the kingpin.

Part Fourteen- Connect the Electrical Cord and Check Air Lines:

Plug the electrical cord into the trailer and fasten its safety catch.

Check both air lines and the electrical line for any signs of damage.

Verify that the electrical lines will not hit any part of the vehicle that will be in motion during transit.

Part Fifteen- Raise the Front Trailer Supports (the landing gear):

Use the low gear range (if so equipped) to begin raising the landing gear. Once it bears no weight, switch to the high gear range.

Raise the landing gear completely, as it is dangerous to move the vehicle if they are not properly secured.

Check that there is sufficient clearance between the top of the tractor tires and the nose of the trailer.

Part Sixteen- Remove the Trailer Wheel Chocks:

Remove the wheel chocks and store them in a safe place.

If You Are Uncoupling Tractor-Semitrailers

Part One- Position The Rig:

- Make sure the surface of the parking area can support the weight of the vehicle you're about to leave on it.
- Line up the tractor with the trailer and do not try to pull out at an angle, as this can damage the landing gear.

Part Two- Ease Pressure Onto the Locking Jaws:

- Shut off the air supply to the trailer so you can lock the trailer brakes.
- Ease the pressure on the fifth wheel locking jaws by backing up slowly and carefully.
- Put on the parking brakes while the tractor is pushing against the kingpin.

Part Three- Chock the Trailer Wheels:

- Chock the trailer wheels if there are no spring brakes on the trailer or if you aren't sure if there are spring brakes on the trailer.

Part Four- Lower the Landing Gear:

- If the trailer has no cargo in it, lower the landing gear until it comes firmly into contact with the ground.
- If the trailer contains a load, you will want to turn the crank in low gear a few extra turns once the landing gear has made contact with the ground.
- Do not lift the trailer off the fifth wheel.

Part Five- Disconnect Air Lines and Electric Cable:

- Disconnect the air lines from the trailer and connect the air line glad hands to dummy couplers at the back of the cab (or you can couple them together).
- Hang the electrical cable with the plug down to prevent moisture from getting inside of it.
- Ensure the lines are supported so no damage will happen during the driving of the tractor.

Part Six- Unlock the Fifth Wheel:

- Raise the handle lock.
- Pull the release handle and move it to the open position.
- Keep your legs and feet clear of the area around the rear tractor wheels to avoid serious injury in case the vehicle moves.

Part Seven- Pull the Tractor Partially Clear of the Trailer:

- Pull the tractor forward until the fifth wheel comes out from under the trailer.
- Stop with the tractor frame under the trailer, which will prevent the trailer from falling to the ground if the landing gear should fail or sink.

Part Eight- Secure the Tractor:

- Apply the parking brake.
- Throw the transmission into neutral.

Part Nine- Inspect the Trailer Supports:

- Ensure the ground is supporting the trailer firmly.
- Ensure that the landing gear is not damaged.

Part Ten- Pull the Tractor Clear of the Trailer:

- Release the parking brakes.
- Ensure the area is clear and then drive the tractor forward until it is cleared.

If You Are Coupling a Pintle Hook

Part One- Inspect Pintle Hook

Check for worn, missing, or damaged parts, and ensure the mount is secure. Pintle hook could separate from the vehicle if not firmly secured to the mounting face.

Part Two- Unlock Lock Pin and Open Hatch

- If applicable, unlock and remove the tethered lock pin.
- Lift lock handle away from vehicle until lock clears lock seat on hook body.
- Rotate the latch assembly upwards until the latch is in the most upright position to open it.
- Release lock handle.

Part Three- Lower Drawbar Into Place

- Position eye of drawbar over horn of pintle hook.
- Lower drawbar into position.

Part Four- Lock Pintle Hook

- Push latch closed. When locked correctly, the lock handle will rotate and move upwards until it is flush with the top of the latch.

- Insert tethered lock in through latch and lock holes.
- If applicable, close tethered wire lock pin.

If You're Uncoupling a Pintle Hook

Part One- Park on Level Surface

- Park trailer on firm level surface.
- Block tires.

Part Two- Disconnect Safety Chains, Electrical Connector, and Breakaway Brake Switch

- Disconnect electrical connector.
- Disconnect breakaway brake switch lanyard.
- Disconnect safety chains from tow vehicle.

Part Three- Unlock Coupler

- Unlock coupler.
- Open coupler.

Part Four- Check Ground Surface for Adequate Support

- Ensure the surface below jack pad can support the tongue load.

Part Five- Rotate Jack Handle

- Rotate the handle to extend jack and transfer the trailer tongue weight to the jack.

Part Six- Raise Trailer Coupler

- Raise trailer coupler above tow vehicle hitch.

Part Seven- Drive Forward

- Drive tow vehicle forward.

If You're Coupling a Drawbar

Part One- Remove Safety Lock Screw and Rotate Safety Cover Bar

- Remove the safety lock screw and set aside the relative self-locking nut.
- Loosen safety lock screw.

- Turn adjustment screw outwards a minimum of five times.
- Rotate safety cover bar outwards so it is completely open.

Part Two- Reverse Truck

- Reverse truck slowly until ball cup drawbar eye is exactly above the drawbar-coupling ball.

Part Three- Lower Drawbeam

- Lower drawbeam until ball cup drawbar eye completely covers drawbar-coupling ball.

Part Four- Rotate Safety Cover Bar

- Rotate the safety cover bar inwards.
- Fit safety lock screw in together with the self-locking nut.
- Tighten both lock screws with their self-locking nuts at a 350 – 400 Newton meters torque wrench setting.

Part Five- Adjust Adjustment Screw

- Adjust screw until there is a 0.3 -0.5 mm vertical clearance between the ball cup and guard disk.
- Lock setting with counter nut.

Part Six- Protect Coupling Ball and Anchor Edge Onto Ball

- Protect the coupling ball's visible part with rubber dustproof bellows protection cover.
- Anchor edge directly onto the ball accurate.

Part Seven- Lubricate Drawbar Eye

- Lubricate inside the drawbar eye ball cup directly through grease nipple.

If You're Uncoupling a Drawbar

Part One- Turn on Trailer Brake

- Ensure that the trailer brake is on.

Part Two- Remove Cover and Loosen Screws

- Remove rubber dustproof bellows protection cover.
- Loosen adjustment screw and counter nut.
- Loosen safety lock screw and remove together with self-locking nut.

Part Three- Rotate Safety Cover Bar and Raise Trailer Drawbeam

- Rotate the safety cover bar outwards until completely open.
- Raise trailer drawbeam until drawbar-coupling ball is completely visible.
- Drive forward very slowly with the trailer.
- Rotate the safety cover bar until it is lodged back into its housing.

Part Four- Lock Safety Screw and Tighten Self-locking Nut

- Fit in safety lock screw and tighten in self-locking nut.

If You're Coupling a Gooseneck Hitch

Part One- Open Clamp Latch on Gooseneck Coupler

- Ensure gooseneck ball is adequately lubricated.

Part Two- Position Coupler and Latch Clamp

- Position trailer coupler directly over the ball.
- Lower gooseneck trailer into place.
- Latch clamp.

Part Three- Attach Safety Chains

- Attach vehicle's safety chains which is a required item by law.

Part Four- Connect Trailer Light Wiring

- Connect trailer light wiring to the vehicle's connector.
- Inspect all lights, including brake lights.

Part Five- Lower and Stow Trailer Jacks

- Lower and stow trailer jacks completely, allowing weight to be on the tow vehicle.

If You're Uncoupling a Gooseneck Hitch

Part One- Remove Safety Pin and Clip

- Detach the safety pin and clip.

Part Two- Rotate Handle and Raise Trailer Off Ball

- Rotate handle.
- Raise trailer off ball which will automatically return coupler to load position.

Part Three- Install Safety Clip and Pin

- Install safety pin.
- Install safety clip.

Inspecting a Combination Vehicle

The seven-point CDL inspection procedure should be used in inspecting your combination vehicle. However, a combination vehicle requires you to inspect more things than you need to on a single vehicle such as the coupling system areas and landing gear. In addition to the checks previously listed, you should also do these:

Coupling System Areas

Check the lower fifth-wheel to be sure that:

- It has no damaged or missing parts.
- It is firmly mounted to the frame.
- The locking jaws are around the shank and not the kingpin's head.
- There is sufficient grease.
- The release arm is properly seated with the safety lock or latch engaged.
- There is no obvious space between the lower and upper fifth-wheel.

Check the upper fifth-wheel to be sure that:

- The kingpin is undamaged.
- The glide plate is securely attached to the trailer frame.

Check the electric and air lines connected to the trailer to be sure that:

- All air lines are properly connected to the vehicle's glad hands with no leaks and are properly secured for turns with sufficient slack.
- The electrical cord is properly plugged in and secured.
- All lines are damage-free.

Check the sliding fifth-wheel to be sure that:

- It is properly greased.
- There are no air leaks if it is air powered.
- The fifth-wheel isn't so far forward to the point of the tractor frame hitting the landing gear, or the cab hitting the trailer during turns.
- It has no damaged or missing parts.
- All locking pins are intact and locked in.

Landing Gear

Check to be sure that:

- The crank handle is secured and in the right place.
- It is fully raised with no missing parts and has no damages or bends.
- There are no hydraulic or air leaks if it is power operated.

Combination Vehicle Brake Check

In addition to the checks you need to do when inspecting air brake systems, you will also need to know how to check the air brakes on your combination vehicle. Bear in mind that the brakes on a double or triple trailer should be inspected just like any other combination vehicle.

Check the Air Flows to all Trailers. Ideally, air should flow to all the trailers and you should start your inspection by chocking the wheels and/or engaging the tractor parking brake. Wait a few moments for the air pressure to rise to the normal level and then press the red knob marked "trailer air supply". Doing this will supply the emergency lines with needed air. The trailer handbrake should be used to supply air to the vehicle's service line. To do this, go to the rig's rear and open the emergency line shut-off valve at the last trailer's rear. When you do this, you should hear air escaping, which is an indication that the entire system is properly charged. Shut the emergency line valve afterward.

Next, open the service line valve to see if all the trailers receive service pressure and then close the valve. You should ensure that your trailer's service brake pedal or handbrake is on as you perform this test. If air is not heard escaping from both lines, it could be as a result of the trailer and dolly valves being shut. Check to see that the valves are in the "OPEN" position. Note that for all your vehicle's brakes to work, there has to be air supply all the way to the back.

Test Tractor Protection Valve. Charge the trailer's air brake system by building up normal air pressure and then pressing the "air supply" knob. Turn off the engine, and step on and off the brake pedal severally to reduce the tanks' air pressure. When the vehicle's air pressure falls within the pressure range (usually 20 – 45 psi), the trailer air supply control or tractor protection valve control should pop out or switch from the "normal" position to the "emergency" position. In case the tractor protection valve malfunctions, all the air from the tractor could be drained due to a trailer brake or air hose leak. When this happens, the emergency brakes will come on, and that could also cause a possible loss of control.

Test Trailer Emergency Brakes. Charge the trailer's air brake system and ensure that the trailer rolls freely. Stop and pull the trailer air supply control out or put it in the "emergency" position. Next, pull on the trailer with the tractor gently to see whether its emergency brakes are on.

Test Trailer Service Brakes. After checking for normal air pressure, release parking brakes and slowly move the vehicle forward. If the vehicle is equipped with the hand control or trolley valve, use it to apply the trailer brakes. As you do this, you should feel the brakes get engaged which shows that they are properly connected and working. You should test the trailer brakes with the hand valve but during normal operation, they should be controlled with the foot pedal which will supply air to the brakes at all wheels.

Vocabulary and Keywords

Chock - A wedge or a block that has been placed against a wheel or other rounded object to stop it from moving or rolling.

Fifth Wheel – A mechanical vehicle component that is designed for the connection to a tractor, truck, or high-traction vehicle.

Gladhand - Also known as a gladhand connector or a gladhand coupler is an interlocking hose that is fitted to transfer pressurized air from a tractor unit to the air brakes on a semi-trailer.

Kingpin – A vertical bolt that allows for pivoting and the connection of a fifth wheel to a trailer and tractor.

CHAPTER - 8

SCHOOL BUSES

Danger Zones

The danger zones of the school bus are the areas on all sides of the bus where students are at the highest risk for injury or accident. These zones stretch out as far as 30 feet from the front bumper with the most danger in those first ten feet. The first ten feet of each and every zone around the bus are the most dangerous in each. Make sure you keep your mirrors poised so you can see as much of these spaces as possible, and make sure you are paying close attention to the students as they get on and off of the bus.

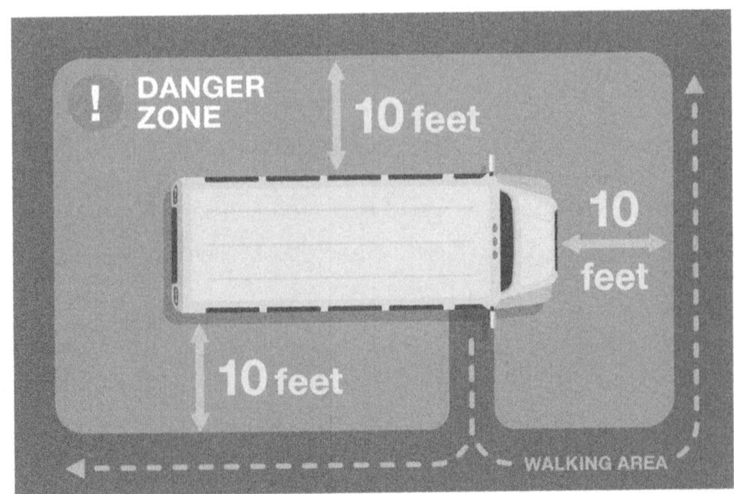

Using Your Mirrors

Using your mirrors when you are driving a commercial motor vehicle can help you to navigate traffic, watch the lanes around your vehicle, and make sure that nothing is going to sneak up on you and cause difficulty for your route. When you are in a school bus, you will be looking in your mirrors just as often, if not more. You will want to be checking your mirrors while you are waiting for students to get on and off the bus so you can see any dangers that could be around the bus and you can do your best to keep the students safe.

Make sure that your mirrors are clean and clear so you can look into them at any and all times when you're driving on your routes. You will need your mirrors for the proper management of and the safety of students in the danger zones of your vehicle.

Make sure that your mirrors are properly adjusted so you can observe the danger zones of your vehicle. You should always check each mirror before you do anything or make any changes in the positioning or handling of the vehicle.

Outside Left and Right Side Flat Mirrors

These mirrors are usually located at the front or side of the windshield on the left and right front corners of the bus. They are used for checking clearances, monitoring traffic, and looking out for students to the bus' rear and sides. Directly in the back of the vehicle's rear bumper and below and in front of each mirror is a blind spot. This blind spot extends between 50 to 150 feet and could even reach up to 400 feet depending on the bus' length and width.

Properly adjusted flat mirrors will allow you to see:

- Up to 200 feet or four bus lengths behind the bus.
- The rear tires where they meet the ground.
- All along the sides of the bus.

Outside Left and Right Side Convex Mirrors

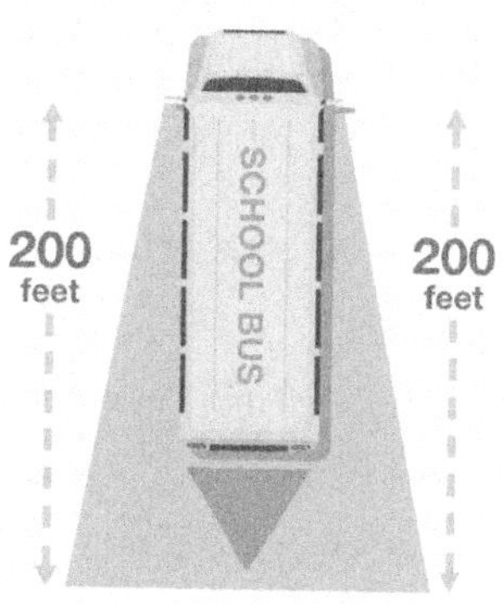

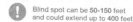

The bus' convex mirrors are located underneath the outside flat mirrors and they are used for monitoring the left and right sides of the vehicle at a wide angle. With them, the driver gets a view of students, clearances, and traffic at the side of the bus. However, the view of people and objects presented by these mirrors is not an accurate reflection of their distance from the bus and size.

Properly adjusted convex mirrors will allow you to see:

- The whole of the bus' side up to its mirror mounts.
- A minimum of one traffic lane on either side of the bus.
- The front of the rear tires where they meet the ground.

Outside Left and Right Side Crossview Mirrors

These mirrors can be found on the left anw mirrors will see:

- The entire area in front of the bus from its front bumper at ground level to a point where there can be direct vision. The mirror and direct view vision are supposed to overlap.
- The left and right front tires where they meet the ground.
- The area from the bus' front to service door.

Overhead Inside Rearview Mirror

This is mounted in the driver's area of the bus directly above the windshield. The mirror is basically for the driver to keep an eye on passenger activity inside the bus. if the bus has a glass-bottomed rear emergency door, there may be limited visibility. Behind the driver's seat is a blind spot area. There is also a large one starting at the rear bumper that could extend up to or above 400 feet behind the bus. The exterior side mirrors can be used to monitor the traffic that comes close to and enters this area.

Properly adjusted rearview mirrors will see:

- The rear window's top in the top of the mirror.
- All the students, including the heads of those directly behind you.

Loading and Unloading

Each year, a higher number of kids are killed while boarding or alighting from a school bus than as passengers inside a school bus. For this reason, it becomes imperative for bus drivers to know what to do before, during, and after loading or unloading students. There are some specific procedures that will help prevent unsafe conditions which could lead to injuries and fatalities during and after loading or unloading.

Approaching Stops

There are official school bus stops and routes for each school district and all stops need to have been previously approved by the district before you make the stop. On no account should you change a bus stop's location without a written note of approval from the appropriate official. Whenever you approach a school bus stop, you need to be very careful because you're automatically placed in a demanding position as you do so. Understanding and also acting in accordance with all state and local regulations about approaching the bus stop is essential. This would involve the correct use of alternating flashing lights, mirrors, the crossing control arm and moveable stop signal arm when equipped.

When you approach a stop, you should:

- Check all mirrors continuously.
- Approach cautiously with the vehicle at slow speed.
- Switch on the right turn signal indicator about three – five seconds before you pull over.
- Check for traffic, pedestrians, or other objects before, during, and after stopping.
- If equipped, activate alternate flashing amber warning lights about five – ten seconds before school bus stop or in line with state law.
- Keep to the right side of the portion of the roadway you're traveling on as much as possible.
- Check mirrors continuously to monitor danger zones for traffic, students and other objects.

When stopping, you should:

- Bring the bus to a complete stop with the front bumper a minimum of ten feet away from students at the stop. Doing this forces students to walk to the bus, allowing you to see their movements better.
- Place transmission in park or in neutral, if there is no park, shift point and set parking brake at each stop.
- Activate alternating red lights when traffic is at a safe distance from the school bus and make sure the stop arm is extended.
- Do a final check to see that all traffic has stopped before opening the door completely and signaling students to board.

Loading Procedures

To perform a safe stop, here are some things that you need to make sure of:

- Students should wait in a set location, facing the school bus as it comes closer.
- Students should only board the bus after being signaled to do so by the driver.
- All mirrors are closely and continuously monitored.

- Count the number of students at the bus stop and ensure they all board the bus. If you can, know the names of students at each stop and ask others for their whereabouts if one student is missing.
- Students should board slowly in single file, and make use of the handrail. When loading in the dark, you should always turn on the dome light.
- Before moving the bus, all students should be seated and facing forward.
- Check all mirrors to confirm no student is running after the bus to catch up.
- If a student is unaccounted for, secure the bus, remove the keys and look around and under the bus. When they are all accounted for, get ready to leave by closing the door, engaging transmission, releasing parking brake, switching off alternating flashing red lights, turning on left turn signal, rechecking the mirrors, and allowing congested traffic to clear up.
- Move the bus, enter traffic flow, and continue on your route when it is safe to do so.
- Essentially, the loading procedure remains the same regardless of where you load students, but there are some minor differences. When loading students at a school campus, you should turn off the ignition switch, remove the key if you're leaving your compartment, and prepare to supervise loading.

Unloading Procedures on Route

To perform a safe stop at marked unloading areas, here are some things to do:

- Let the students be on their seats until they're told to exit the bus.
- All mirrors should be checked.
- Count numbers of students during unloading to be sure of every student's location before you pull away from the stop.
- Tell students to leave bus and walk a minimum of 20 feet away from the side of the bus to a position where you can plainly see them all.
- All mirrors should be checked again, ensuring no students are around the bus or returning to it.
- Secure the bus, remove the key and look around and under the bus if a student is unaccounted for.
- When they are all accounted for, get ready to leave by closing the door, engaging transmission, releasing parking brake, switching off alternating flashing red lights, turning on left turn signal, rechecking the mirrors, and allowing congested traffic to clear up.

Note that you are not to back up the vehicle if you miss an unloading stop. Instead, follow the local procedures for dealing with such situations.

Additional Procedures for Students Crossing Roadway

If a school bus is stopped in a private road or highway to load or unload at an area where traffic isn't controlled by a traffic control signal or officer, here are some things you need to do as the driver:

- Escort all pre-kindergarteners, kindergarteners, or students in grades one through eighth who need to cross where the school bus stopped. You should use a handheld "STOP" sign while doing this.
- Require all students crossing to walk in front of the bus as they cross.

- Make sure that all students crossing where the school bus is stopped do so safely, and that all other students or pedestrians are at a safe distance from the bus before moving it.

Bear in mind that as the driver, you are required to enforce all local or state regulations regarding the actions of students outside the bus.

Unloading Procedures at School

The local and state laws and regulations concerning unloading students at school are usually different from unloading along the bus' route. This is especially so in situations where there are activities in the school's parking lot or any other location away from the traveled roadway. As the driver, it is very crucial that you understand and also obey all local and state laws and regulations. Generally, you are to follow the procedures below when unloading:

- Stop safely at a designated unloading area.
- Secure the bus by turning off the ignition switch and removing the key if you're leaving the driver's compartment.
- Have the students remain on their seats until told to leave the bus.
- Position yourself to monitor the unloading process.
- Escort any pre-kindergarteners, kindergarteners, or students in grades first through eighth who need to cross the highway where you're stopped with a handheld "STOP" sign.
- Let students exit in an orderly manner.
- Watch students as they alight from the bus to ensure they all move away from the unloading area quickly.
- Walk through the bus to inspect for sleeping or hiding students as well as items left behind by students.
- Check all mirrors to confirm no student is returning to the bus.
- When they are all accounted for, get ready to leave by closing the door, engaging transmission, releasing parking brake, switching off alternating flashing red lights, turning on left turn signal, rechecking the mirrors, and allowing congested traffic to clear up.
- Pull away from the unloading area when it is safe.

Special Dangers of Loading and Unloading

Forgotten or Dropped Objects- You should always monitor students closely and they approach the bus and look out for any who you may lose sight of. Note that sometimes during loading and unloading, a student may drop an object around the bus. Stopping or returning to retrieve the object may cause a student to disappear from your line of sight at a moment that can be very dangerous.

You should tell all students to leave all dropped objects and move to a safe point away from the vehicle's danger zones. They should then try to catch your attention or inform you in order to retrieve the said object.

Handrail Hang-Ups- Having accessories, clothing, or even body parts caught in the door or handrail when exiting has resulted in a number of injuries and even death. All students exiting the bus should be closely observed so be sure they are in a safe location before you move the bus.

Inspecting Your School Bus

In addition to the checks listed in Chapter 2 of this handbook, school bus drivers also have to inspect the following areas of the vehicle:

Emergency Equipment

School bus drivers must inspect the following emergency equipment in addition to extra electrical fuses if equipped, three red reflective triangles, six fuses or three liquid burning flares, and a properly charged and rated fire extinguisher:

- A first-aid kit.
- A kit for cleaning up bodily fluids.

Lighting Indicators

The following lighting indicators (internal panel lights) must also be checked by school bus drivers:

- If present, alternately flashing amber lights signal.
- Alternately flashing red lights indicator.
- If fitted, a strobe light indicator.

Lights and Reflectors

School bus drivers must check the following (external) lights and reflectors in addition to the vehicle's lights and reflective devices:

- If provided, the strobe light is working and not broken.
- If equipped, a stop arm light.
- If installed, alternately flashing amber lights are functional and not damaged.
- The vehicle's alternately flashing red lights on the front and back are working and unbroken.

Student Mirrors

School bus drivers must examine the internal and external mirrors used for monitoring students in addition to the external mirrors. You should:

- Make sure everything is in working order.
- Ensure that all internal and external mirrors, as well as mirror mounts, are in good condition and have no loose fittings.
- Make sure that your visibility isn't obstructed by dirty mirrors.

Stop/Safety Arm

Check the stop arm, if it's provided, to make sure it's properly attached to the vehicle's frame. You should also check for loose fittings and damage as well, and when the stop arm is operated, make sure it fully extends.

Passenger Lift/Entry

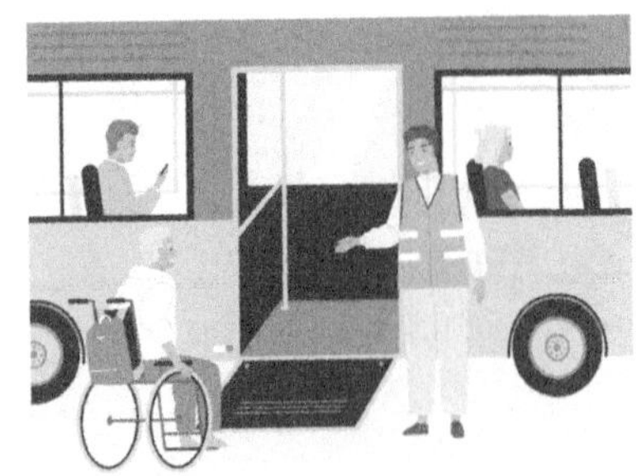

- From the inside, ensure the entry door is not broken, that it works properly, and that it shuts securely.
- Verify that the handrails are secure and that the step light, if fitted, is operational.
- Confirm that the entry steps are clear and the treads aren't loose or worn out.
- Look for leaking, broken, or missing parts if your vehicle has a handicap lift, and explain how to inspect a lift for proper operation.
- The lift must be completely retracted and properly secured.
- Verify that the lift control interlock(s) is/are working properly.

Emergency Exit

Show that at least one emergency exit is not damaged, that it functions correctly, and that it closes firmly from the inside.

- Make sure you can operate the release handle properly from both inside and outside the vehicle.
- Identify and describe the operations of all other emergency exits.
- Confirm that any emergency escape warning devices are operational.

Passenger Seating

- Look for defective seat frames and make sure they're securely fastened to the floor.
- Make sure the seat cushions are firmly attached to the seat frames.

Post-trip Inspections

After completing your route or school activity trip, you need to do a post-trip inspection of your bus. This would involve walking through and around the bus to look for sleeping students, forgotten articles, open doors and windows, mechanical problems especially with mirror systems, stop signal arms etc., and vandalism or damage. If there are any special situations or problems, you should report to the school authorities or your supervisor immediately.

Emergency Procedures

Emergency situations can happen at any time and to anyone, so it is best to be completely prepared for just such an event. This could be in the form of a medical emergency to a student on the bus, a stalled bus in a high-speed intersection or on railroad-highway crossing, an electrical fire in the bus' engine compartment, or an accident. Planning for these things can be hard, but it is important that you keep your emergency signaling equipment and first aid kits up to date and in good working order.

Planning for Emergencies

Determine if there is a need to evacuate the bus due to immediate danger. The primary and most important thing during emergencies is to recognize the hazard. If you have enough time to do so, you should get in touch with your dispatcher to explain the situation before you decide whether to evacuate the bus or not.

As a general rule, keeping students on the bus in an emergency and/or potential crisis situation is the best way to maintain student safety and control, as long as they're not exposed to unnecessary injury or risk. However, bear in mind that you need to quickly decide whether to evacuate the bus or not before it gets too late. Things that should be considered before choosing to evacuate or not are:

- Has hazardous material spilled?
- Is there a fire or a threat of one?
- Is there an odor of leaking or raw fuel?
- Is there a chance of the bus getting hit by other vehicles?
- Is there a sighted tornado or rising waters in the bus' path?
- Are there downed power lines?
- Would evacuating students expose them to severe weather, speeding traffic, or a dangerous environment?
- Would moving students worsen injuries like fractures, back and neck injuries?

Mandatory Evacuations - There are certain situations in which you are mandated to evacuate the bus. They are when:

- The bus is on fire or on the verge of catching fire.
- The bus' position may change and increase the level of danger.
- The bus is adjacent to or stalled on a railroad-highway crossing.
- There is a pending danger of an accident.
- There is a spill of hazardous materials which necessitates a speedy evacuation.

Evacuation Procedures

Plan ahead and be prepared. Whenever possible, you should assign two older and responsible student assistants to man each emergency exit. They should be taught how to help other students when they're leaving the bus. Another student assistant should be responsible for leading students to a "safe place" after evacuation. However, you may not have older and responsible students on your bus during the time of emergency, and must therefore explain the emergency evacuation procedures to all students.

Explaining to them includes knowing how to operate the emergency exits as well as mentioning the importance of listening to and obeying all instructions you give.

To determine a safe place for evacuation, you can make use of these tips:

- A safe place will be a minimum of 100 feet away from the road in the direction of oncoming traffic.
- If there is a fire, students should be led upwind of the bus.
- Lead students as far away from railroad tracks as possible and in the direction of an oncoming train, if any.
- If there is a HAZMAT spill risk, lead students upwind of the bus for a minimum of 300 feet.

If a bus is in the path of a sighted tornado and evacuation is ordered, students should be escorted to a nearby culvert or ditch if no building shelter is available. There, they should be instructed to lie face down with their hands covering their head. Areas that are prone to flash floods should be avoided, and you should lead the students as far away from the bus as possible so it cannot topple on them.

General Procedures.

You have to determine whether evacuating the students is the best way to get them to safety. To do this, here is a useful procedure you can follow:

Decide on the best evacuation type be it window, roof, rear, front, side door, or a combination of doors.

Get the bus secured by putting the transmission in park or in neutral, if no shift point; setting parking brakes; shutting engine off; removing key, and activating hazard-warning lights. If time permits, inform your dispatch office of the conditions, evacuation location, and the kind of assistance you need.

Dangle telephone or radio microphone out of your window and if it is operable, take your cell phone for later use.

Dispatch an area resident or passing motorist to get help if a cell phone or radio is absent, or inoperable. 2 older, responsible students should be sent to get help as a last resort.

Order evacuation.

Lead students out of the bus. Unless their life is in immediate danger, avoid moving a student who may have a spinal or neck injury. This is because there are special procedures for moving such victims to prevent further injury.

Instruct student assistants to lead students to the closest safe place.

Walk through the bus to be sure no students remain and retrieve emergency equipment.

Join the waiting students while accounting for them all and checking for their safety.

Keep the scene of the incident protected and set up necessary emergency warning devices as appropriate.

Collate information for emergency responders.

Recommended Procedures for Crossing Railroad-Highway Crossings

All buses must operate at crossings in line with the laws and regulations that have been set by the state. Generally, all school buses are required to stop at crossings, and as a driver, it is up to you to ensure the crossing is safe before you start across the tracks. Note that the specific procedures required vary from state to state so you need to be aware of what your state requires. Although a school bus is one of the safest vehicles on a highway, it does not have any edge at all when involved in a train accident. This is simply because a train's weight and size prevent it from stopping quickly like a vehicle, and there are no emergency escape routes. The recommended procedure for preventing school bus and train accidents is highlighted below:

Approaching the Crossing

- Slow down the vehicle, shifting to a lower gear if you're driving a manual transmission bus, and test brakes.
- Switch on the hazard lights about 200 feet before getting to the crossing and make sure that your intention to cross is known.
- Scan surroundings and look out for traffic behind your vehicle.
- If possible, keep to the right side of the roadway.
- In case of a brake failure or any problem behind you, choose an escape route.

At the Crossing

- Stop the vehicle a maximum of 15 feet to, and 50 feet from the nearest rail to you, where you can see the tracks clearly.
- Place transmission in park or in neutral if there is no park shift point, and press the service brake or set parking brakes.
- Switch off all noisy equipment such as radios, and silence the students.
- Open the driver's window and service door, and watch and listen for approaching trains.

Crossing the Track

- Before proceeding, check crossing signals again.
- Only stop the vehicle before the first set of tracks at a multiple-track crossing. Drive across all the tracks until completely cleared when you're sure there are no approaching trains on any track.
- Cross tracks in low gear and ensure you don't switch gears while you cross.
- Even if it means breaking the gate, drive through it if it comes down after you have already started across the tracks.

Special Situations

Bus Gets Trapped on Tracks or Stalls - If your bus stalls or gets stuck on the tracks, evacuate everyone from the bus and get them off the tracks immediately. Everyone should be moved far away from the bus at an angle that is toward the train and away from the tracks.

Police Officer at Crossing - You are required to obey all directions if there's an officer at the crossing. In case there is none and you think the signal isn't working properly, report the situation to your dispatcher and get instructions on how to proceed.

Obstructed View of the Tracks - At railroad-highway crossings, you should always plan your route so that you get maximum sight distance. You should never try crossing the tracks unless you can see far enough down them to be certain that there are no approaching trains. Passive crossings which do not have any traffic control device will require extra care on your part. However, you must also watch and listen to be doubly sure even if there are railroad signals that show the tracks are clear.

Storage or Containment Areas - At railroad-highway crossings on your route or any crossing you approach during a school activity trip, always know your bus' length and size of the containment area. When you encounter a crossing that has a stop sign or signal on the opposite side, pay close attention to the amount of room available. Ensure that there is sufficient containment or storage area to clear the tracks completely on the other side if you need to stop. A general rule says you should add about 15 feet to the bus' length in order to determine a sufficient amount of containment area.

Student Management

As a school bus driver, your concentration needs to be on the driving task for you to get them to and from school safely and in a timely manner. When you load and unload passengers, you should be careful not to take your eyes off what is happening outside. Even if one of your passengers has a behavior problem on the bus, wait until the unloading students are off the bus and have moved away safely before you address it. You can pull the bus over to handle such a problem if the situation warrants it.

Handling Serious Problems

For serious problems regarding student management, here are some tips to make use of:

- The school's procedures for discipline or refusal of bus-riding rights.
- Stop the bus in a safe location away from the road such as a driveway or parking lot.
- Secure the bus and if you have cause to leave your seat, take the vehicle's ignition keys along with you.
- Stand and speak to the offending student or students firmly in a courteous manner. Remind them of the kind of behavior they are expected to show while on the bus in a way that indicates you mean business.
- If you need to change their seating position, ask them to move to a seat close to you so you can keep an eye on them.
- Never unload students anywhere apart from their designated school bus stop, or at school. In case of a serious offense that may hinder you from driving safely, call the police or a school administrator to remove the student.
- Follow all state or local procedures for getting assistance.

Special Safety Considerations

Strobe Lights - Some buses have white strobe lights mounted on their roofs to help with visibility. If your bus is equipped with these, it implies that you cannot see in front, beside, or behind the school bus easily. Visibility could either be slightly limited or so bad that you can't see anything at all. The bus' strobe lights should only be used in poor atmospheric conditions such as snow, dust, snow, fog, etc. when visibility falls to or below 500 feet.

Driving in High Winds - Driving in strong winds can be tricky as they affect the bus' handling. The side of your bus functions like a sail on a sailboat, and strong winds can push the bus sideways. In some situations, the bus can be moved off the road or even worse, tipped over.

If you ever find yourself caught in strong winds, you should grip the steering wheel strongly and try anticipating gusts. Slow down the vehicle to reduce the wind's effect or if possible, pull off the roadway for some time until the strong wind stops. If you need more information on how to move your bus, get in touch with your dispatcher.

Backing

Any time you drive a school bus, it is highly recommended that you do not back it as it is dangerous and increases the chances of an accident. Backing should only be done when there is no other safe way to move the vehicle. However, backing is never an option when there are students outside the bus. In situations where you have no choice but to back the vehicle, follow these procedures:

- You may flash the bus' hazard lights when backing to warn pedestrians or other motorists.
- Post a lookout to warn you about other vehicles, obstacles, and persons. They should not give traffic directions.
- If there is no lookout, set the parking brake, switch off the engine and remove keys, and walk to the bus' rear to ensure the way is clear.
- Signal for silence on the bus.
- Check rear windows and mirrors constantly.
- Back the bus smoothly and slowly.
- If you have to back up at a student loading point, double check that you pick all students up before you do so and always watch out for latecomers.
- Ensure all students are inside the bus before backing.
- If you have to back up at a drop-off point, ensure you unload students after, and not before backing.

Tail Swing

A school bus' tail swing can measure up to 3-foot in length. Before and while making any turning movements, you have to check your mirrors carefully and this is even more important when driving away from loading or unloading points.

CHAPTER - 9

DOUBLES AND TRIPLES

Pulling Doubles and Triples

When pulling two and three trailers, you have to be extra careful. This is because there can be more issues while driving, and these kinds of vehicles are generally less stable compared to other commercial motor vehicles. Below are some areas of concern that you need to be extra careful about:

Prevent trailer from rolling over. To prevent a roll over, you need to steer the vehicle gently and reduce speed around curves, off ramps, on ramps, and around corners. Bear in mind that a speed that may be safe for a single trailer combination vehicle or a straight truck may be too high for a set of doubles or triples.

Watch out for the crack-the-whip effect. Due to this effect, doubles and triples have a higher tendency to turn over so you should always steer gently when you pull trailers.

Do a thorough inspection. With two or three trailers, you have more critical parts to look out for, be sure to check all of them carefully.

Look far ahead. To prevent jackknife or rollover, you need to drive doubles and triples smoothly. The best way to ensure you do this is by looking far ahead enough so you know when you slow down or switch lanes before it gets too late.

Manage your space. Expectedly, doubles and triples use up more space compared to other commercial motor vehicles. Aside from the added length, they also cannot be stopped or turned suddenly and so require more allowance. Therefore, you should always allow extra following distance and ensure the gaps available are large enough before you cross or enter traffic. Changing of lanes too should only be done when you are very sure that the vehicle's sides are clear.

Adverse conditions. Adverse conditions like mountain driving, slippery conditions and bad weather will require you to be even more careful when driving vehicles like these. You will have more length and dead axles to pull with the drive axles compared to drivers of other vehicles. As a result of this, there is a higher risk of skids and traction loss.

Parking the Vehicle

Be sure that you do not park in a spot that you can't pull straight through when leaving. Know the arrangements of parking lots so that you don't have to go through a difficult and long escape.

Coupling and Uncoupling

Knowing the correct way to couple and uncouple doubles and triples is a basic step to operating them safely. If they are not properly coupled and uncoupled, it can be very dangerous. If you need to couple or uncouple doubles and triples, here are the steps you should follow:

Coupling Double Trailers

SECURE REAR TRAILER

Drive the tractor near the trailer, connect the emergency line, charge the trailer air tank, and disconnect the emergency line if the rear trailer doesn't have spring brakes. As long as the slack adjusters are properly adjusted, doing this should set the trailer's emergency brakes. If you're not sure whether the brakes will hold, you can chock the wheels. For safe handling, the lighter trailer should come last while the more heavily loaded trailer should come immediately after the tractor.

POSITION CONVERTER DOLLY IN FRONT OF REAR TRAILER

On a dolly is a converter gear which is a coupling device that has one or two axles and a fifth wheel. It is used for coupling semi trailers to the rear of a tractor-trailer combination to form a double rig. To use this device:

Open air tank petcock to release dolly brakes or use the parking brake control if the dolly is equipped with spring brakes.

Wheel dolly into position by hand if the distance isn't too far so that it aligns with the kingpin.

You can also use the tractor and the first trailer to pick up the converter dolly. To do so:

- Position the combination to the converter dolly as close as possible.
- Move dolly to rear end of the first semi trailer and couple to trailer.
- Lock pintle hook.
- Secure dolly support in raised position.
- Pull the dolly as close as possible to the front end of the second semi trailer.
- Lower dolly support.
- Unhook dolly from the first trailer.
- Wheel dolly into position in front of the second trailer to align with the kingpin.
- Connect converter dolly to front trailer.
- Back first trailer into position before the dolly tongue.
- Hook dolly to front trailer by locking pintle hook and securing converter gear support in raised position.

CONNECT CONVERTER DOLLY TO REAR TRAILER

- Ensure brakes are locked and/or wheels chocked.
- Make sure trailer height is accurate. Ideally, it should be a bit lower than the fifth wheel's center so that pushing the dolly under the trailer will raise it up slightly.
- Back converter dolly under rear trailer.
- Raise landing gear off the ground slightly to prevent damage in case the trailer moves.
- Test coupling by pulling against the second trailer's pin.
- Visually inspect the coupling to make sure locking jaws are closed on the kingpin, and there is no space between the lower and upper fifth wheel.
- Connect air hoses, light cords, and safety chains.
- Shut the converter dolly's air tank petcock and shut off the valves at the second trailer's rear.
- Open shut-off valves at the second trailer's rear and on the dolly as well, if equipped.
- Raise landing gear completely.
- Charge trailer brakes by pushing in the "air supply knob" and then check air at the second trailer's rear. There is a problem if air pressure is absent and that will prevent the brakes from working.

Uncoupling Double Trailers

UNCOUPLE REAR TRAILER

- Park rig in a straight line on a firm level surface.
- Apply the vehicle's parking brakes to avoid movement of the rig.
- Chock the second trailer's wheels if there are no spring brakes equipped.

- Lower second trailer's landing gear enough to take some weight off the dolly.
- Close air shut-offs at the first trailer's rear, and on the dolly if equipped.
- Disconnect all dolly electrical and air lines and secure them.
- Release dolly brakes.
- Release converter dolly's fifth-wheel latch.
- Pull the tractor, first trailer, and dolly forward slowly to get the dolly out from under the trailer at the rear.

UNCOUPLE CONVERTER DOLLY

- Lower dolly landing gear.
- Disconnect safety chains.
- Chock vehicle wheels or apply converter gear spring brakes.
- Release first trailer's pintle hook.
- Pull clear of the dolly slowly.

You should never unlock the pintle hook when the dolly is still underneath the rear trailer. Doing so may cause the tow bar to lift up, increasing the risk of injury and making recoupling difficult.

Coupling and Uncoupling Triple Trailers

COUPLE TRACTOR OR FIRST TRAILER TO THE SECOND OR THIRD

- Couple tractor to first trailer.
- Move converter dolly into position and couple the first trailer to the second one with the method used to couple doubles in order to complete the triples rig.

UNCOUPLE TRIPLE TRAILER RIG

- Uncouple the third trailer by pulling dolly out and unhitching it with the method used to uncouple doubles.
- Uncouple the rig's remainder the same way you would any double-bottom rig.

CHAPTER - 10

TRANSPORTING HAZARDOUS MATERIALS

Who Does What?

Shipper

The shipper sends the transport from one location to another through airplane, rail, truck, or vessel. They will also make use of HAZMAT regulations to determine the product's ID number, proper shipping name, hazard class, packing group, correct packaging, correct placards, and correct label and markings. They must also prepare shipping papers; package, mark, and label materials; supply placards, and provide emergency response information. The shipper has the responsibility of certifying on the paper that the shipment has been prepared according to HAZMAT rules unless the cargo tank being pulled is supplied by you or your employer.

Carrier

The carrier plays the role of taking the shipment from the shipper to the correct destination. Before transporting, they check that the shipment has been properly described, labeled, marked, and prepared by the shipper for transporting. They are also to refuse any improper shipments.

Driver

The driver ensures that the shipper has properly identified, labeled, and marked the HAZMAT. They refuse leaking shipments and packages, and if required, placard the vehicle during loading. The driver plays the role of transporting the shipment in a safe and timely manner. All special rules concerning the transportation of HAZMAT are strictly followed and they properly keep all HAZMAT emergency response information and shipping papers. In case of any accident or incident while in control of the shipment, the driver is required to report to the appropriate government agency.

Loading and Unloading Hazardous Materials

Shipping HAZMAT is an especially tricky task that requires a high level of care and precision. As the driver, you should always do all that is possible to protect the containers of HAZMAT you're chipping. Hooks, as well as any other tool that can damage packaging when loading should be avoided.

General Loading Requirements

Before you load or unload HAZMAT you need to set the parking brake and ensure that the vehicle doesn't move.

HAZMAT should be loaded away from heat sources as heat increases the hazardousness of many products.

Inspect for leaks or damaged containers as leaking is a huge sign of trouble. You should never transport leaking packages because you, the material, the truck as well as other people might be in danger. Doing this is illegal and could get you into problems with the law.

To keep packages from moving while they're being transported, all HAZMAT containers must be properly braced.

You or people nearby are not allowed to smoke around hazardous materials. All fires should be kept away during loading and unloading. Smoking around explosives, flammable gas, flammable liquids, flammable solids, and oxidizers is totally prohibited.

Containers should be secured against moving to prevent falling, sliding, or bouncing around as they are being transported. Containers with valves and other fittings require extra caution during loading. After you load, you should avoid opening any package during the course of your trip. HAZMAT should never be transferred from one package to another while in transit and while a cargo tank may be emptied, no other package may be emptied while on the vehicle.

Cargo Heater Rules

There are some special cargo heater rules that apply when loading explosives, flammable gas, and flammable liquids. Usually, cargo heaters, as well as automatic cargo heater or air conditioner units, are forbidden from being used. Unless all related rules have been carefully read, these three hazard classes should never be loaded in a cargo space with a heater.

Overhang or tailgate loads of explosives, flammable solids, and oxidizers are prohibited and you should use a closed cargo space instead. Unless all the packages are covered with a fire and water-resistant tarp or are fire and water resistant, these materials have to be loaded in a closed cargo space.

Precautions for Specific Hazards

– Class 1 Materials (Explosives). Before you load or unload any explosive, the vehicle's engine must be turned off. Afterward, check the cargo space and do the following things:

- Disable the cargo heaters. Disconnect the heater's power sources and drain the heater fuel tanks.
- Ensure that there are no sharp points that can damage your cargo such as bolts, nails, broken floorboards, broken side panels, and screws.
- Floor linings should be used with explosives in Division 1.1., 1.2, and 1.3. The floors must be tight and the liner should be made of either non-ferrous metal or non-metallic material.
- Extra care should be used to protect explosives and they should never be dropped, thrown or rolled. All explosive packages should be kept away from other cargo that may damage them.

A Division 1.1, 1.2, or 1.3 explosives should not be transferred between vehicles on a public road unless it is an emergency. In case an emergency transfer is necessary for safety, three bi-directional emergency reflective triangles should be set out and other people on the road alerted. You should avoid transporting damaged packages of explosives including packages that show an oily stain or dampness.

Division 1.1 or 1.2 explosives should not be transported in vehicle combinations if there is a placarded or marked cargo tank in the combination. They also should not be transported if another vehicle in the combination is carrying initiating explosives; packages of radioactive materials marked "Yellow III"; poisonous materials or poisonous gas; and hazardous materials in a DOT Spec 106A or 110A tank or portable tank.

– Class 4 and Class 5 (flammable solids and oxidizers) Materials. Materials in the Class 4 category are solids that react to air, water, and heat or even spontaneously. Such materials including those in Class 5 must be securely covered or completely enclosed within a vehicle. As for materials that become unstable and harmful when they're wet, they must remain dry during loading and unloading and while in transit. Those that are prone to spontaneous heating or combustion should only be carried in vehicles with adequate ventilation.

– Class 8 (corrosive) Materials. If you're loading the vehicle by hand, breakable containers of corrosive liquid should be loaded one after the other with their right sides up. Do not roll or drop them and the surface they are loaded on should be even. Carboys should only be stacked if the tiers below can safely bear the weight of the upper tiers. Nitric acid should not be loaded above other products and when loading charged storage batteries, do so in such a way that the liquid does not spill with their right sides up.

Corrosive liquids should not be loaded above or next to explosives C, flammable solids, dangerous when wet materials, oxidizers, and poisonous gases. When loading corrosive liquids, avoid loading them alongside explosives A, explosives B, blasting agents, poisonous gases, spontaneously combustible materials, and poison liquids.

– Class 2 (compressed gases) Including Cryogenic Liquids. When transporting these materials, the cargo space floor must be flat if there are no racks for holding cylinders in your vehicle. The cylinders must be held upright and should either be inside boxes that will prevent them from turning over or in racks that are attached to the vehicle. If the cylinders are designed in a way that the relief valve is in the vapor space, they may be loaded horizontally.

Division 2.3 or 6.1 (poisonous gas or poisonous) materials. These materials should never be transported in containers that have interconnections. Packages that are labeled POISON or POISON INHALATION HAZARD should not be loaded in the driver's sleeper or cab, or with food material for animal or human consumption. Special rules apply to loading and unloading Class 2 materials in cargo tanks and you must be specially trained to do so.

– Class 7 (radioactive) Materials. Some Class 7 material packages have a number known as the "transport index" on them. The shipper will label such packages Radioactive II or Radioactive III and print its transport index on the label. Each package is surrounded by radiation and this also passes through other packages nearby. In order to prevent this problem, the number of packages that can be loaded together including their closeness to animals, people and unexposed film is controlled. The degree of control that you need when transporting these materials is stated on the transport index. The total transport index of all packages in one vehicle must not be above 50.

– Mixed Loads. Some products are required to be loaded separately and cannot be loaded together in the same space. Below are some examples of such products alongside materials they should not be stored with:

1. Division 6.1 or 2.3 (materials with POISON or POISON INHALATION HAZARD) should not be loaded in the same vehicle with human or animal food unless the poison is carefully packed in a way that is approvable.

2. Division 2.3 (Poisonous gas zone A) or 6.1 (poisonous liquids, PGL zone A) explosives, oxidizers, flammable liquids, corrosive liquids, organic peroxides, blasting agents, flammable gases, and flammable solids.

3. Charged storage batteries should not be loaded with explosives.

4. Class 1 (detonating primers) should not be loaded with any other explosives except for those in authorized packages or containers.

5. Division 6.1 (cyanides or cyanide mixtures) should not be loaded with corrosive materials, acids, or other acidic materials that can release hydrocyanic acid such as sodium cyanide and silver cyanide.

6. Nitric acid (Class 8) should not be loaded with other materials unless it is not placed above another material.

Bulk Packaging Marking, Loading and Unloading

When it comes to bulk packaging of hazardous materials, cargo tanks and portable tanks are the two main types that are used. Cargo tanks are bulk packaging that is permanently fixed to a vehicle. This means that they remain on the vehicle during loading and unloading. There are different types of cargo tanks in use but the most common ones are the MC331 for gases and MC306 for liquids. As for portable tanks, they are bulk packaging which do not have a permanent attachment to the vehicle. For them, loading and unloading of products only take place when the tanks are off the vehicle. Afterward, they are placed on a vehicle to be transported.

Markings

Whenever you're shipping HAZMAT in cargo tanks, portable tanks, or any other type of bulk packaging like dump trucks, the ID number must be clearly displayed. The rules require black numbers measuring 100 mm on orange panels and placards, or a white diamond-shaped background if you are not required to use placards. Specification cargo tanks must display markings of their retest date. As for portable tanks, the owner or lessee's name must be displayed including the contents' shipping name on two opposing sides. On portable tanks with capacities above 1,000 gallons, the shipping name letters must be a minimum of two inches tall while those on tanks with capacities below 1,000 gallons should be 1 inch tall. The ID number must be seen on each side and end of a portable tank or any other bulk packaging that holds up to or above 1,000 gallons, and on two opposing sides if the tank holds below 1,000 gallons. Even while on the vehicle, the ID numbers on the portable tank must be visible. If they aren't, it must be displayed on both sides and ends of the vehicle.

Intermediate bulk containers or IBCs are also bulk packaging but are not required to display owner or shipping name, unlike tanks.

Loading Tanks

Whoever is in charge of loading and unloading cargo tanks should always ensure that a qualified person watches. They must be alert, see the cargo tank carefully, be within 25 feet, know the hazards of involved materials, know appropriate

emergency procedures, and be able to and authorized to move the cargo tank. Cargo tanks that are transporting anhydrous ammonia and propane have special attendance rules to be fooled.

Before you move a tank containing HAZMAT, you need to close all valves and manholes regardless of how short the distance or how small the amount is. Closing valves and manholes is necessary to prevent leaks and it is illegal to move cargo tanks with open covers or valves unless empty.

Flammable Liquids

Before loading or unloading, the first step is to turn off the vehicle's engine, and you should only run it if you need to operate a pump. Cargo tanks should be correctly grounded before filling through an open filling hole. Ground the tank before the filling hole is opened, and maintain it until after closing the hole.

Compressed Gas

On a compressed gas tank, liquid discharge valves should always be closed except during loading and unloading. Your engine should be turned off when loading or unloading unless it uses a pump to transfer products. If you use the engine, turn it off after the product has been transferred, and before unhooking the hose. Note that before you move, couple, or uncouple a cargo tank, all loading and unloading connections must be unhooked first. When you uncouple from the power unit, be sure to chock trailers and semi trailers at all times to prevent them from moving.

Driving and Parking Rules

Parking with Division 1.1, 1.2, or 1.3 Explosives

You should never park Division 1.1, 1.2, or 1.3 explosives within five feet of the part of the road you are traveling on. Except you're only parking for a short time for vehicle operation necessities such as fueling, you are not to park within 300 feet of an open fire, place where people gather, tunnels, bridges, or buildings. If you need to park to do your job, make the stop as brief as possible.

You also should not park on private property unless the property owner is aware of the risk. Someone has to keep an eye on the vehicle at all times and you can only let someone else do this for you if your vehicle is on the shipper's, carrier's, or consignee's property.

Your vehicle can be left unattended in a safe haven which is a place approved for parking unattended vehicles carrying explosives. Local authorities are usually in charge of designating authorized safe havens.

Parking Placarded Vehicle Not Transporting Division 1.1, 1.2. Or 1.3 Explosives

Placarded vehicles that are not laden with explosives may only be parked briefly within five feet of the part of the road you are traveling on if work requires you to. Whenever you park on a public roadway or shoulder, there must always be someone to watch it for you. You should never uncouple a trailer with HAZMAT and leave it on a public street nor should you park within 300 feet of an open fire.

Attending Parked Placarded Vehicles

Anyone who is attending to a placarded vehicle must:

- Remain in the vehicle and awake, and not inside the sleeper berth, or within 100 feet of the vehicle with the vehicle in their clear view.
- Know about the hazards of the materials being shipped.
- Know emergency procedures.
- Be able to move the vehicle, if necessary.

Avoid the Use of Flares

Occasionally, the vehicle may break down and you'll have to make use of stopped vehicle signals. Red electric lights or reflective triangles are a good option in such situations, burning signals like fuses or flares should never be used around a tank for flammable liquids or flammable glass regardless of whether it is empty or loaded. They should also not be used around vehicles carrying Division 1.1, 1.2, or 1.3 explosives.

Route Restrictions

In certain states and countries, you are required to hold a permit before you can transport hazardous materials or waste. These areas could also limit the number of routes available to you. However, local rules concerning routes and permits are subject to change and it is up to you to find out if you must make use of special routes, or need permits. If you need a permit, be sure that you have gathered all the necessary papers before you start.

If you are employed by a carrier, you can ask your dispatcher about permits and route restrictions. If you're an independent driver with plans to use a new route, get in touch with state agencies where you want to travel. In certain localities, drivers are prohibited from transporting hazardous materials over bridges, through tunnels, or other roadways. Be sure to check and get accurate information concerning this before starting a trip.

Whenever you're driving a placarded vehicle, you should avoid crowds, narrow streets, tunnels, alleys, and populated areas. Even if it is not convenient, you should use an alternative route, unless there isn't any. Placarded vehicles should never be driven close to open fires unless you can pass safely without stopping the vehicle.

To transport Division 1.1, 1.2, or 1.3 explosives, there must be a written route plan for you to follow. Carriers are responsible for preparing this plan beforehand and providing the driver a copy. However, you can plan out the route yourself if the explosives are picked up at a location aside from your employer's terminal. The route plan should be written in advance and you should hold on to a copy while transporting explosives. Shipment of explosives should only be delivered to authorized persons, or they should be left in a secure room designed for storing explosives.
The carrier should choose the safest route for transporting placarded radioactive materials and after doing so, tell the driver about the materials, and show the route plan.

No Smoking

You are not to smoke within 25 feet of a placarded cargo tank carrying flammable liquids or Division 2.1. Smoking or carrying lighted cigars, pipes, or cigarettes within 25 feet of a vehicle containing explosives, flammable liquids, flammable solids, spontaneously combustible materials, or oxidizers is also prohibited.

Turn off Engine during Refueling

Before you fuel a vehicle that contains hazardous materials, you should always turn off your engine. At all times, there should be someone at the nozzle controlling fuel flow.

Fire Extinguisher

Placarded vehicles' power units must have a fire extinguisher with an Underwriters Laboratories (UL) rating of up to or above 10 B:C.

Check Tires

- Ensure that the vehicle's tires are properly inflated.
- Each tire on your vehicle must be examined at the start of each trip and whenever you park the vehicle.
- The use of a tire pressure gauge is the only acceptable way to inspect tire pressure.

Avoid driving with a flat or leaking tire except to the closest safe place to get it fixed. Any overheated tire should be removed and placed at a safe distance away from the vehicle. Until the cause of the overheating is determined, avoid driving the vehicle and follow the rules about attending and parking placarded vehicles. Bear in mind that these rules are applicable even when you're repairing, replacing, or checking tires.

Shipping Papers and Emergency Response Information

A HAZMAT shipment that does not have a shipping paper that is properly prepared should never be accepted. This is why it is essential that you know all the sections on a shipping paper, as well as the correct information to be written in each. A shipping paper for hazardous materials must be easily recognized at all points m and should be kept in a place where other people can quickly find it after an accident.

Shipping papers for hazardous materials should be clearly distinguished from others by keeping them in separate tabs or placing them on top of your paper stack. You should be able to reach the papers with your seatbelt on and they must be seen easily by anyone entering the cab. Always remember to leave shipping papers on your seat or in your door pouch. Emergency response information and the shipping paper should be kept in the same location.

PAPERS FOR DIVISION 1.1, 1.2, OR 1.3 EXPLOSIVES

Each driver that is transporting Division 1.1, 1.2, or 1.3 explosives must be given a copy of the Federal Motor Carrier Safety Regulations, Part 397 by the carrier. Along with this should also be written instructions on what the driver should do if there is a delay or an accident. These instructions should include the nature of the explosives being transported, names and number of people to contact including shippers or carrier agents; and precautions to be taken during emergencies of leaks, accidents, or fires. When you receive these documents, remember that you are required to sign for them.

While you drive, you should have good knowledge of, and possess shipping papers, written emergency instructions, a written route plan, and a copy of Part 397 of the FMCSR.

Chlorine Equipment

If you're transporting chlorine inside cargo tanks, you need to have an approved gas mask inside the vehicle. You must also have an emergency kit to control leaks in the cargo tank's dome cover plate fittings.

HAZMAT Emergencies

Emergency Response Guidebook (ERG)

The Emergency Response Guidebook or ERG is a guidebook provided by the DOT for firefighters, industry workers, and police to learn how to protect the public and themselves from hazardous materials. This guide is indexed by the HAZMAT's ID number and proper shipping name which emergency personnel will look for on the shipping paper. This is why it is crucial that the placards, label, ID number, and shipping names entered in the shipping papers are accurate.

Accidents/Incidents

In case you're involved in an accident or an incident takes place, your job at the scene as a professional driver is to keep people away from the scene while limiting the spread of the material if you can safely do so. You are also to share the HAZMAT's danger with emergency response personnel and give emergency responders the shipping papers along with the emergency response information. Below is a checklist you should follow in situations like this:

- Check to ensure your driving partner is alright.
- Carry the shipping papers with you.
- Keep people far away from and upwind of the vehicle.
- Warn other people of the danger.
- Call for help.
- Follow employer's instructions.

Fires

Minor truck fires that take place on the road might have to be controlled by you. However, do not try fighting HAZMAT fires unless you have the right equipment and training to do so safely. This is because fires like this require protective gear and special training.

You should call for help as soon as you discover a fire, and use a fire extinguisher to prevent a minor fire from spreading to cargo before the arrival of a firefighter. Before you open a trailer door, you should always feel them for signs of heat. If it is hot to touch, there may be a cargo fire and you should leave the doors closed. This is because opening the doors will allow air in which may cause the fire to flare. Many fires only smolder until the arrival of firefighters when denied air, and end up doing less damage. If your cargo is already burning, don't try to fight the fire on your own as it isn't safe to do so. Instead, have shipping papers handy so that you can hand them to the emergency personnel immediately they arrive. While they are on their way, you should alert people of the danger and keep them away from the scene.

You should also call for help if you discover a leak from the cargo you're transporting. Use the shipping papers, package location, or labels to identify the hazardous material that is leaking. By all means, avoid touching leaking materials as you can injure yourself by doing so. You also should not try to find the source of a leak or identify the material by smelling it. This is because toxic gases can injure, kill, or destroy your sense of smell even if they cannot be perceived. Drinking, eating, or smoking around a spill or leakage is totally prohibited in HAZMAT transportations.

A HAZMAT spill from your vehicle is another situation that also requires you to get help as soon as possible. You should not move the vehicle any more than is required for safety when this happens. If doing so will ensure safety, you may move it off the road and away from locations where people are gathered. Note that the vehicle should be moved only if you can do so without endangering yourself and other people.

If there is HAZMAT leaking from your vehicle, you should never continue driving to find help, a truck stop, phone booth, or any similar reason. Bear in mind that the carrier will have to pay for the cleanup of contaminated drainage ditches, roadways, and parking lots. These costs are very high, so try to make the contamination trail as short as possible. If HAZMAT is spilling, take the following steps:

- Park the vehicle.
- Get the area secure.
- Remain with the vehicle.
- Use your Citizens band Radio (CB) or cell phone to place a call for help.
- If Citizens Band Radio or cell phone does not work, send someone else to get help.

When sending someone to get help, provide the person with a description of the emergency; the exact location and travel route; your name and carrier's name, and city or community where the terminal is loaded; and the proper shipping name, hazard class, and HAZMAT ID number, if known. This information can be a lot for one person to remember so it is always advisable to write it all down for the person being sent to get help. It is important to do this because this information must be available to the emergency response team for them to know the best way to locate you and handle the emergency. Getting to the scene may require traveling for several miles on their part, so giving them all the necessary information will enable them to bring the correct equipment along on the first trip. If you're pressed for time, it may be quicker to snap your shipping papers and emergency contact information with the cell phone of the person getting help than to write them out.

In situations where moving the vehicle will either damage the vehicle or lead to contamination, avoid doing so. Keep the vehicle upwind and far away from businesses, cafes, truck stops, and roadside rest stops. You should never try repacking or repairing leaking HAZMAT containers unless you have the right training and equipment to do so safely. If you're caught up in such a situation and do not know what to do, call your supervisor or dispatcher and, if needed, emergency personnel to get instructions.

Responding to Specific Hazards

Class 1 (Explosives) - If there is a vehicle breakdown or accident while carrying explosives, you are to alert other road users of the danger and keep bystanders away from the scene. Do not allow anyone to smoke or build an open fire anywhere close to the vehicle. If there is a fire, alert everyone of the danger of an explosion. If a vehicle or more is involved in an incident with the vehicle transporting HAZMAT, all the explosives should be carefully removed before the vehicles are separated. After removing them, they should be placed about 200 feet away from occupied buildings and vehicles. Always keep a safe distance away from the explosives.

Class 2 (Compressed Gases) - Other people should be alerted of the danger if there is compressed gas leaking from your vehicle. It is only those that are involved in the removal of the hazard or wreckage that should be allowed to get close. The shipper must be notified immediately if there is any accident involving compressed gas. Note that a flammable compressed gas should not be transferred between tanks on a public roadway unless you are fueling machinery used for road maintenance or construction.

Class 3 (Flammable liquids) - If you're transporting flammable liquid and there is an accident or the vehicle breaks down, do not allow bystanders to gather around the scene. People should be warned of the danger and smoking of any kind should be discouraged. At no point should you transport a leaking cargo farther than you need to reach a safe place. If you can safely do so, get off the roadway. Flammable liquids should only be transferred between vehicles on a public roadway during emergencies.

Class 4 (Flammable Solids) and Class 5 (Oxidizing Materials) – If there is a spill of an oxidizing material or flammable solid, you need to alert others of the fire hazard. Smoldering packages of flammable solids should never be opened, but should only be safely removed from the vehicle if you can do so. You can also remove undamaged packages if doing so will reduce fire hazards.

Class 6 (Poisonous Materials and Infectious Substances) – Your job as a driver is to protect yourself, others, and property from harm when transporting these materials. Bear in mind that a lot of products that are categorized as poison are flammable as well. You need to take added precautions for flammable gases or liquids if you think a Division 2.3 or 6.1 HAZMAT may be flammable. Welding, smoking, or the use of an open flame near the vehicle should be disallowed. Warn people around of the hazards of fire, inhaling vapors, or coming in contact with the poison.

A vehicle carrying Division 2.3 or 6.1 materials must be inspected for stray poison before you use it again if it is involved in a leak. If a Division 6.2 package gets damaged while you're handling or transporting it, your supervisor should be contacted as soon as possible. Do not accept any package that looks damaged or shows leakage signs.

Class 7 (Radioactive Materials) - You should tell your supervisor or dispatcher as soon as possible if the material's package gets broken or leaks. In case of a spill, or damage to an internal container, avoid inhaling or touching the material. The vehicle should not be operated until it has been properly cleaned and checked using a survey meter.

Class 8 (Corrosive Materials) - During a spill or leakage when transporting these materials, you should be careful not to injure or damage them further when handling their containers. If any parts of the vehicle are exposed to a corrosive liquid, they must be washed with water thoroughly. After unloading the cargo, wash out the vehicle's interior as soon as you can before you reload it. In situations where continuing to transport a leaking tank could be dangerous, you are to get the vehicle off the road. If transporting is safe, you should try to contain the liquid escaping from the vehicle. Bystanders should be prevented from getting close to the liquid and its fumes, and you should do all you can to prevent injury for yourself and others.

Required Notification

The National Response Center is responsible for coordinating emergency response to various chemical hazards. It serves as a resource for firefighters and police, and has a 24-hour toll-free line that you can call which is **1-800-424-8802**. When any of the occurrences listed below take place due to a HAZMAT incident or accident, you or your employer are required to phone:

- A person gets killed.
- A person gets injured and requires hospitalization.
- There is damage to property estimated above $50,000.
- The general public is evacuated for a period of time longer than 1 hour.
- One or more major transportation facilities or arteries remain closed for a period of time longer than or up to 1 hour.
- There is an occurrence of a breakage, fire, spillage, or suspected radioactive contamination.
- There is a breakage, fire, spillage, or suspected contamination of a shipment of infectious substances such as toxins or bacteria.
- A marine pollutant above 882 pounds for a solid or 119 gallons for a liquid is released; or there is a situation that the carrier thinks should be reported to the National Response Center.

If you phone the National Response Center, the information you should be ready to provide include:

- Your name.
- Carrier's name and address.

- Your phone number where you can be reached.
- Location, time, and date of incident.
- Extent of injuries, if any.
- If such information is available, the name, classification, and quantity of the HAZMAT involved.
- The of incident, nature of HAZMAT involvement, and whether there is a continuous danger to life at the scene.

Shipper's name and quantity discharged if a reportable quantity of hazardous substance is involved in an incident or accident.

Your employer should also be given all required information. When there is an incident, the carrier is required to write detailed reports within 30 days of the occurrence to the Chemical Transportation Emergency Center (CHEMTREC) on **1-800-424-9300**.

HAZMAT Glossary

Bulk packaging- Packaging other than a vessel or barge, such as a transport vehicle or freight container, in which HAZMAT are loaded with no intermediary form of containment and has:

1. A liquid receptacle with a maximum capacity of more than 119 gallons (450 L).

2. A receptacle for solids with a maximum net mass of 882 pounds (400 kg) and a maximum volume above 119 gallons (450 L)

OR

3. A receptacle for a gas with a water capacity larger than 1,000 pounds (454 kg) as described in CFR, Title 49, Section 173.115.

Cargo tank- A bulk packaging that is:

1. A tank designed primarily for the transportation of liquids or gases, which contains appurtenances, reinforcements, fittings, and closures.

2. Is permanently attached to or forms a part of a motor vehicle, or is not permanently attached to a motor vehicle but, due to its size, construction, or attachment to a motor vehicle, is loaded or unloaded without being detached from the vehicle.

3. Not designed in line with a specification for portable tanks, tank cars, cylinders, or multi-unit tank car tanks.

Division- A subdivision of a specific hazard class.

EPA- United States Environmental Protection Agency.

Freight container- A container with a volume up to, or above 64 cubic feet, designed to be lifted with its contents and primarily for holding packages in unit form when transporting

Fuel tank- A tank aside from a cargo tank that is used to move combustible or flammable liquid or compressed gas, to

supply fuel for operating another equipment on the vehicle, or the vehicle itself.

Gross weight or mass- The total weight of the packaging including its contents' weight.

Hazard class- The hazard category assigned to a HAZMAT based on the CFR, Title 49, Part 173 defining criteria and the CFR, Title 49, 172.101 table. Although a substance may match the basic criteria for more than one hazard class, it is only allocated to one.

Hazardous materials/HAZMAT- A substance or material that has been recognized by the United States Secretary of Transportation as having the potential to pose an undue risk to health, safety, or property when moved in commerce. Hazardous substances, hazardous wastes, marine pollutants, elevated temperature materials, and materials designated as hazardous in CFR, Title 49, Part 172.101, as well as materials that meet the definition criteria for hazard classes and divisions in CFR, Title 49, Part 173, Subchapter C, are all included in this definition.

Hazardous substance- A substance, including its mixtures and fluids, that meets the following criteria:

1. Appears in Appendix A to CFR, Title 49, Section 173 & 172.101.

2. Is in a quantity that is up to, or above the reportable quantity (RQ) indicated in Appendix A of CFR, Title 49, Part 173 and 172.101 in one package.

AND

3. When used in a combination or solution for the following purposes:

– Radionuclides, in accordance with paragraph 7 of CFR, Title 49, Part 173 and 172.101.

– Is in a concentration by weight that equals or surpasses the concentration corresponding to the RQ of the material, excluding radionuclides.

This term does not apply to lubricants or fuels made from petroleum.

Hazardous waste- This includes any substance subject to the EPA's Hazardous Waste Manifest Requirements, as defined in CFR, Title 40, Section 262.

Intermediate bulk container- A stiff or flexible portable container different from a portable tank or cylinder that is meant for mechanical handling.

Limited quantity- The maximum amount of a hazardous material for which special labeling or packaging exceptions may apply.

Marking- The descriptive name, ID number, instructions, cautions, weight, specification, United Nations (UN) marks, or combinations thereof necessary on a HAZMAT product packaging.

Mixture- A substance that contains more than one chemical ingredient or element.

Name of contents- The HAZMAT's proper shipping name as stated in Title 49, Section 172.101 of the Code of Federal Regulations.

Non-bulk packaging- A package that includes:

1. A liquid receptacle with a maximum capacity of 119 gallons (450 L) or less.

2. A solid receptacle with a maximum net mass of 882 pounds (400 kg) or less and a maximum capacity of 119 gallons (450 L).

OR

3. A receptacle for a gas with a water capacity greater than 1,000 pounds (454kg) or less, as specified in CFR, Title 49, Section 173.115.

4. A maximum net mass of 400 kilograms (882 pounds) or less for a bag or box complying with the applicable standards for specification packing, including the maximum net mass limits, set out in CFR, Title 49, Part 178, Subpart L, regardless of the definition of bulk packaging.

N.O.S.- Not otherwise specified.

Outage or ullage- The amount by which a container falls short of being filled with liquid, commonly represented in percent by volume. The amount of outage necessary for liquids in cargo tanks is determined by how much the material expands in response to temperature shifts during transit. The expansion rates of various materials vary. There must be enough of a power outage so the tank does not fill up at 130 degrees Fahrenheit.

PHMSA- Pipeline and Hazardous Materials Safety Administration, U.S. Department of Transportation, Washington, DC 20590.

Portable tank- Bulk packaging (excluding a cylinder with a water capacity of up to, or lower than 1,000 pounds) that is designed to be loaded onto, on, or temporarily attached to a transport vehicle or ship, and that is fitted with skids, mountings, or accessories to make mechanical handling of the tank easier. A freight tank, tank car, multi-unit tank car tank, or trailer transporting 3AX, 3AAX, or 3T cylinders is not included.

Proper shipping name- The name of the HAZMAT in Roman numerals, not italics in CFR, Title 49, 172.101.

P.s.i or psi- Pounds per square inch

P.s.i.a. or psia- Pounds per square inch absolute

Reportable Quantity (RQ)- The quantity provided in Column 2 of Appendix A to CFR, Title 49, Section 172.101 for each substance named in Column 1 of Appendix A,

Shipper's certification- A declaration on a shipping form signed by the shipper stating that the shipment was correctly prepared in accordance with the regulations. As an illustration:

"This is to verify that the above-mentioned materials are correctly classified, described, packaged, marked, and labeled, and are in proper shipping condition, as per applicable Department of Transportation regulations."

OR

"I hereby declare that the contents of this consignment are fully and accurately described above by the proper shipping name, and that they are classified, packaged, marked, labeled/placarded, and are in all respects in proper condition for transportation by (insert mode of transportation, such as rail, aircraft, motor vehicle, or vessel) in accordance with applicable international and national government regulations."

Shipping paper- A shipping order, bill of lading, manifest, or other shipping document prepared for a similar purpose in compliance with CFR, Title 49 172, Subpart C.

Technical name- A recognized chemical or microbiological term being used in scientific and technical handbooks, journals, and publications.

Transport vehicle- A cargo-carrying vehicle, such as a car, van, tractor, truck, semi-trailer, tank car, or rail car, that is used for cargo transportation by any method. Each cargo-carrying body (trailer, train car, etc.) represents a different transport vehicle.

UN standard packaging- Packaging criteria that are in compliance with UN recommendations.

UN- United Nations

CHAPTER - 11

TANK VEHICLES

Driving Tank Vehicles

Due to the high center of gravity and liquid movement, transporting liquids in tanks demands relevant skills. Certain vehicles that transport liquids or gases require an "N" endorsement. It is not necessary for the liquid or gas to be a HAZMAT. If you want to haul a liquid or liquid gas in a tank or tanks with an individual rating capacity of more than 119 gallons and an aggregate rated capacity of 1,000 gallons or more that is either permanently or temporarily attached to the vehicle or chassis, you'll need an "N" endorsement.

A tank vehicle is not a commercial motor vehicle (CMV) that transports an empty storage container tank that is not designed for transportation with a rated capacity of at least 1,000 gallons and is temporarily coupled to a flatbed trailer.

You should always inspect a tanker before loading, unloading, or driving it. This ensures that the vehicle is both safe to drive and safe to transport the liquid or gas. It is illegal for a CLP holder with an "N" endorsement to operate a tank vehicle unless it is empty. In addition, the tanker must be purged if it formerly contained HAZMAT.

A commercial skills test is necessary if a candidate is only applying for a Class C CDL with an "N" endorsement. The applicant must be tested in a representative Class C CMV designed to transport liquid or gaseous materials in a tank or tanks with an individual rated capacity of more than 119 gallons and a tank or tanks with an aggregated rated capacity of up to, or above 1,000 gallons temporarily or permanently attached to the chassis or vehicle.

Leaks

With the completion of all applicable knowledge examinations, an "N" endorsement can be added to a current Class C CDL; the commercial skills test is not necessary. Leaks are the most crucial thing to look for in any tank vehicle. Look for signs of leaking under and around the vehicle. A leaking tank should not be used to transport liquids or gases and it is criminal to do so. You'll get a ticket and won't be able to drive any further. You could also be held accountable for any spill cleaning. In general, keep the following in mind:

Look for dents or leaks in the tank's body or shell.

Make sure the intake, discharge, and cut-off valves are all in good working order.

Before loading, unloading, or driving the vehicle, double-check that the valves are in the proper position.

Check for leaks in pipes, connections, and hoses, especially around joints.

Examine the vents and manhole covers. Check to see if the lids have gaskets and that they close properly.

Keep the vents clear so they work correctly.

Inspect Special Purpose Equipment

Check to see if any of the following items are in good condition in your vehicle:

- Vapor recovery kits
- Cables for grounding and bonding.
- Emergency shutoff systems.
- Built-in fire extinguisher.

Note that driving a tank vehicle with open valves or manhole covers is never a good idea.

Special Equipment

Check your vehicle's emergency equipment requirements. Find out what kind of equipment you'll need and ensure you have it and that it works.

High Center of Gravity

The load's high center of gravity causes much of \d on ramp/off ramp curves.

CHAPTER - 12

THE ROAD TEST

The latest version of the CDL road test, at the time of writing, is about two and a half hours long. It is made up of three sections that will assure the evaluator that you are ready for your commercial driver's license. The three parts of the test are:

- The Pre-Trip Inspection
- Parking
- Driving on Roadways and Highways

Each of these sections takes a variable amount of time with the most focus on your abilities to inspect and park your vehicle. In this chapter, we will explain each portion of the road test and what will be expected of you to get a passing grade on your examination.

Just like with any test or exam, you will need to make sure that you have studied properly. While logging hours of study or driving school are not requirements for licensure, these are the best ways to make sure that you're getting out onto the road with the most confidence and with as much useful knowledge as possible.

Part One of the Road Test: The Pre-Trip Inspection

This section of the exam typically takes about an hour to complete. The examiner or evaluator may ask you to begin your pre-trip inspection at a different point of the vehicle, but for the sake of ease, I will begin this walkthrough from the very front of the vehicle, through the inspection of the under-hood elements, then along the driver's side toward the back, along the back of the vehicle, then back up toward the front.

You will notice that some sections are repeated a couple of times. This is absolutely intentional. Your examiner will want you to cover things as they come up along your inspection because you will be expected to inspect these elements in each instance. You cannot inspect the brakes for one set of tires and assume that all the others are in exactly the same condition.

It will be imperative for your evaluator to be confident in your ability to properly assess the working order and the overall safety of your vehicle before you take it out onto the road with other motorists.

Once you have read this section of this manual, familiarize yourself with your own vehicle as there very well may be differences between the vehicle referenced in this section and your own vehicle. If you are not sure what the parts of your vehicle look like or how to find them, there are many resources available online, and you can also enroll in a local driving course that will teach you what all of these technical parts are, what they do, and how to tell at a glance that they're in good working order. They will also teach you what parts cannot be evaluated simply at a glance and will

subsequently teach you how best to evaluate them.

I will mention this in the next section as well, but another thing to bear in mind is that it is important for you to take your road test and to do all practical learning exercises in the same type of vehicle that you will be operating, if not in the actual vehicle you intend to use. While you can practice and learn on someone else's vehicle, the DMV will prefer that the vehicle you use for the test is the very one that you are being licensed to operate.

Further requirements for the exam extend to the vocabulary. You want to make sure that you refer to the parts of the vehicle and the requirements for each of those parts in just the right way so the evaluator can be certain that you know what you're looking for and that you are capable of determining the working order and condition of your vehicle and its components.

You will walk around the vehicle with your evaluator and point to each of the areas of the vehicle while stating what you're looking at and what signs you're watching for in each of them. In some cases, the evaluator will ask you about these parts of the vehicle, but many times, it will be up to you to tell the evaluator what you know.

Starting from the very front of your vehicle, looking straight at the windshield, you should be able to see the clearance lights on top of the cab. They should be amber or yellow in color and they must be clean, and functional with no breaks or damage.

The windshield wipers must be securely mounted, smoothly operational, with functional and clean rubber seals.

The headlights of the vehicle must be clean and functional with no breaks or cracks, and proper coloring regulations dictate that they should be clear.

The fog lights on the front of the vehicle should be clean and functional with no breaks or cracks, and proper coloring regulations dictate that they should be clear.

Mirrors are clean, securely mounted on functional brackets. No breaks in the mirrors and they're properly adjusted.

When standing at the front of the vehicle, there should be no puddles beneath the vehicle that would indicate dripping from the engine or the transmission.

Open the hood and indicate the parts of the vehicle that require pre-trip inspection and what you're looking for in each of them. You will need to make sure that you know as much as possible about what's under the hood of your vehicle so you're not pointing to things that aren't there, missing things that are there, etc. The following are examples of parts that are under the hood of one sample vehicle but make sure that you make your own list of under-hood components and study and familiarize yourself with them thoroughly.

Now that the hood has been opened and you have another vantage point to the ground beneath the engine, make sure that there are no puddles of fluid on the ground that would indicate dripping fluid from the engine or the transmission.

Hoses must be in good working condition, securely fastened, and not leaking on either end or in between.

The power steering fluid must be at the safe operating range in the reservoir, above the refill mark.

Check the oil dipstick with the engine off to make sure that your oil level is at a safe operating range and above the refill mark. You do not have to pull the dipstick out for the test, just indicate to the evaluator that you know how to do that when conducting your own pre-trip inspections. If you do choose to pull the dipstick out for the test, just make sure you don't drip oil and make sure that any spills or drips are properly cleaned before proceeding.

The power steering box must be mounted securely, with no leaks or damage, and there must be no missing nuts or bolts. All the hoses to and from the power steering box must be securely fastened, not broken, and not leaking.

Next, you will want to check the steering linkage. The pitman arm, drag link, and tie rod must be in good, working condition with no breaks or damage. Make sure they are not worn or cracked, that the connections are not worn or loose, and there are no missing nuts, bolts, or cotter keys (also known as split pins, or cotter pins).

Air compressor must be operating properly, not damaged or leaking, and securely mounted.

Alternators must be operating properly, not damaged or leaking, and securely mounted. The belt on the alternator must have no more than ¾ inch of play and must have no cracks or frays.

The power steering pump must be operating properly, not damaged or leaking, and must be securely mounted.

Come around to the passenger's side of the vehicle and check all the hoses and make sure that they are in good condition and not leaking.

Once again, from your new vantage point to the area underneath the engine, make sure that there are no puddles of fluid on the ground that would indicate dripping fluid from the transmission or engine.

Make sure that the coolant is at the safe operating range, above the refill mark. If you do not have a clear plastic coolant reservoir, make certain that the engine is off and has cooled before you remove the cap to check the coolant level. Taking the cap off of the coolant reservoir when the engine is off can cause problems, so it's best to do this when the engine has been off for some time.

The water pump must be operating properly, not damaged or leaking, and securely mounted.

Come back around the front of the vehicle and begin to work your way back along the driver's side for the remainder of this portion of the test.

There are a lot of tires on your vehicle, which means that you have suspension and brakes for each set of those. You want to make sure that you have this section down because if you miss the same item for each tire on this portion of your exam, that will cost you a lot of points and could set you back.

We're going to begin with the suspension components on the front end of the vehicle, on the driver's side. These portions will be repeated throughout this section so you can hear them, become familiar with them, and know what you're looking for and what you should be communicating to your examiner when that time comes for you.

The leaf springs must not be shifted, cracked or broken.

The spring hangers must be securely mounted to the frame and must not be cracked or broken.

The U bolts that hold the leaf spring in place must be securely mounted to the axle and must not be missing any nuts or bolts, and must not be broken in any way.

The shock absorber must be securely mounted and must not be leaking.

Bushings on the top and bottom of the shock absorber must be securely mounted to the frame and axle with no breaks or missing bolts.

The slack adjuster and pushrod must not be missing any parts and cannot move more than one inch with the brakes released when pulled by hand.

The brake chamber must not be dented, cracked, broken, or leaking. It also must not be missing any clamps, nuts or bolts.

The brake hoses, lines, and couplings must not be cracked, worn, or leaking.

The brake drums must not be cracked or broken and must be free of contaminants such as debris, oil, and grease.

The brake lining must not be worn or dangerously thin.

Tread depth must be no less than 4/32 of an inch, the tire must be evenly worn, and there must be no cuts or damage to the tread or sidewall of the tire.

The rim must not be cracked or damaged and must have no evidence of welding repair or damage.

Mirrors and mirror brackets must be secure and properly adjusted and there must be no broken or loose fittings.

The driver's side door must open and close properly from the outside. The seal must be intact and the hinges must be secure.

The turn signal light must be yellow or amber in color, clean and functional and must not be cracked or broken.

The steps up to the cab must be solid, clear of objects, and securely mounted to the tractor frame.

The steps up to the catwalk must be solid, clear of objects, and securely mounted to the tractor frame.

Air/electric lines must not be cut, chaffed, spliced or worn. Electric lines must have no steel braid showing through.

Gladhand connectors on the lines to the attached trailer must be secure, not leaking, and properly seated in place on either end of the connection.

Electrical plugs must be firmly seated and in place on either end of the connection.

Frame members and cross members must have no cracks, holes, or damage.

Catwalk must be clear of any objects and must be secured to the frame.

Drive shaft must be secure, not bent, and the couplings must be free of any foreign objects.

Exhaust must be securely mounted, free from any leaks or damage. Must not be leaking materials such as carbon soot or rust.

Header board on the trailer must have no holes, bulges or cuts and must be strong and secure enough to properly hold the cargo inside.

Reflective tape must be clean, functional, and proper color (white and red).

The reflectors must be clean and functional, no severe damage, amber or yellow in color.

Important note: The reflective strips, reflectors, and lights must be mentioned each time you pass one on your way around the vehicle. If you see a reflector, check that everything is in good condition and state that you have checked this out loud. I won't list it several times here, because it would be just about every other item, but your examiner will be glad to know you're paying attention to each visibility component of your vehicle.

The splash guards in front of your tires must not be broken or frayed and must be securely mounted.

For dual tires, check your spacers. Budd spacers have to be evenly centered, the tires must be evenly separated, and the space between the tires and the area around the budd spacers must be free of any debris.

Splash guards or mud flaps must be securely mounted to the tractor frame.

The fifth wheel connection locking jaws must be fully locked and secure around the kingpin, which must not be bent or damaged. The fifth wheel skid plate must be properly lubricated, and the fifth wheel must be properly secured to the platform. The fifth wheel platform must be properly secured with no cracks or damage and must be secured to the frame of the vehicle. If you have a sliding fifth wheel, you must make sure that all the pins are securely in place. Trailer apron must not be damaged and there must be no gap between the trailer apron and the fifth wheel skid plate. The release arm must be in the engaged position and the safety latch must be locked in place.

Tail lights must be red and free of breaks or cracks, and should be clearly visible.

Air ride suspension components cannot be damaged or leaking.

Leaf springs must not be shifted, cracked, or broken and must be securely in place.

Make sure the spring hangers are securely mounted to the frame and are not cracked or broken.

The U bolts that hold the leaf spring in place must be securely mounted to the axle and must not be missing any nuts or bolts, and must not be broken in any way.

The bushings located on the top and bottom of the shock absorber must be securely mounted to the frame and axle with no breaks or missing bolts.

Any reflective tape you pass on your inspection should be pointed out and verified to be clean, not damaged, and properly placed. You must also do this for plastic reflectors and for lights that line the top of the trailer as well.

The landing gear underneath your trailer must be locked securely into the fully-raised position. Support frames and landing pads should be in good condition with no breaks or damage, and the crank handle for the landing gear must be securely locked into place. Door ties, if present, should be secure and free of damage.

If your trailer has a side door, make sure that it opens and closes properly from the outside and that hinges and door seal are secure and functional (though, your testing examiner will not require that you demonstrate the working order of the hinges and the seal; only that the door properly opens, closes, and locks from the outside). The door chain should be securely mounted as well, with no breaks or damage.

At the back of the vehicle, you must verify that your tail lights and turn signals are the proper color, are not broken or damaged, are properly functional, and are clearly visible.

You must verify that your clearance lights are the proper color, are not broken or damaged, are properly functional, and are clearly visible.

The rear door should open and close properly from the outside, though you do not need to open the door all the way. All door locking mechanisms should be functional and not broken or damaged.

Making your way back up the passenger's side of the vehicle, once again check all the tires, brakes, and suspension components for each set of tires.

The brake lining must not be worn or dangerously thin.

The fuel tank underneath the passenger's side door should be secured with straps that are connected to the tractor frame. The cap should be securely fastened and there should be no leaks from the tank or from the fuel lines.

The final stop on the pre-trip inspection is to inspect the front passenger's side tire.

Tire tread depth on tires in the front of the vehicle must not be any less than 4/32 of an inch, the tire must be evenly worn, there must be no cuts or damage to the tread or sidewall of the tire.

The brake lining must not be worn or dangerously thin.

This concludes the pre-trip inspection of your vehicle.

Part Two of the Road Test: Parking

Follow the instructions of the examiner, ask if you have any questions.

Back up straight for 100 feet. (Get out once and pull up once)

Off-set backing. Right or left, they will tell you. Figure out your start and end points and get to know them before moving. Take your time, do not rush. This section isn't timed.

Parallel park to the driver's side

Parallel park to the passenger's side

Alley docking. When you dock your vehicle, you will be lining your truck up between two sets of cones and stopping short of a third line of cones that runs parallel to your bumper. If you are not between the cones or if you are outside that line, that will cost you 10 points on your test, if not failing you the whole maneuver.

On every maneuver except for straight backing, you can get out twice to look and you can pull up twice for free. Pulling up means moving forward, such as to straighten yourself out so you can back up again. Save at least one get-out-and-look for the end of each maneuver so you can make sure that you've done everything properly. Put the vehicle in neutral, apply the parking brake, then get out and look around. Getting out of the vehicle more than these two times is an automatic failure.

Part Three of the Road Test: Driving on Roadways and Highways

This is arguably the easiest part of the CDL test because it puts all the focus on your ability to drive the truck along with traffic. Just mind your mirrors, keep the local laws in mind, keep your eyes on the road, and drive safely.

Turns

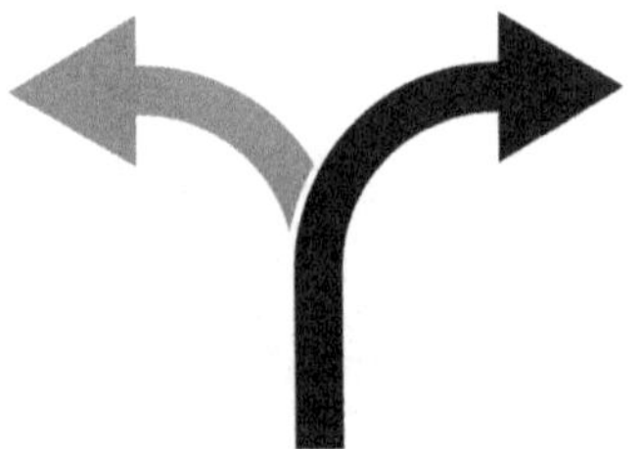

When the examiner asks you to make a turn:

Look in all directions for incoming traffic

Use your turn signals before safely getting into the lane you need to make the turn.

As you approach the turn:

Warn other road users by switching on your turn signals

Slow down the vehicle smoothly and switch gears as needed but avoid coasting unsafely.

Unsafe coasting takes place when the vehicle's gearshift is in neutral or the clutch is depressed for more than the vehicle's entire length.

If you need to make a stop before turning:

Bring the vehicle to a smooth stop without skidding

Stop the vehicle completely behind the stop sign, crosswalk, or stop line.

If you're stopping behind another vehicle, stop at a point from which you can see the rear tires of the vehicle in front of you.

Stop carefully to prevent the vehicle from rolling

The vehicle's front wheels should always be aimed straight ahead

When you're ready to turn the vehicle:

Check for incoming traffic from all directions

Place both hands on the steering wheel as you turn

Check your mirrors frequently while turning to ensure the vehicle doesn't hit anything

Prevent the vehicle from moving into incoming traffic

Steer carefully so the vehicle finishes the turn in the right lane

After making the turn:

Ensure that your turn signal is turned off

Meet up with traffic speed, switch on turn signals, and move into the rightmost lane when safe

Use mirrors to check for traffic

Intersections

As you approach the intersection:

Check thoroughly for traffic in all directions

Bring the vehicle to a slow speed

Apply brakes smoothly and switch gears if needed

If needed, bring the vehicle to a complete stop behind a stop signal, stop line, stop sign, or sidewalk, and keep a safe gap between your vehicle and the one in front of you.

Prevent the vehicle from rolling forward or backward

Note that you should never enter an intersection if there isn't enough space for your vehicle to clear it.

When driving through an intersection:

Look in all directions for traffic

Decelerate and give way for any traffic and pedestrians at the intersection

Avoid changing lanes while driving through the intersection

Place your hands on the wheel at all times

After driving through the intersection:

Keep checking mirrors for traffic

Speed up smoothly and switch gears as needed

Urban Business

At this point during your test, you are to make frequent traffic checks and keep a safe following distance. You should center your vehicle in the rightmost lane and keep up with traffic flow, but be sure not to exceed the stated speed limit.

Changing Lanes

The examiner will ask you to switch lanes to the left and back to the right during multiple lane portions of the test. Before doing so, make the needed traffic checks and use the correct turn signals. Wait for a safe gap before you move into a lane and leave a safe following distance between you and the preceding vehicle.

Before you drive into the expressway:

Look for traffic

Make use of the correct turn signals

Merge the vehicle smoothly with the accurate traffic

Once you're on the driveway:

Remain on the correct lane, keep sufficient distance between you and the vehicle in front of you, and ensure that you drive within the stated speed limit.

Continue checking for traffic properly in all directions

When leaving the expressway:

Carry out the needed traffic checks

Make use of the correct signals

Slow down smoothly in the exit lane

As soon as you're on the exit ramp, keep decelerating within the lane markings, and keep enough spacing between your vehicle and others.

Stop/Start

To do this maneuver, the examiner will ask you to pull over at the roadside and park like you wanted to get out and inspect something on your vehicle. When doing this, you must check thoroughly for traffic in all directions before moving to the shoulder of the road or rightmost lane.

When you're about to stop:

Look out for traffic

Switch on your right turn signal

Slow down the vehicle smoothly, apply brakes evenly, and switch gears as needed

Bring the vehicle to a complete stop without coasting

As soon as you stop the vehicle:

The vehicle must be parallel to the road's shoulder or curb and safely out of the flow of traffic

The vehicle should not block off any signs, driveways, intersections, fire hydrants, and so on

Switch off the turn signal

Engage the 4-way emergency flashers

Use the parking brake

Shift the gear stick to Park or Neutral

Step off the brake and clutch pedals

When you're asked to resume:

Use mirrors to check thoroughly for incoming traffic from all directions

Switch on the 4-way emergency flashers

Switch on the left turn signal

Release parking brake and drive straight ahead when traffic allows you to conveniently do so

Avoid turning the wheels before the vehicle moves

Check for traffic coming from all directions, especially the left side of the vehicle

Steer the vehicle and speed up smoothly into the correct lane when it is safe to do so

Switch off the left turn signal as soon your vehicle joins the flow of traffic.

Curve

When you're approaching a curve:

Check for traffic thoroughly in every direction

Reduce the vehicle speed before driving into the curve to eliminate the need for further shifting or braking

Steer the vehicle properly so that it remains in the same lane

Check continuously for incoming traffic from all directions

Railroad Crossing

Before you arrive at the crossing, you should:

Slow down, apply brakes smoothly, and switch gears as needed

Check and listen for the presence of trains

Check for incoming traffic from all directions

Keep the vehicle in the rightmost lane if you're driving on multiple lanes

Avoid stopping, changing gears, overtaking another vehicle, or changing lanes while any vehicle part is still in the crossing

If you're driving a school bus, vehicle with placards, or bus, the following procedures should be observed at all railroad crossings, unless they are exempt:

Activate the vehicle's 4-way emergency flashers as you approach a railroad crossing

Stop the vehicle within 50 feet from the nearest rail, but not less than 15 feet away

Look in both directions along the track and listen for approaching trains or signals indicating a train's approach. If you're driving a bus, you may also need to open up the doors and windows before you cross the tracks

As you drive the vehicle across the tracks, be sure to place both hands on the steering

Avoid switching gears, changing lanes, or stopping while any vehicle part is still across the train tracks

Deactivate the vehicle's 4-way emergency flashers after crossing the tracks

Check mirrors continuously for incoming traffic.

It is important to bear in mind that it isn't all road test routes that will have a railroad crossing. If you use such a route, the examiner may just ask you to explain and also demonstrate the correct crossing procedures at a simulated location.

Bridge/Sign/Overpass

The examiner may ask you to tell them the posted height or clearance after driving underneath an overpass. They may also ask you to say the posted weight limit after you drive over a bridge. If your test route doesn't have an overpass or bridge, the examiner may ask you about any other traffic sign present. When you're asked, be ready to identify said sign, and also explain its meaning to the examiner.

Student Discharge

If you're trying to get a school bus endorsement, the examiner will ask you to demonstrate the procedures for loading and unloading students at stops.

General Driving Behaviors

Your overall performance in the general driving categories below will influence how the examiner will score you during the road test. They are:

Clutch usage (For vehicles with manual transmission)

Always make use of the clutch when shifting

You must always double-clutch when shifting if your vehicle has a manual transmission that is unsynchronized. Avoid revving the engine or lugging it

Avoid coasting while the vehicle clutch is still depressed, riding the clutch as a means to control vehicle speed, or "popping" the clutch

Gear usage (For vehicles with manual transmission)

Avoid clashing or grinding the gears

Switch to a gear that does not lug or rev the engine

Avoid shifting at intersections and when making turns

Brake usage

Avoid pumping or riding the brake

Avoid slamming down on the brakes. To brake, do so smoothly with steady pressure

Lane usage

Avoid driving the vehicle over lane markings, sidewalks, or curbs

Always stop the vehicle behind stop signs, crosswalks, or stop lines

On multiple lane roads, the turn should be completed in the right lane i.e., a left turn should be finished in the lane that is directly to the center line's right side

Complete a right turn in the rightmost lane

Remain in, or switch to the rightmost lane unless there is a blockage on the lane

Steering

Avoid under-steering or over-steering the vehicle

Unless you're shifting, always place both hands on the steering wheel. After shifting, return both hands to the wheel immediately.

Regular traffic checks

Look out for traffic frequently

Use the vehicle mirrors regularly

Use mirrors to check for traffic before, while in, and after driving through an intersection

Scan and look out for traffic in high volume areas and highly populated spaces where there will be many pedestrians

Using turn signals

Make proper use of the vehicle turn signals

Engage the turn signals when needed

Always make use of the turn signals at the right times

Remember to switch off turn signals after completing a lane change or turn

The Points System

The fewer points, the better. 12 points fails. 0-11 passes. Using your pull ups and get-outs can cost you points. Hitting the cones and lines on the course will cost multiple points, the values for which are determined by your evaluator, the local DMV guidelines, and the severity of the cross. Not following directions can also cost you multiple points.

CHAPTER - 13

THE PRACTICE TEST

1. What should you do to make sure that you are as alert as possible throughout your trips in your vehicle?

- ☐ A. Maintain a daytime schedule for your driving
- ☐ B. Get 8 to 9 hours of sleep the night before your trip
- ☐ C. Avoid any medications that might cause drowsiness or fatigue
- ☐ D. Do all of the above

2. The maximum GVW or Gross Vehicle Weight specified by the manufacturer for a single vehicle (including the weight of its cargo), is the ___________

- ☐ A. Gross Vehicle Weight Rating
- ☐ B. Gross Combination Weight Rating
- ☐ C. Gross Vehicle Weight
- ☐ D. Gross Combination Weight

3. How can you be certain that your vehicle is equipped with an Anti Lock brake system (ABS)?

- ☐ A. Check that your vehicle was manufactured after March 1, 1998, because vehicles made after that are required to have a panel light that indicates them
- ☐ B. Check the instrument panel for a yellow ABS malfunction light
- ☐ C. Look for sensor wires coming from the rear of your brakes that are for the wheel speed sensors.
- ☐ D. All of the above will work

4. Is it easier to brake in a truck with no load than in a truck with a full load?

- ☐ A. No
- ☐ B. Yes
- ☐ C. Yes, but only on wet surfaces
- ☐ D. Yes, but only if the truck was manufactured after 1998

5. When traveling at 55 miles per hour in a vehicle that is 30 feet long, how many seconds of following distance should you leave?

- ☐ A. 3 seconds
- ☐ B. 4 seconds
- ☐ C. 9 seconds
- ☐ D. 12 seconds

6. Why is it that when you do your pre-trip inspections, you should always have the starter switch key in your pocket?

- ☐ A. Because someone could start and move the truck while you're inspecting it
- ☐ B. Because it could damage the starting mechanism
- ☐ C. Because someone could steal your vehicle while you're conducting your inspection
- ☐ D. Because any of the above can happen

7. Which of these items is NOT a necessary component for your emergency kit?

- ☐ A. Spare electrical fuses
- ☐ B. Warning devices
- ☐ C. A functional fire extinguisher
- ☐ D. A spare jacket

8. When you conduct a walk-around inspection of your vehicle using the 7-Step Inspection Method, what should you be looking for on the left side of the vehicle?

- ☐ A. Clean window on the driver's side door
- ☐ B. Any missing, bent, or broken clamps, studs, or lugs
- ☐ C. Properly inflated tires and properly secured valve stem caps
- ☐ D. Properly functional door latches and locks
- ☐ E. All of the above

9. Which of the following is the most important hand signal for you and your helper to agree upon before it's needed?

- ☐ A. "Stop"
- ☐ B. "Go"
- ☐ C. "Turn up the music"
- ☐ D. "Speed up"

10. If there is an obstruction in the road and you are blocked on both sides of the vehicle, what should you do?

☐ A. Brake hard and hold the wheel straight

☐ B. Steer right

☐ C. Brake lightly and hold the wheel straight

☐ D. Steer left

11. What is the minimum depth for front tire treads?

☐ A. 1/32 inch

☐ B. 1/2 inch

☐ C. 3/8 inch

☐ D. 1/8 inch

12. What constitutes a hazard on the road?

☐ A. Something you must stop for

☐ B. Something you can safely ignore

☐ C. Something you can easily avoid

☐ D. A road user or road condition that presents a possible danger

13. The color of your vehicle's turn signal at the rear should be ________

☐ A. Red

☐ B. Amber

☐ C. Yellow

☐ D. Any of the above

14. Why should you always try to back toward the driver's side of the vehicle?

☐ A. Because you can see better, watching the rear side of the vehicle from the driver's side window

☐ B. Because your vehicle will likely be pulling toward the driver's side

☐ C. Because it's more comfortable for turning your neck

☐ D. All of the above

15. If you're on the road and you experience a tire failure, which of the following should you AVOID?

☐ A. Holding the steering wheel tightly

☐ B. Keeping your foot off the brake pedal

- ☐ C. Being aware that a tire has failed
- ☐ D. Braking hard and immediately

16. If you swing wide to the left before you turn right in your commercial motor vehicle, what might happen?

- ☐ A. You might cause damage to the leaf springs in your vehicle
- ☐ B. Someone may attempt to pass you on your left and may become a collision risk
- ☐ C. Someone may attempt to pass you on your right and present an obstruction or collision risk
- ☐ D. All of the above are possible

17. When ensuring that you are safely transporting your cargo, which of the following does NOT fall under your responsibility?

- ☐ A. Making sure that cargo is properly secured
- ☐ B. Recognizing possible overloads
- ☐ C. Inspecting the cargo
- ☐ D. Verifying and ensuring the freshness of the contents of sealed cargo

18. If an aggressive driver confronts you on the road, you should ___________

- ☐ A. Avoid making eye contact with the aggressive driver
- ☐ B. Call the police using your cellular phone if you are in the position to do so safely
- ☐ C. Ignore any rude gestures or comments and refuse to react in a negative manner
- ☐ D. Do all of the above

19. How far ahead of you should you look when you're on the road?

- ☐ A. 5 to 10 seconds
- ☐ B. 7 to 12 seconds
- ☐ C. 10 to 12 seconds
- ☐ D. 12 to 15 seconds

20. Why should the cargo in your vehicle be covered?

- ☐ A. Because many states make cargo coverings a requirement
- ☐ B. To keep individuals safe in the event of any spilled cargo
- ☐ C. To keep the cargo clean and safe in the event of inclement weather
- ☐ D. For all the reasons listed above

21. What are hazardous materials placards?

- ☐ A. Hazardous materials placards are signs posted on the inside of the vehicle to remind the driver of what he or she is carrying
- ☐ B. Hazardous materials placards are signs posted on the outside of the vehicle to identify the hazard class of the cargo within
- ☐ C. Hazardous materials placards are signs that help tax collectors and auditors to determine how much to tax the hazardous cargo
- ☐ D. Hazardous materials placards are signs that warn other motorists to keep a safe distance of at least 1,000 feet from the vehicle

22. When you are driving and it has just reached freezing temperatures, which of the following areas might be slippery?

- ☐ A. An area that is shaded
- ☐ B. A road that looks wet
- ☐ C. A bridge
- ☐ D. All of the above

23. How many seconds does it take for a typical tractor-trailer to cross a double railroad track?

- ☐ A. More than 15 seconds
- ☐ B. More than 30 seconds
- ☐ C. 10 seconds
- ☐ D. 14 seconds

24. An Anti Lock Braking System will allow you to ___________

- ☐ A. Drive at a higher speed without worrying about braking times
- ☐ B. Brake hard without the wheels locking up
- ☐ C. Brake in a much shorter distance
- ☐ D. Stop your vehicle with more power

25. Choose the item below that is a key component of the steering system in your vehicle.

- ☐ A. Bearing plate
- ☐ B. Torque rod
- ☐ C. Leaf spring
- ☐ D. Gear box

26. When driving your vehicle at night, which of the lights on your truck should you be using as often as possible?

- ☐ A. Hazards or emergency flashers
- ☐ B. High beams
- ☐ C. Novelty lights
- ☐ D. Low beams

27. If you are in a situation in which you must stop on a one-way road or a divided highway, where should you place your warning devices around your vehicle to signal other motorists?

- ☐ A. 20 ft., 50 ft., and 100 ft. facing the approaching traffic
- ☐ B. 50 ft., 100 ft, 150 ft., facing the approaching traffic
- ☐ C. 10 ft., 100 ft., 200 ft. facing the approaching traffic
- ☐ D. 100 ft., 200 ft., and 300 ft., facing the approaching traffic

28. An example of a key suspension part is the ___________

- ☐ A. Drag link
- ☐ B. Spindle
- ☐ C. Hydraulic shock absorber
- ☐ D. None of the above

29. Your wheel bearing seals should be inspected for _________

- ☐ A. Leaks
- ☐ B. Twisted axles
- ☐ C. Broken leaf springs
- ☐ D. Tears

30. What is the importance of using a helper when backing up your vehicle?

- ☐ A. Doing so provides a job for someone else
- ☐ B. Doing so helps you to mind your blind spots
- ☐ C. Doing so makes others feel more comfortable
- ☐ D. All of the above

31. Why must air tanks be drained?

- ☐ A. The air can get stale
- ☐ B. Because water and oil can cause brake failure
- ☐ C. Animals can get inside the tank
- ☐ D. So you can fill them up again

32. How can you tell if your commercial motor vehicle is equipped with Anti Lock Brakes?

- ☐ A. Drive forward at 40 mph, then slam on the brakes to see if they lock up
- ☐ B. Call the manufacturer and ask
- ☐ C. If the vehicle was manufactured after March 1st, 1998, it has Anti Lock Brakes
- ☐ D. Check the dashboard for an ABS signal lamp

33. For what is the supply pressure gauge used?

- ☐ A. The supply pressure gauge tells you what your tire pressure is
- ☐ B. The supply pressure gauge tells you how much air pressure is in the air tanks for your air brake system
- ☐ C. The supply pressure gauge tells you how pressurised the cabin is becoming while going up and down mountain roads
- ☐ D. The supply pressure gauge tells you how much pressure your cargo is under in the trailer

34. Every commercial motor vehicle ***must*** have a warning signal for low air brake pressure. True or False?

- ☐ A. True
- ☐ B. False

35. What happens if you do not put even weight on the front axle of your vehicle?

- ☐ A. If it's not weighed down enough, it could fail to steer the vehicle properly
- ☐ B. If it's not weighed down enough, your gas mileage will be way better
- ☐ C. If it's not weighed down enough, you could break it
- ☐ D. If it's not weighed down enough, the fifth wheel could break

36. When you're inspecting the exhaust system for defects, which of the following requires servicing and attention?

- ☐ A. Leaking exhaust system parts
- ☐ B. Missing mounting brackets or clamps
- ☐ C. A broken exhaust pipe, muffler, or tailpipe

☐ D. All of the above

37. Which of these is most likely to cause a fire in your commercial motor vehicle?

☐ A. Flammable cargo with appropriate ventilation
☐ B. Driver smoking at a rest area
☐ C. Loosened connections and short circuits
☐ D. Fuel that has been spilled, then quickly and properly cleaned up

38. If you increase your speed to double, how much more distance will you require in order to brake to a full stop?

☐ A. Twice as much distance
☐ B. Three times as much distance
☐ C. Four times as much distance
☐ D. Five times as much distance

39. Which of these skills is NOT among the four basic skills that are required of someone who wishes to operate commercial motor vehicles

☐ A. Steering
☐ B. First Aid certification
☐ C. Accelerating
☐ D. Backing safely

40. If you find that you're feeling drowsy while you're driving a commercial motor vehicle, what should you do?

☐ A. Pull off of the roadway and get some sleep before returning to the driver's seat
☐ B. Drink a strong cup of coffee
☐ C. Open the windows and let the fresh air wake you up
☐ D. Drink a caffeinated energy drink

41. Which of these methods is NOT basic for shifting up?

☐ A. Letting up on the clutch while simultaneously pushing down on the accelerator
☐ B. Pressing in the accelerator while pushing in the clutch and turning toward the driver's side
☐ C. Releasing the clutch
☐ D. Pressing in the clutch and shifting up at the same time

42. How frequently should you be stopping to check on your cargo during a route?

- ☐ A. Every three hours or 150 miles
- ☐ B. After every break you take while you're driving
- ☐ C. Within the first 50 miles
- ☐ D. All of the above

43. Which of these statements about retarders is correct?

- ☐ A. Retarders help to slow the vehicle down, which reduces the need for using the brakes
- ☐ B. When you have poor traction with your wheels, the retarder may cause them to skid
- ☐ C. It is best to turn off the retarder whenever there are dangerous road conditions such as ice, wetness, or snow cover
- ☐ D. All of the statements listed above are correct

44. Which of the below options is a common cause of tire fires?

- ☐ A. Underinflation of the truck tires
- ☐ B. Overinflation of the truck tires
- ☐ C. Tires that are too cold
- ☐ D. All of the above

45. Before you transport a load that is sealed, you must:

- ☐ A. Take a small sample of whatever is inside the sealed cargo to ensure that it is safe
- ☐ B. Check that you do not exceed the gross weight limit or the axle weight limits for your vehicle
- ☐ C. Take a picture of whatever is inside so you can prove to the recipient that it hasn't been tampered with
- ☐ D. All of the above

46. What is the formula for total stopping distance?

- ☐ A. Braking distance plus stopping distance
- ☐ B. Reaction distance plus braking distance
- ☐ C. Perception distance plus reaction distance plus braking distance
- ☐ D. Reaction distance plus viewing distance plus braking distance

47. Being a distracted driver is a definite NO in the industry. In order to avoid being a distracted driver, you should:

- ☐ A. Eat, drink, and smoke only while you're on straight portions of the road
- ☐ B. Avoid using your cell phone until you have reached your destination or a rest area
- ☐ C. Make sure to get all the emotionally difficult conversations out of the way during the first hour of your travel
- ☐ D. Read maps or use your phone only when there are no other vehicles on the road around you

48. Which of the following statements about letting air out of hot tires is true?

- ☐ A. Letting air out of hot tires will have no effect at all
- ☐ B. Letting air out of hot tires is a good idea because any extra pressure from the heating will be relieved
- ☐ C. Letting air out of hot tires is a bad idea because when the tires finally cool back down, the pressure will be too low
- ☐ D. Letting air out of hot tires will allow the tires to cool down and you will be able to continue the trip sooner

49. Which of these correctly describes how to use the brake pedal when going down a steep downgrade?

- ☐ A. Apply light and steady pressure
- ☐ B. Apply more pressure as the vehicle travels downhill
- ☐ C. Release the brake pedal when the vehicle is at 5 mph below your safe speed and allow the vehicle speed to come back to your safe speed. Repeat braking afterward to 5 mph below safe speed

50. Drivers should avoid using the trailer hand brake to adjust a trailer that is jackknifing because:

- ☐ A. It will be too hard to reach the brake handle
- ☐ B. The skidding occurred as a result of the brakes on the trailer wheels in the first place
- ☐ C. The brakes on the trailer wheels will stop responding to the hand brake

51. When driving on a slippery road, you should:

- ☐ A. Make quick stops
- ☐ B. Make turns as fast as you can
- ☐ C. Avoid passing slower vehicles

52. Which of the statements about the use of turn signals below is correct?

- ☐ A. Drivers should always use turn signals to mark their vehicles when it is parked by the side of the road
- ☐ B. Drivers should signal early on when they want to turn
- ☐ C. Drivers do not need to make use of their turn signals when they change lanes in traffic on four-lane highways

53. What happens as the blood alcohol concentration or "BAC" rises in a person?

- ☐ A. They can see more clearly how alcohol affects them
- ☐ B. They need a longer period of time to sober up
- ☐ C. Their self-control and sense of judgment are affected

54. ____ is the process of turning the vehicle wheel back in the opposite direction once a traffic emergency or hazard has been cleared.

- ☐ A. Oversteering
- ☐ B. Countersteering
- ☐ C. Counterturning

55. While driving a combination vehicle, what will happen immediately if the emergency line remains together but the service line comes apart?

- ☐ A. Nothing will likely happen until the driver tries applying the brakes
- ☐ B. The tractor's emergency brakes will be engaged
- ☐ C. The trailer's air tank will get exhausted through the open line

56. If you're driving a placarded vehicle, how many feet before the closest rail at a railroad crossing should you stop?

- ☐ A. 5 to 20
- ☐ B. 15 to 50
- ☐ C. 10 to 35

57. The best drivers are those who prepare for and also watch out for hazards. This kind of driving is referred to as:

- ☐ A. Objective
- ☐ B. Defensive
- ☐ C. Offensive

58. The majority of users die or lose consciousness with a blood alcohol concentration of ____

- ☐ A. 0.4%
- ☐ B. 0.16%
- ☐ C. 0.1%

59. In order to release the brakes on a converter dolly with spring brakes, you need to:

- ☐ A. Make use of the converter dolly's parking brake control

- ☐ B. Open up the air tank petcock
- ☐ C. Do both options above

60. Which of the statements about tankers and their center of gravity below is true?

- ☐ A. Tankers can overturn at speed limits that are posted for curves
- ☐ B. The majority of the cargo's weight is lifted high up off the road
- ☐ C. Both options above

61. What could happen to the vehicle brakes if water and oil accumulate inside the air tanks?

- ☐ A. The brakes could lock up
- ☐ B. There could be brake failure
- ☐ C. The brakes could start heating up

62. Letting air out of hot tires:

- ☐ A. Will cool them down and allow you to continue your journey faster
- ☐ B. Will have zero effect
- ☐ C. Is unadvisable because the pressure will drop too low after the tires cool off

63. Hospital supplies, emergency drug shipments, and even small-arms ammunition may sometimes be hauled on a school bus. The total weight of such hazardous materials must not be higher than:

- ☐ A. 100 pounds
- ☐ B. 500 pounds
- ☐ C. 300 pounds

64. Why is texting while driving especially dangerous?

- ☐ A. Because the driver may receive an upsetting message
- ☐ B. Because it is physically and mentally distracting
- ☐ C. Because people enjoy reading and the driver may become too engrossed in what they're reading

65. Empty trucks:

- ☐ A. Need shorter stopping distance compared to full ones
- ☐ B. Are the easiest ones to stop as there is no shifting cargo
- ☐ C. May have poor traction resulting from wheel lockup and bouncing

66. In the event that your bus is disabled and there are riders aboard, you may push or tow your bus to a safe place only:

- ☐ A. By a tow truck that is 27,000 lbs. GVWR or larger
- ☐ B. If the distance is not up to 500 yards
- ☐ C. If leaving the bus poses a higher risk to the riders

67. A converter dolly is made up of ____ axles and a ____ wheel

- ☐ A. Two or three; fifth
- ☐ B. One or two; fifth
- ☐ C. Two or three; third

68. The crack-the-whip effect common in trucks with trailers has the highest tendency to tip over:

- ☐ A. A triple's rear trailer
- ☐ B. A full trailer at the back of a truck
- ☐ C. A double's rear trailer

69. To know that your test of the tractor protection valve is successful:

- ☐ A. The vehicle's low air pressure warning will come on
- ☐ B. The vehicle parking brake valve will pop out
- ☐ C. The tractor protection valve control will switch from "normal" to "emergency" or pop out

70. As a general rule, where should a school bus driver keep the students on a bus in an emergency?

- ☐ A. In a field some distance away from the bus
- ☐ B. On the bus
- ☐ C. On the roadside close to the bus

71. You need to ____ in order to uncouple a loaded trailer after the landing gear makes firm contact with the ground

- ☐ A. Safely secure crank handle
- ☐ B. Turn crank a few more times to take some weight off the tractor
- ☐ C. Turn the crank a few more times until the trailer lifts off the fifth wheel

72. After deciding on the best kind of evacuation, what must a driver do next?

- ☐ A. Get the bus secure
- ☐ B. Inform the dispatch office about the evacuation

☐ C. Hang the microphone or radio telephone outside the driver's window to be used later

73. During high winds, all of the following should be done by a driver except:

☐ A. Use extra care when operating lighter vehicles

☐ B. Pay extra attention to the force of wind when leaving a tunnel

☐ C. Brake frequently to make the wind less effective against the vehicle

74. When they are properly adjusted, a bus' outside right and left side convex mirrors will allow drivers to see:

☐ A. A minimum of one traffic lane on either of the bus' sides

☐ B. Ahead of the rear tires touching the ground

☐ C. Both options above are correct

75. The trailer hand valve is responsible for engaging the brakes. Which of the statements about it below is true?

☐ A. The trailer hand valve should only be used when testing trailer brakes

☐ B. The foot brake transmits air to all the vehicle brakes, including the trailer(s)

☐ C. Both options are true

76. When you're driving a more recent truck that has a manual transmission, and you come across a long and steep downgrade, you will have to use ___ gear that you used in climbing the hill

☐ A. A neutral

☐ B. A lower

☐ C. A higher

77. During an emergency, a driver should reconsider evacuating students from their school bus:

☐ A. If moving them may worsen their injuries

☐ B. If evacuating them would expose them to hazards like downed power lines

☐ C. In either of the situations above

78. Before driving through a railroad crossing, you need to ensure that the bus will have sufficient containment to clear the railroad tracks completely. How long is adequate containment as a general rule?

☐ A. The total length of the bus plus 25 feet

☐ B. The total length of the bus plus 15 feet

☐ C. The total length of the bus plus 10 feet

79. Aside from electrical fuses, if equipped, there should be a functioning fire extinguisher and three red reflective triangles. What other emergency equipment should be present on a school bus?

- ☐ A. A body fluid cleanup kit and a first aid kit
- ☐ B. A bolt cutter and three flares
- ☐ C. Alcohol and a first aid kit

Answers

ANSWER 1: D- Do all of the above. It is imperative for drivers to be aware of a condition called sleep debt. This is a condition that manifests when someone is chronically getting less sleep than they really need. Getting six hours or less per night can increase your risk of having an accident by up to 300%. The percentage of trucking accidents and crashes believed to be caused by lack of sleep or driver fatigue is nearly 15%. Try to get 8 to 9 hours of sleep the night before you embark and, if possible, maintain a healthy sleep schedule when you're not driving as well so you are not in sleep debt. One should also carefully plan one's driving route so that stopping points along the way are easily accessed so you can refresh as often as you need to in order to stay alert and vigilant to hazards on the roads. If you are on a medication that causes drowsiness or fatigue, speak with your doctor about alternatives, as driving while under these effects isn't particularly safe.

ANSWER 2: A- Gross Vehicle Weight Rating. It is the sole responsibility of the driver to ensure that cargo is safely and securely loaded into the vehicle before motion on the road. Unsecured cargo can present a severe danger to the driver and to other motorists. The Gross Vehicle Weight Rating is specified by the manufacturer for a single vehicle, plus the weight of its load so there isn't too much strain on the vehicle components.

ANSWER 3: D- All of the above will work. Today, most vehicles have indicators on the instrument panel that will light up briefly when the battery is engaged to alert you about the ABS. You can check for the wires as well. Additionally, the owner's manual should have information on the brakes system in your vehicle.

ANSWER 4: A- No. Trucks will often stop most effectively when they are used as they are designed to be used. Trucks are meant to hold an evenly-distributed and properly balanced load, and are manufactured to stop in time with the traction offered by that load. If a truck is not loaded, it will often have a longer stopping distance and less traction.

ANSWER 5: B- 4 seconds. In order to figure out the appropriate following distance, you will want to figure on one second for every ten feet of your vehicle, plus an extra second if you are driving at a speed over 40 miles per hour, which is typical for interstate travel. Therefore, someone driving a 30-foot vehicle at the standard interstate speed limit of 55 miles per hours, should leave 4 seconds of following distance.

ANSWER 6: A- This is because someone could start and move the truck while you're inspecting it. If you have the starter key in your pocket, it makes it impossible for someone like a helper or co-driver to hop into the driver's seat and start the vehicle without knowing your location. Such an event could cause injury and it is safest to avoid it entirely.

ANSWER 7: D- A spare jacket. While having a jacket on hand in your vehicle is a good idea for comfort or during inclement weather, it is not an essential part of your emergency kit. Your emergency kit should contain items that can help you return yourself and your vehicle to safe, working conditions, should something happen to put that at risk.

ANSWER 8: E- All of the above. During step five of the seven-step inspection method, you will check the rear of the vehicle and make sure that all the lights and reflectors are functioning and clean enough to signal clearly to other motorists. See chapter 2, section one for more information on the 7-step Inspection Method and what exactly to look for when conducting your own.

ANSWER 9: A- Stop. Accidents cannot be reversed once they happen, but being able to signal the need for a stop can help you to prevent them. Knowing that your partner is signaling you to stop can save a lot of time, trouble, damage, and money. Make sure that you and your helper are on the same page with your signals before you embark so you're prepared for any event.

ANSWER 10: B- Steer right. Stopping when you encounter an obstruction may not always be the best option or the safest thing, as you can always turn your vehicle more quickly than you can stop it, particularly if you are carrying a load. Steering right and doing your best to avoid the obstruction while clearly signaling your intention to move to the right.

ANSWER 11: D- 1/8 inch. Sometimes expressed as 4/32 of an inch. All of the other tires on the vehicle should have at least 2/32 or 1/16 inch tread depth.

ANSWER 12: D- A road user or road condition that presents a possible danger. A hazard can cause trouble if not properly avoided. If you stay vigilant, you should be able to avoid most hazards. Spotting them early and reacting properly is key.

ANSWER 13: D- Any of the above. During step five of the seven-step inspection method, you will check the rear of the vehicle and ensure that all the lights and reflectors are functioning and clean enough to signal clearly to other motorists. See chapter 2, section one for more information on the 7-step Inspection Method and what exactly to look for when conducting your own.

ANSWER 14: A- Because you can see better, watching the rear side of the vehicle from the driver's side window. If you can more easily see a side of the vehicle, then you should use that side of the vehicle to lead you into a spot. The comfort of your neck should not affect this process, as it is a very small part of the process and safety takes priority over the comfort of the driver. If your truck is pulling to one side or another, it is in need of service and should receive that before embarking with your next load.

ANSWER 15: D- Braking hard and immediately. Slamming on the brakes in the event of a tire failure could cause you to lose control of the vehicle, so you must take your foot off the gas. It's important to brake gently and gradually once the vehicle has come to a slowed speed and once you have regained control of the vehicle.

ANSWER 16: C- Someone may attempt to pass you on your right and present an obstruction or collision risk. Swinging wide to the left when you're attempting to turn right could give other motorists an opening to try to pass you on the right. Doing so would allow them to get into your blind spots and present a serious hazard. Instead, make right turns keeping the rear of your vehicle as close as possible to the curb and turn wide as you complete your turn. This will keep that opening from presenting itself to other motorists and will allow you to maneuver safely.

ANSWER 17: D- Verifying and ensuring the freshness of the contents of sealed cargo. You are not permitted to open and inspect cargo, so you are not held responsible for the freshness or quality of what you're transporting. It is your responsibility to make sure that the cargo is safely secured in place, that it is properly balanced, that you have not overloaded the vehicle, and that your cargo does not obstruct any emergency equipment.

ANSWER 18: D- Do all of the above. If you find that an aggressive driver is trying to confront you following an incident, you must not give that person the confrontation they want. Instead, get the help of police officers, keep the peace, and stay safe.

ANSWER 19: D- 12 to 15 seconds. When you're on the road, you should keep your eye on the distance it will take your commercial motor vehicle (CMV) to travel in 12 to 15 seconds. If you are traveling at a speed of 60 miles per hour, your CMV will travel up to a quarter of a mile in just 15 seconds. That is also a distance of about 1,320 feet.

ANSWER 20: D- For all of the reasons listed above. There are quite a few reasons for drivers to cover their cargo that include the protection of the cargo and the protection of individuals. Additionally, covering your cargo will help you to stay within and comply with state regulations

ANSWER 21: B- Hazardous materials placards are signs posted on the outside of the vehicle to identify the hazard class of the cargo within. There are four regulated placards on the outside of the vehicle that signal the type of materials being carried. Emergency service personnel and those who are tasked with loading and unloading the cargo must know these things to conduct themselves properly.

ANSWER 22: D- All of the above. As soon as the outside temperature reaches freezing, some areas will become icy before others. Shady areas and bridges are often the first areas to become icy and if the road ahead appears wet, it could be a layer of black ice, a very thin layer of extremely slippery ice through which you can easily see the road beneath it. It is best to proceed with caution through these areas during freezing weather.

ANSWER 23: A- More than 15 seconds. A typical tractor-trailer can take upwards of 15 seconds to fully clear a double railroad track and it can also take up to 14 seconds to clear a single railroad track. Always ensure you have ample time and space to clear them.

ANSWER 24: B- Brake hard without the wheels locking up. You should always be conscious of the space you need to slow your vehicle and come to a stop safely. If you need to brake hard, your ABS will allow you to do so without the wheels locking up on you, which can increase the possibility of a skid. Having an Anti Lock braking system in your vehicle does not change the way you brake normally and should not be considered a substitute for normal, careful, cautious braking and driving tactics on the road. Your brakes should be regularly serviced and maintained to ensure they work properly.

ANSWER 25: D- Gear box. The gear box is a key component and an integral part of the steering system in your commercial motor vehicle. All other parts listed are components of the suspension system in your vehicle.

ANSWER 26: B- High beams. When you are driving at night, you should be using your high beams so you can see as far ahead of yourself as possible without putting yourself in danger or without blinding other drivers. Some states recommend in their commercial driver's license Manuals that you dim your headlights whenever you are within 500 feet of another vehicle.

ANSWER 27: C- 10 ft., 100 ft., 200 ft. facing the approaching traffic. The Federal Motor Carrier Safety Regulation 49 CFR 392.22 specifies that your warning devices should be placed at 10 feet, 100 feet, and 200 feet from your vehicle, facing toward oncoming traffic so motorists are given plenty of notice and space to give clearance to your vehicle. This regulation also stipulates where these devices must be placed on other types of roadways as well, so familiarize yourself with that so you can maintain vehicle and driver safety on curved roadways and undivided two-way roadways.

ANSWER 28: C- Hydraulic shock absorber. Some other key parts of the suspension are: leaf spring, spring shackle, vehicle frame, main spring, front axle hanger, axle, bearing plates, torque rod, and auxiliary spring.

ANSWER 29: A- Leaks. It is most likely that the problem with a wheel bearing seal is leaking. Check for grease on the wheels or any visible evidence of things like leaks or cracks.

ANSWER 30: B- Doing so helps you to mind your blind spots. commercial motor vehicles have far larger and more blind spots than the average vehicle, so it is important to have another pair of eyes from another angle to help you know when to stop, go, reverse, straighten out, or perform other maneuvers to back in safely. Before starting, it is advised that you and your helper agree on a set of hand signals for such maneuvers so you know exactly what is being communicated to you at all times.

ANSWER 31: B- Because water and oil can cause brake failure. Compressed air typically has a bit of water and compressor oil in it, which can build up and cause issues for your brakes. The water that gets into the air tank could freeze, which has the potential to cause brake failure. In order to avoid this, make sure you drain all of your air tanks completely before leaving your truck overnight. Each air tank must be equipped with a drainage valve on the bottom of it. There can be more than one type of drainage valve, however, so make sure you read the manuals for your vehicle and understand how to operate these. A manually-operated drainage valve is typically activated by using a quarter turn or a pull cable and this should be done at the end of each day of driving. An automatic drainage valve will drain those tanks on their own, but may have a manual mechanism in case of failure. It is also possible to get an air tank with electric heating devices that prevent and reverse freezing of the automatic drain during freezing weather.

ANSWER 32: C- If the vehicle was manufactured after March 1st, 1998, it has Anti Lock Brakes. You can check your owner's manual and the dashboard as well, but it is a legal requirement of all commercial motor vehicles to have ABS if they were manufactured anytime in the last two decades.

ANSWER 33: B- The supply pressure gauge tells you how much air pressure is in the air tanks for your air brake system. If a vehicle has an air brake, then it will have a pressure gauge attached to the air tank. Vehicles with a dual air brake system will either have a gauge for each half of the system or they will have two needles on a single gauge. These gauges tell you how much air pressure is in the air tanks.

ANSWER 34: A- True. It is a legal requirement that your vehicle provide a visible warning signal if the pressure in the air tanks for your air brake system has fallen below 55 PSI. On older vehicles, this requirement can also be one half of the compressor governor cutout pressure. This signal is usually a red light and may have an accompanying buzzer to draw your immediate attention. There is also an alarm device called a "wig wag" that may come with this alert. A mechanical arm will drop into your view when the system drops to dangerously low levels and when the pressure level is fixed, it will automatically rise back out of your view. Some are manual and will need to be placed back into the initial position, but it will not stay in place so long as that pressure is too low. If your commercial motor vehicle is a bus, it is common for this alert to trigger at 80 to 85 PSI.

ANSWER 35: A- If it's not weighed down enough, it could fail to steer the vehicle properly. Balance is key so the wheels and suspension are bearing equal weight, because you could overload one or more axles and cause them to malfunction. In addition to this, if the front axle of your vehicle is not properly weighed down from the load you're carrying, it could be too light to allow the vehicle to steer properly.

ANSWER 36: D- All of the Above. Defects in the exhaust system can be extremely serious because they can lead to poisonous fumes leaking into the cab or the sleeper berth. When you're doing your pre-trip inspection, check the exhaust for anything that is loose, broken, missing, or leaking. This includes exhaust pipes, mufflers, mounting brackets, bolts or nuts, clamps, and vertical stacks. Make sure to also watch for parts that could be bumping or rubbing up against parts of the fuel system, the tires, or other moving parts of the vehicle.

ANSWER 37: C- Loosened connections and short circuits. Smoking while in a rest area, spilled fuel that has been quickly tended to, and flammable cargo can all present their own problems, but if they are all managed properly, then a fire should not break out in the vehicle. A special circumstance such as loosened connections and short circuits can cause a fire in the presence of these other factors.

ANSWER 38: C- Four times as much distance. If you increase your speed to double, your braking distance will increase by about as much as the square of the speed increase, which comes to about four times as much as before. As an example, if you are traveling from 15 to 30 miles per hour, you will need to increase your stopping distance from 46 feet to 184 feet.

ANSWER 39: B- First Aid certification. Depending on the state, the four basic skills required for safe operation of commercial motor vehicles are: accelerating, steering, stopping, and backing safely. While having a certification and working knowledge of first aid is incredibly helpful while you're on the road, it is not one of the four basic skills that is needed for the safe operation of commercial motor vehicles.

ANSWER 40: A- Pull off of the roadway and get some sleep before returning to the driver's seat. Caffeinated drinks and the rushing fresh air on your face may make you feel alert for a short period of time, but the drowsiness will settle back in within the hour. The only true cure for drowsiness and sleepiness is sleep, so you will need to make some time to remedy it before you put yourself and others in danger on the roadways.

ANSWER 41: B- You must let up on the accelerator, press in the clutch and shift into neutral gear at the same time, let up on the clutch, allow the engine and gears slow to the required RPM for the next gear, press in the clutch, and shift into a higher gear simultaneously. Then release the clutch and press in the accelerator at the same time. Acceleration should not be involved until the very end , and it should not be pressed while the clutch is being pressed in.

ANSWER 42: D- All of the above. Checking on your cargo every three hours or 150 miles allows you to make sure that nothing has shifted during that time in transit. Checking on your cargo before you get back on the road after each break you take helps you to make sure that nothing has happened while you were away from the vehicle. Checking on your cargo within the first 50 miles of your trip allows you to see how the road is affecting your cargo and if any adjustments need to be made to the weight distribution or securement.

ANSWER 43: D- All of the statements listed above are correct. While retarders are excellent for reducing one's need to apply the brakes, there are some drawbacks that you should be aware of. Using them in certain weather and road conditions can affect your traction and your ability to control the vehicle, therefore they should be turned off in inclement weather.

ANSWER 44: A- Underinflation of the truck tires. Two of the most common causes for tire fires are underinflated tires and dual tires that are mounted too close together. This is because of heightened friction, so make sure your tires are inflated to the appropriate PSI during your pre-trip and post-trip inspections.

ANSWER 45: B- Check that you do not exceed the gross weight limit or the axle weight limits for your vehicle. If your cargo is sealed, you are not permitted to open it or inspect it. You must simply load it properly and carefully, secure it safely while respecting weight limits, and take it to the destination. Make sure that you are bearing weight limits and restrictions in mind when you are preparing to embark and securing your load.

ANSWER 46: C- Perception distance plus reaction distance plus braking distance. The total stopping distance in your commercial motor vehicle is the sum of the perception distance, which is how far your vehicle will travel from the time you spot the hazard to the time your brain processes it, reaction distance, which is how far your vehicle will travel from the time your brain orders your foot to take action to the time your foot actually hits the brake, and the braking distance, which is how far your vehicle will travel once you've applied the brakes, until a complete stop is reached.

ANSWER 47: B- Avoid using your cell phone until you have reached your destination or a rest area. When you're on the road, a distraction is a distraction, no matter how small it might seem to you at the time. With stopping time and reaction to hazards being calculated down to the very portions of a second that it takes for your brain to process the hazard in front of you, it's imperative that your eyes stay on the road and that all your mental power be trained on getting your load and your vehicle safely to its destination, letting all else take lower priority. If you need to have a deep conversation, deal with something, consult a map, text someone, or have something to eat, you should find a safe place to pull off the road and handle it there.

ANSWER 48: C- Letting air out of hot tires is a bad idea because when the tires finally cool back down, the pressure will be too low. When your tires heat up, the air pressure does increase. However, if you relieve that extra pressure while the tires are hot, then you will not have enough pressure to get back on the road once the tires cool down. Once again, having too little pressure in your tires can cause a tire fire or a blowout. If your tires are too hot for you to touch, then you should stop until they have a chance to cool down and the pressure drops.

ANSWER 49: C- When driving on steep or long downgrades, avoid applying brakes continuously as it may cause them to get less effective. Instead, the brakes should only be applied as a supplement to engine braking. To do this, decide on a 'safe' speed and allow your vehicle to reach that speed. Afterward, brake just hard enough that the vehicle goes 5 mph slower and then let the speed climb back to your 'safe' speed. Continue alternating speed up and down this way until you reach level ground. This method, known as snubbing or snub braking, is the safest way to brake on steep downgrades.

ANSWER 50: B- The trailer hand valve controls the trailer brakes as well as the tractor brakes. If the vehicle is already jackknifing as a result of the trailer wheels locking up, the situation can be worsened by applying the trailer brakes using the hand valve. Instead of doing this, it is best to stop braking so that the rear wheels can resume rolling, and you can steer the vehicle to correct the skid.

ANSWER 51: C- You should always drive smoothly and slowly when under slippery conditions. Your turns should be as gentle as possible, and you should not pass other vehicles unless you need to.

ANSWER 52: B- Drivers should always start signaling well in advance and continue until the maneuver has been completed. Afterward, they should turn off the turn signal if it has flicked off by itself.

ANSWER 53: C- Although alcohol affects the human body in various ways, the first areas that are affected are a person's judgment and self-control. Due to this, they may not realize how drunk they are getting and may start making dangerous decisions as a result.

ANSWER 54: B- When a driver countersteers, they are redirecting the vehicle in the opposite direction they steered while attempting to avoid a hazard or any other hazard. This action is part of the singular driving action of steering and countersteering.

ANSWER 55: A- If a leak develops in the service line, the air tank pressure may remain around the normal level until the driver tries to use the brakes. The loss of air from the leak will cause air pressure to drop rapidly and if it drops far enough, the vehicle's emergency brakes will be engaged.

ANSWER 56: B- Your vehicle must stop between 15 to 50 feet from the closest rail at a railroad crossing if it is placarded. After doing this, proceed when you are sure there is no approaching train, and avoid shifting while on the tracks.

ANSWER 57: B- Defensive driving is driving that is aimed towards saving time, money, and lives, regardless of the actions of other people and surrounding conditions. It is about pre-empting situations that are potentially dangerous, including mistakes of other motorists and driving conditions, and deciding on the best way to deal with such situations. To be a defensive driver, you should constantly check for hazards around your vehicle. If you do spot one, consider the kinds of emergencies that it may cause and come up with plans on how to deal with it.

ANSWER 58: A- Most people who have a BAC that is up to 0.4% will pass out, while some will die.

ANSWER 59: C- To attach the first semitrailer to the converter dolly, the dolly's brakes need to be released in order to be moved. Opening the air tank petcock or making use of the parking brake control if the dolly has spring brakes will release the dolly's brakes.

ANSWER 60: C- Tank vehicles typically have a high center of gravity which is usually between five to six feet above the ground. Due to this, a tanker will be top-heavy making it more prone to rollovers than any other kind of vehicle. Tests have also shown that tank vehicles can rollover at the speed limits posted for curves. Drivers need to slow down properly below the posted speed limit in order to safely navigate an upcoming curve.

ANSWER 61: B- Accumulation of oil or water can build up and lead to the brakes failing so air tanks need to be drained on a daily basis.

ANSWER 62: C- Air pressure increases when vehicle tires get hot. However, attempting to relieve that extra pressure will leave the air pressure too low when the tires cool, which may cause them to blow out or even catch fire. If you notice your tires are too hot to be touched during a trip, stop somewhere until they cool down.

ANSWER 63: B- Some hazardous materials like small-arms ammunition and consumer commodities that are labeled as ORM-D (limited hazard may be carried by buses. However, they should not carry above 500 pounds in total or above 100 pounds of any hazard class.

ANSWER 64: B- Texting and driving is particularly dangerous because it poses a physical and mental distraction to the driver. Apart from diverting their mental attention off the road, texting also requires the driver removing at least one hand from the vehicle's controls.

ANSWER 65: C- A truck's brakes will only perform at their optimum when used as intended i.e. carrying properly balanced cargo. On the contrary, empty trucks have longer stopping distances than loaded ones because of their lesser traction.

ANSWER 66: C- Unless exiting the bus would be more dangerous for the passengers, passengers should not remain on a bus while it is being towed. It is only after the bus has been pushed or towed to the closest safe location that the passengers are allowed to be aboard.

ANSWER 67: B- Similar to the rear of a traditional tractor, a semitrailer has one or two axles and a fifth wheel, and can therefore be attached to a converter dolly.

ANSWER 68: A- In every double or triple combination, each trailer has a higher likelihood of rolling over than the one preceding it. A triple's rear trailer is 3.5 times as likely to overturn as a five-axle tractor-trailer. This occurrence is known as the crack-the-whip effect or rearward amplification. To ensure safety, the lightest trailer should be positioned in the rear and the heaviest in front.

ANSWER 69: C- when testing the tractor protection valve, the tractor protection valve control which is also known as the trailer air supply control should pop out or switch to the "emergency" position from "normal" position. This indicates that the valve has been closed automatically in order to prevent the air pressure from dropping too low.

ANSWER 70: B- In most crisis or emergency situations, it will be easier to control school students and also ensure their safety by keeping them on the bus than evacuating them. However, if remaining on the bus will get the students exposed to injury or risk, the bus driver must escort them to a location that is safe.

ANSWER 71: B- After landing gear makes firm contact with the ground, the crank should be turned in low gear a few more times to take some weight off the tractor, but not to the extent of lifting the trailer off the fifth wheel. This way, it will be much easier to couple the trailer and unhook the fifth wheel when next it is needed.

ANSWER 72: A- After determining a need to evacuate and deciding on the evacuation type, the bus needs to be secured so that it doesn't move. The transmission should be placed in Park or in Neutral if there is a Park shift point is absent. Parking brakes should be set, engine turned off, and ignition key removed. The hazard warning lights should also be activated.

ANSWER 73: C- Typically, winds are stronger when exiting a tunnel and against lighter vehicles. As it can make steering difficult, driving right beside another vehicle is also best avoided. However, braking more frequently will do little to nothing in suppressing the wind's effects.

ANSWER 74: C- The bus' outside left and right side convex mirrors should be set in a way that allows the driver to see the bus' left and right sides up to its mirror mounts, ahead of the rear tires touching the ground and a least one traffic lane on each side.

ANSWER 75: C- Also known as a Johnson bar or trolley valve, the trailer hand valve controls the trailer brakes alone and not the tractor brakes. While it can be used in testing the trailer brakes, it should not be used while driving as applying it will brake the trailers and not the tractor, which can cause skidding. It is best to use the foot brake instead which sends air to the tractor brakes, and the trailer brakes as well.

ANSWER 76: B- When navigating a downgrade in a more recent truck model, most drivers will need to downshift to a gear lower than that which they used in climbing the hill.

ANSWER 77: C- A school bus should not be evacuated if doing so would expose the students to external dangers such as a downed power line. Students with injuries like back or neck fractures should also not be evacuated as moving them could worsen their conditions.

ANSWER 78: B- Before proceeding through a railroad crossing, drivers should ensure that the containment area i.e. the space on the crossing's opposite side is big enough for your bus to pass through. As a general rule, the containment area should at least be up to the total length of your bus plus an additional 15 feet.

ANSWER 79: A- In addition to the usual safety gear required for commercial motor vehicles, a school bus must also be equipped with a body fluid cleanup kit and a first aid kit.

Dear reader,

We understand that preparing for the CDL exam can be a daunting task, and that's why we want to offer you additional tools to support you in achieving your goal. By **scanning the QR code below**, you can easily download not only our **CDL Flashcards but also the Audiobook Version of our study guide.**

Our Flashcards are an invaluable resource for anyone preparing for the CDL exam. They are designed to help you memorize vital information quickly and efficiently. Each card has been meticulously crafted to provide all the necessary information in a concise and easy-to-understand format.

Utilizing our Flashcards will allow you to review the material more frequently and in manageable portions, thereby improving your retention of the information. You can use them anytime and anywhere, whether you're on a work break or waiting for the bus.

Adding to the flashcards, we are excited to introduce our **Audiobook Version.** This tool brings an extra dimension to your study routine by allowing you to learn on-the-go. Whether you're commuting, doing chores, or just relaxing, the Audiobook Version lets you immerse yourself in the study material at your convenience, reinforcing what you've learnt and making the most of your time.

Remember, our Flashcards and Audiobook Version are not meant to replace our CDL study guide or practice test book; rather, they are designed to complement your study routine and provide that extra push to your preparation.

So why wait? **Scan the QR code below** and start using our **Flashcards and Audiobook** today to help you achieve your goal of passing the CDL exam!

CHAPTER - 14

NAVIGATING THE TRUCKER WORLD AS A NEWBIE

Without a doubt, life on the road would require you to make a number of adjustments to your normal lifestyle. As an inexperienced driver who is only starting to get the hang of the trucking world, aspects like cooking, personal care, grooming, and so on may be confusing. In this section, here are some areas where you might need extra help, along with tips on how to handle them.

Cooking and Eating

When on a long trip, healthy food will likely be the last thing on your mind as you try to complete your haul. However, it is an aspect that should never be completely ignored as drivers live a largely sedentary life. This kind of lifestyle, paired with an unhealthy diet can lead to a series of medical issues if care is not taken. For one, it can make it very easy for you to gain weight- hopping in the car and spending hours on the road or in traffic implies that your body does not get so much exercise while working. This, in turn, will cause a buildup of unwanted body fat. The presence of rest areas and gas stops with various unhealthy snacks along the way make it easy to expose yourself to a huge amount of calories.

Eating healthy is paramount as it will help to prevent diseases like stroke, cancer, heart disease, and obesity. With optimal health, your focus and productivity levels are also heightened. This will go a long way in improving your trucking skills as you'll be able to make swifter driving decisions when needed. Although being on the road for a long stretch at once may not be very convenient, here are some tips to remain healthy and in shape that you can apply below:

Cooking and Eating Tips

Keep exercise equipment inside the cabin. The most common reason for excessive weight gain is a lack of activeness. Having exercise equipment that you can easily grab from your cabin will help you remain fit during those long hauls. The equipment does not need to be a heavy one which will take up a lot of space such as a treadmill but can be jump ropes, resistance bands, and other small ones. You can even take your bike with you, and ride it around truck stops for some time when possible. Riding a bike this way, for example, will ease your lower body which may be cramped from being in one position for a long time.

Eat a healthy breakfast. Breakfast is a very important meal because the way you start your morning will largely determine your mood throughout the rest of the day. Your breakfast should be filled with healthy fats, protein and complex carbs so that you can get energy that will last for a longer period of time. On the other hand, sugary food will only give you a sugar rush that will stop suddenly resulting in a system crash, along with fatigue. Egg whites, cottage cheese, low-fat yogurt, and hard-boiled eggs are good options for a trucking day breakfast. Omelets are also a good choice as long as there is little to no grease in it.

Buy a good amount of healthy snacks. Snacking typically presents a challenge for most people on the road to eating healthy. Even at home, it is common to feel a craving or urge to munch on a food item. On the road as well, you may feel the urge to munch on something, and having some healthy snacks handy will reduce your chances of pulling over at a stop for some high-calorie snack. Bananas, vegetables, nuts, low-salt popcorn, raisins, raw pumpkin seeds, raw nuts, dark chocolate, and berries can provide a healthy mix of snacks for you to carry along with you on long trips and also overcome the snack cravings.

Eat a light dinner. Most people love a big dinner but that is not very healthy as dinner should ideally be the lightest meal. Your dinner portions should always be kept small and make sure you do not eat right before going to bed. If you really want to enjoy healthy food, you can consider getting a slow cooker with which you can enjoy healthy and tasty meals like stew, barbeque chicken, pot roast, etC. Bear in mind that half of your plate should always be covered in vegetables and include canned goods like beans or spinach. This is a good way to help you get the maximum amount of nutrients from your food. There are also specially formulated vitamins and supplements that you can get if you think you're still lacking certain nutrients.

Get a healthy eating app on your phone. There are countless free apps that can be downloaded on your mobile device that will provide guidance on how you can eat healthily. These apps can also help you to keep track of the number of calories you're consuming by setting a calorie goal based on your body mass index. As long as you remain within that count, you won't gain weight and even if you do go over it, some exercise will get you back in shape in no time. Apps like these are readily available for your use, and they can be quite beneficial to the health and wellbeing of truck drivers.

Maximize your cabin space. As a truck driver, it can be quite easy to store food mostly because of a lack of cabin space. However, getting rid of cardboard food packaging is one way to deal with this. Cardboard packaging occupies space and has no specific usefulness after you open it. If you have packaged meats in Styrofoam containers, take them out and transfer them into sealed bags to save space. The next step to keeping your food fresher for longer is through vacuum-sealing food storage to keep out air. This will save space inside the truck and will also preserve your food for much longer.

Consider a fridge. If you can afford it, a mini-fridge can be a useful investment as it can help to store and also preserve food. Although it can be quite costly when getting one at first, the purchase will be very worth it and the machine will 'pay for itself' in the long run. Note that it might take up some floor space if you do not have a top bunk where you can strap it down.

Store fruits and vegetables properly. Note that it is not all fruits and vegetables that are supposed to be refrigerated. Be sure to find out if a specific item needs to remain cold before deciding on how to store it. If you're keeping any in the fridge, wrap them up in paper towels to keep out moisture.

Sleeping

After or during a long driving day, you need to find somewhere convenient to pull up and get some rest for a minimum of about 10 hours. Not only is it responsible to do this for your safety and that of other road users, but it is also legal to do so. Getting adequate and quality sleep plays a very important role in any driver's lifestyle as a fatigued driver can be a liability and potential danger on the road. Even though lack of sufficient sleep and fatigue are common issues for many people all over the world, truck drivers are more prone to getting inadequate and low-quality sleep. A recent study from the Center for Disease Control in the United States shows that over half of the total number of transport workers is sleep deprived. As a lot of drivers spend days or weeks on the road at once, it can be hard to establish a regular sleep pattern which is very important. The reason truck drivers are mandated to follow such strict hours of service regulations is so that they can have sufficient time to rest.

Your most preferred place to park when you need some rest will likely be a truck stop as they are primarily designed for that purpose. These stops are built to handle heavy commercial vehicles, and also have the necessary equipment to provide such services. Truck drivers who are more experienced will try maximizing their working hours by sleeping in their customers' parking lot when possible. While it may sound much more convenient to stay over at an inn every night, that kind of lifestyle will be quite expensive and will take up a large chunk of your earnings. In order to ensure safety behind the wheel and also boost your sleep, here are some tips you can use:

Sleeping Tips

Find somewhere quiet to park. Oftentimes, it can be hard to find a quiet and safe parking spot considering the shortage of truck parking spaces. However, you should always try doing so as much as possible. If you come across an empty truck stop, try parking far away from all the activity. As you have no control over the noises made around you, avoiding them is the best step to take.

Block all light coming from outside. Sleeping inside your truck implies that it will be practically impossible to block all outside light. As you'll mostly be close to a 24-hour truck stop, other drivers may want to keep awake while you're trying to fall asleep. The outside light can disrupt your sleep and also make you take longer to fall asleep. One way to manage this situation is by covering up your truck's windows with shades or curtains. If this still doesn't work, wearing a sleep mask when going to bed can be helpful.

Stay away from screens before sleeping. There has been a push in recent times to limit screen time not just for truck drivers, but for everyone as well. Although LED screens are not particularly harmful on their own, the blue light they emit can keep you from falling asleep quickly. Having to sleep inside your truck is already hard enough, and there is no need to make it even harder. Sinking into a restful slumber will happen quicker when you avoid all screens for some time before bed.

Buy a high-quality mattress pad. Undoubtedly, your bed back at home will be far more comfortable than the one inside your truck. However, you can make your cab more comfortable by investing in a high-quality mattress pad to help improve your sleep.

Regulate cab temperature. Be it during the summer or winter, extreme temperatures can affect your sleep negatively. While you cannot control the weather, a personal heater or fan for your cab will do a lot in preventing sweat when hot, and shivers when cold.

Avoid excessive eating or drinking before sleep. Finding time to sit and savor a meal can be hard for drivers due to time constraints. This can make it extra tempting to eat just before shutting down for the night. However, doing this right before going to bed can keep you up or result in frequent restroom breaks in the middle of the night. The digestive system requires between 30 minutes to 1 hour to thoroughly break down food so ensure that you allow enough time for that to happen before getting some rest.

Showering

Although trucks may have a bed, refrigerator, storage space, cooking appliances, or even a television, they do not have showers. Some people think truck drivers shower inside their trucks but as there is no running water, that isn't possible. Truck drivers shower at rest or truck stops along interstates where they park and then use the shower. The majority of truck drivers prefer showering at truck stops because staying over at a motel just a few times weekly would mean wasting a lot of money. It would be more efficient for you to sleep inside the truck and then head over to the truck stop in the morning for a shower. Experienced drivers who really want to shower every day will usually do so on their break or during their 10-hour rest period. If you do choose to stop at some point, bear in mind that the higher the number of stops, the less distance you can travel. Anywhere you go, you will surely find facilities for showering, restroom breaks, and even quick walks.

Truck stop showers are usually free if you fill up a certain amount of fuel. You get a fuel or reward card which is loaded with shower credits each time you fuel up your truck. When you have a sufficient amount of credits, you are entitled to take a free shower. However, shower credits may expire after about 7 days, depending on the truck stop. You can also pay for a fee of around $10 to take a shower but most drivers choose to acquire shower credits when fueling. Some trucking companies also reimburse drivers for showers or even offer free ones which will be limited to specific stops.

A shower stall typically contains a toilet, a sink with cold/hot water, a mirror, an AC outlet, a towel, and a hair dryer sometimes so you will need to bring anything else you might need. Consider getting a showering bag to keep your things in, shower shoes or flip flops, shampoo, soap, wipes, a bag for dirty laundry, a change of clothes, hair dryer, or a small bag or purse that can be hung on a hook. Below are some tips you can make use of at a truck stop shower stall:

Showering Tips

Always keep your feet covered up. Be sure to cover your feet at all times inside the shower stall to avoid catching a fungus. Getting a pair of flip flops or shower sandals is a good way to keep your feet protected. Note that flip flops can be slippery and hard to walk with in a dirty parking lot. Shower sandals are sturdier and will provide better traction to prevent you from slipping and falling.

Go with your own towel. Although many truck stops have towels available, bringing your own is a good option because you can always be sure it is clean. Besides, having your towel helps in case you're at a truck stop where there are no towels.

Pack your soap and shampoo separately. When packing your shower bag, put your shampoo and soap in a separate sealable plastic bag. This will prevent shampoo from getting all over the rest of your items in case of a spill.

Use wipes. Baby and/or Clorox wipes will come in handy for cleaning handles and countertops as needed. You could also use them to do a quick wipe on days you cannot or do not want to shower.

Pack a small hairdryer. A small hair dryer can be very useful when you're at a stop that does not provide one. By having yours, you can avoid having to deal with cold or moist hair during cold weather.

Have a change of clothes with you. Always remember to put some clean clothes into your bag so you're not stuck with only the dirty ones and nothing else to change into.

Managing Your Expenses on the Road

Planning ahead is the best way to minimize the cost of traveling on the road. For example, you can stock up on good and healthy groceries with a fridge. You can also avoid buying expensive items at truck stops by going to a big store to get all you may need before hitting the road. While you will only need to make a few expenses, be careful of any additional spending as it can rob you of your earnings.

The spending at truck stops when using bathrooms or getting something to eat there will likely be the cost that affects your earnings the most if you let it. Discipline plays a huge role and your paycheck will likely be exhausted by the end of the week if care isn't taken. There are certain expenses that you can expect while on the road and they include:

Food. You need proper nourishment while on the road and food can easily become your largest monetary expense. Taking food along with you will not only save you precious time but will also save you a lot of money.

Phone. You will likely have your cell phone with you while on any trip so you will need to pay phone bills. Even if you do not have your cell phone with you, you may still need to use a payphone and phone card at a truck stop. You could check with your carrier to find out whether they have discounts with any phone companies.

Laundry. The majority of large truck stops have washers and dryers that you will have to pay for. Unless you plan to store your dirty clothes in your truck until you're back home, this is a necessity and there's really no way around it.

Showers. You will only need to pay for showers if you do not have a fuel receipt or have never purchased at the stop before. A shower usually costs around $9 but you should not have to pay for it so often. To minimize the cost of taking showers, plan your trips so that you can shower at stops you have previously fueled at and/or have shower credits.

Internet access. If you do not have your own wifi, many truck stops allow you to use their wifi connections with daily, hourly, monthly, and unlimited plans for a fee. However, you may save more by adding a data plan and hotspot to your cell phone instead.

Tolls. The majority of companies will pay for tolls upfront while many large ones will have an automatic electronic payment system. All the same, certain companies will prefer you to pay the toll in cash and then reimburse you the amount spent. If this is your company's method, make sure you have some extra cash with you when approaching regions with tolls.

Lumper fees. This should be covered by the company as well, but some very small carriers might want you to pay first and be reimbursed.

Tips on Saving Money on the Road

- Open a savings and checking account. Set up an automatic draft each pay day from your checking into your savings account.
- Use a budget. Make your own budget and ensure that you stick to it. It will help to know the extra amount of money you have before starting the trip.
- List all your pending bills. Make a list of all the bills that need to be paid especially if you're not making use of a budget. Doing this may help keep you focused and less likely to spend on unnecessities.
- Plan ahead. The importance of this in cutting costs cannot be overemphasized. Always make sure that you buy everything you will need on the road in time.
- Use cruise control when possible. Adjusting your vehicle speed manually every time would consume more fuel than leaving it to your truck. It is most efficient to keep your speed at about 60 mph, allowing you to control your speed and also avoid any expensive speeding tickets.

- Maintain your vehicle. Making sure that your truck is safe can save you a lot of money. Always inspect all bolts and nuts before driving and pay attention to oil changes and tire air pressure. It can be very inconvenient and frustrating to run into mechanical problems as they can greatly put you behind schedule.
- Find out about discounts. Truck drivers usually enjoy many discounts while on the road and this can come in handy. A lot of restaurants and hotels have discounted prices just for truckers, while some truck stops offer rewards cards and loyalty programs. You can even get discounts on showering, coffee, fuel, and so on. By making the most of these rewards systems and discounts, you can save some money.

Tips and Tricks for New Truck Drivers

Just like with any other job, being a truck driver and driving a trick has a learning curve. While a CDL school will show you how to get your license, it won't train you on how to be a truck driver. The majority of the things you'll learn about trucking will be learnt on the job, and not in a classroom. Most times, preparing for their first driving job can be confusing for many new truck drivers. You may worry about the items or tools to bring along, how to survive your first year, and so on. The tips and tricks below will help you to make your first driving job a pleasant one.

Don't start during winter- Driving trucks during winter can be hard or even dangerous if you spend much time in places with lots of ice and snow. If you can, try timing the end of your training to end in any season aside from winter. This way, you won't have to deal with freezing brakes or air lines, slippery conditions, snow, or sub freezing temperatures that can cause uncomfortable driving and sleeping. Starting during summer or spring is ideal so that you have one or two seasons of driving experience before winter.

Keep your truck clean- The exterior, as well as interior of your truck should always be clean. By taking time to clean up daily or even weekly, you'll be keeping your work and living space free from dirt. Wash the exterior as often as possible to keep it clean and ensure you do not neglect the interior which will serve as your home as well if most of your time is spent on the road. Try sweeping out the floor of the truck with a little dust broom that you can keep in the pocket of the driver's door. How frequently this will be done will depend on the weather, where you live, and how often you enter and exit the vehicle. Sweeping is one good way to maintain a clean truck that does not take much time. As much as possible, endeavor to clean up after yourself immediately after sleeping, eating, delivering load, or shopping for food so that everything remains organized. Avoid letting dirty clothes and garbage pile up- always dispose of items you do not need.

Keep an eye on weather conditions- As you drive from one region to another through the country, you may move into winter conditions or torrential southern rainstorms in the northern region in contrast to the warm conditions in the south. Always pay attention to the weather and be ready to adjust your driving and schedule as necessary to accommodate the weather.

Observe low clearance and weight warnings- If you ever make a wrong turn and approach a bridge that cannot support your vehicle weight, or is too low to allow your vehicle to pass through, the best line of action is to stop. Instead of proceeding, switch on your flashers, apply the brakes, and get in touch with local law enforcement to guide your truck out of the situation safely

Save money- With every chance you get, be sure to spend wisely and save up as much as you can. Avoid spending money on things that you do not really need. Truck and rest stops usually sell expensive tools and food so be wary of overspending at these locations. Make proper plans, purchase food items beforehand, and always cook your own meals. Rather than buying tools that will likely be overpriced at a stop, buy them ahead of time when you can conveniently research the most friendly prices. To manage your earnings properly, only spend on things that are absolutely necessary and save the rest towards an investment goal.

Do regular exercise- As mentioned before, being a truck driver involves a lot of sitting. This, coupled with unhealthy eating habits means that you are prone to gaining some weight. It can be very easy to completely neglect exercising because you're not close to a gym or your home. However, a simple exercise routine of some sit ups and pushups after each trip can make a significant difference, and is recommended by many drivers.

Always perform the pre-trip inspection- Asides from knowing the procedures in order to pass your CDL test, you should always inspect your vehicle before each trip. Stepping out to do a walk-around check on your trailer and truck to ensure everything is in order will only take you a few minutes. This short period of time could save you from getting a ticket, or even worse. You can get the most out of your inspection by getting or making a checklist that will help you make this routine and keep you from neglecting a potential safety issue.

Care for your health- Spending long hours on the road can make remaining healthy challenging for truck drivers. However, you need to develop good health habits so that you can maintain ideal weight, and also remain in peak physical condition. Having good habits will minimize or even prevent injury and illnesses that can stop you from driving and impede your career. When you keep fit, you can handle longer routes and harder assignments, which will make you more desirable and suitable for high-paying jobs.

Always keep your vehicle locked- Truck stops are usually close to areas with high traffic so there can be a large number of unscrupulous individuals trying to trick or prey on unsuspecting drivers. Even if you're not very far away from your vehicle, always take some extra minutes to ensure your vehicle is locked up.

Keep yourself entertained on the road- Although physical health matters, you should avoid neglecting your mental health as well. Being on the road for long periods may cause you to feel bored very quickly so feel free to take along items or things that will keep you entertained on the journey. You can read, listen to podcasts, draw, play online chess, watch television, and so on. Regardless of what it is, just make sure you have one or two activities to do when you're away from the wheel.

Always keep records- Doing paperwork might not be very enjoyable, but it can be a very useful habit to build. While on the job, keep organized records of all expenses, trip reports, receipts, and the likes.

Don't go to sleep sitting up- Some truckers think that sleeping while sitting up can help get the body adapted to sleeping in that position. However, sleep quality can be adversely affected by this which can lead to drowsiness. There is no reason to sleep this way because you are mandated by the law to make use of the mattress in your cabin, not the driver's seat.

Get all necessities before starting a trip- Bear in mind that making stops on the road implies that you will also lose time and money. You don't have to wait until you start driving before you get everything you need. Whether it is your first or tenth trip, always get everything ahead of time to avoid the need to stop on the way.

Have cleaning supplies handy- Maintaining a clean interior is just as important as maintaining a clean exterior. With items like soap, rags, a bucker, paper towels, and air freshener, you can clean up the inside of your truck at any time.

Have a career plan- As you start your career, think about the kind of career you'd like to develop. Reflect on whether you'd like to drive for a company for some time, or you'd want to own your own truck and be independent. If you're seeking long-term employment under a company, you should consider factors like financial stability, pension plans, and benefits. On the other hand, consider factors like learning potential and initial salary if your goal is to own your truck. Drivers who want to work independently should note that the business sides of trucking like tax reporting, profit/loss calculation, fuel mileage tracking, accounting, expense tracking, and so on are essential and should be learnt. Having some knowledge about these terms will also be useful if working for a company long-term.

Sign up for reward cards- All major truck stop chains as well as many smaller businesses offer reward cards to professional drivers. Each time you make a purchase or you refuel, points are added to your reward card which you can then save up and use to buy items, get free showers, and many other benefits. Living on the road can be very expensive and these reward programs are a good way to help you save more money.

Work at your own pace- During the first year of driving especially, it is recommended that you take your time when carrying out assignments. Be it to pick up goods, unhook air lines, or raise and lower landing gear, you will need to be extra careful and patient. Working too quickly can cause you to make mistakes that slowing down a little will easily prevent. The more experience you gain, the faster your pace will get so there is no need to rush during the early days.

Get some tools- Booster cables, good gloves, flashlight, rags, small hand tool kit, windshield washer fluid, a large water jug, DOT reflective triangles etc. are items that you should always have with you. The right tools will not only save you time but will also allow you to make more money. Try to know how to use the tools beforehand so that you can make simple repairs while on the road, and also avoid getting violations during inspections.

Pack clothing for all weather- As a driver, you may start your trip somewhere sunny and end it in a snowy region. No matter where you are, having suitable clothes for the weather will go a long way in keeping you comfortable, and allowing you to focus better. This will also save you the expense of buying extra clothes that suit the weather.

Have a pair of clean and professional-looking clothes with you- While it does not necessarily have to be a fancy suit, a clean polo or button up shirt will leave a better impression on your clients and customers than a dirty band shirt. The majority of truck stops have laundry and shower services that can still help you keep a clean, professional look even if you're driving long distance.

CHAPTER - 15

FREQUENTLY ASKED QUESTIONS

What Is a CDL?

All drivers operating large commercial motor vehicles must have a Commercial Driver License (CDL). By possessing a CDL, you demonstrate that you have undergone training and testing and are qualified to operate such vehicles.

What Kind of Training Do I Need to Get My CDL?

At the time of writing, there is no formal training required to obtain a commercial driver's license. The written test for your state must be passed with a grade of 80% or higher and the driver must be able to demonstrate under testing conditions that they understand how to operate their vehicle safely.

For safety reasons, it is required that a driver take their CDL test in the vehicle they anticipate operating with their new license. This allows the driver to ensure they're acquainted with the right type of vehicle and it allows the testing official to be certain they are preparing the newly licensed driver as thoroughly as possible for safe and efficient travel on the roadways.

In addition to these testing requirements, you will need to seek out a medical professional that is listed on the National Registry of Certified Medical Examiners who can administer an extensive physical exam and forward the results to your local licensing bureau. The federal government requires that commercial drivers be of a certain level of health in order to legally operate these vehicles.

Once you've completed these testing requirements and have been issued your commercial driver's license, you may apply for the testing needed for the required endorsements.

How Quickly Can I Get My CDL?

This largely depends on you and how quickly you would like to push through all the necessary testing and appointments to get your license. That being said, you can complete the licensing process in as little as two weeks. The average time from beginning of study to full licensure is about three to seven weeks.

Do I Need to Take Practice Tests before I Am Eligible to Take the Official Written and Driving Tests for the CDL?

In a word, no. There is no requirement for practice testing or study hours before you can take the CDL written test and driving test. It can be very helpful to take practice tests that will show you the types of things you ought to know before going to take them. Studying your manuals and knowing the laws in place for your state are strongly advised so that you can get the best possible grade on your exam and so that you can drive as safely and efficiently as possible.

You can find practice tests for your state online, and you can also take the practice test in chapter 12 of this book to prepare yourself.

What Types of CDL Can I Get?

Class A

A Class A CDL allows the holder to drive vehicles weighing more than 26,001 pounds and/or more than 10,000 pounds when towed.

Class B

A Class B CDL allows the licensee to drive vehicles weighing more than 26,001 pounds but less than 10,000 pounds when towed. A Class B license also allows the holder to transport 24 or more passengers, including the driver.

Class C

A Class C CDL allows the holder to drive vehicles that are not classified as Class A or B, such as transport vehicles that carry 16 to 23 passengers, including the driver. Hazardous goods may also be transported by Class C CDL holders.

How Can I Get a Class A commercial driver's license?

The requirements for the Class A CDL are as follows:

- A passing grade on the commercial driver's license General Knowledge Test
- A passing grade on the commercial driver's license Driving Test
- Passing grades on one or more endorsement tests and requirements
- Secured endorsements and passing grades for Air Brakes, Combination Vehicles, and Pre-Trip Inspection
- A passing medical examination that certifies your physical wellness and fitness to perform all the duties deemed necessary by the federal government

How Can I Get a Class B commercial driver's license?

The requirements for the Class B CDL are the same as a Class A CDL including:

- Passing grades for Air Brakes and Pre-Trip Inspection

How Can I Get a Class C commercial driver's license?

The requirements for the Class C CDL are the same for a Class A and B CDL including:

- Secured endorsements and passing grades for HAZMAT, Passenger Transport, and Pre-Trip Inspection

Is There a Difference between the Class C and Class D Licenses?

Yes. A Class C license is a classification of the commercial driver's license, the requirements and specifications for which are specified and provided by the federal government. The Class C commercial driver's license is required for the operation of any vehicle which doesn't meet or exceed the requirements of Class A or Class B vehicles, but is designed to transport upwards of 16 passengers including the driver or which is clearly labeled and suited for the transport of hazardous materials (HAZMAT).

A Class D license is a license provided to drivers for **non-commercial** purposes. The requirements for this vary from state to state and a Class D license should not be considered appropriate for anyone in operation of a commercial motor vehicle. For more details about the Class D license and how to obtain one, see your local state's driver handbook for details.

How Many Questions Will I Have to Answer on the Commercial Driver's License General Knowledge Test?

The official commercial driver's license General Knowledge Test contains 50 questions that pertain to things like the components of your vehicle, safety measures and precautions, and general vehicle operation standards. Study guides for your state's commercial driver's license test can be found online at www.driving-tests.org/cdl-handbooks.

How Long Am I to Hold a Commercial Learner's Permit (Clp) Before Taking a Road Test?

Before taking the road test, you must have held your CLP for at least 14 days. This will provide you the opportunity to practice driving and prepare for your CDL.

What Should I Know for My CDL Test?

Vehicle Inspection (Pre-trip) Test: This aspect tests potential CDL holders on their understanding of vehicle safety before operating a vehicle.

Basic Vehicle Control Test: This section assesses CDL candidates' ability to maneuver big commercial vehicles, including turns, moving forward and backward, and other maneuvers.

Road Test: This section puts potential CDL holders through a series of traffic situations to see if they can drive safely and efficiently in both ordinary and unusual settings.

What Is a CDL Endorsement?

You may be required to obtain specific endorsements on your CDL license in addition to getting the necessary CDL license. You will be able to transport liquids, marked hazardous goods, and passengers with these endorsements. They are as follows:

H - Allows you to transport hazardous items.

N - Allows you to carry liquids using a tanker trailer.

P - Allows you to operate a vehicle that transports people.

S - Allows you to operate school buses.

T - Allows you to move two or three trailers that weigh more than a certain amount.

X - Allows the transportation of hazardous goods in a tanker trailer.

How Can I Get a HAZMAT Endorsement?

Apply for a CDL HAZMAT endorsement, a medical screening, a CDL HAZMAT exam, and TSA security clearance.

How Can I Get a Tanker Endorsement?

Visit your local DMV for the tanker endorsement test to get your CDL tanker endorsement. Depending on the state you live in, the CDL tanker test normally consists of between 0-30 questions.

What CDL Endorsements Can Fetch Me the Highest Earnings?

HAZMAT, Tanker, and Trailer endorsements are generally the most lucrative CDL endorsements.

What Is the Difference between Intrastate and Interstate Commerce?

When acquiring your CDL, it's crucial to know what kind of driving you'll be doing and where you'll be doing it. This information will be required on forms and at other points during your test.

You'll need an interstate commercial driver's license if you're going to be driving between states or across the country. If you're only going to be driving within one state, you will need an intrastate CDL.

Where Can I Get a Medical Certification?

The majority of doctors will be able to certify your medical fitness and eligibility for a CDL. However, note that if you have any of the following conditions, you may be unable to obtain a CDL:

Diabetes that necessitates the administration of insulin to maintain control

Chronic respiratory problems

Serious heart problems

High blood pressure that is uncontrollable by medication

Epilepsy

A history of substance misuse, particularly alcohol abuse.

How Much Time Do I Have to Take the CDL Test?

The validity of your commercial learner's permit is 180 days. You'll be able to drive a commercial vehicle under supervision throughout that period in order to practice and learn how to operate one. If you don't pass your Commercial Skills test within that time frame, you'll have to start over.

What Is the Meaning of Dot in Trucking?

There are various DOT definitions in the trucking sector. DOT stands for the Department of Transportation, This is a federal government department in charge of maintaining and improving the country's transportation system. There are various other DOT definitions to be aware of, including DOT certifications, inspection, and number, among others.

What Is a DOT Certification?

The Federal Motor Safety Carrier Administration verifies that you have the skills and knowledge to properly operate a commercial vehicle when you obtain your DOT certification. You must complete a group of written and driving tests to acquire your DOT certification. A DOT physical will also be required of you. The DOT physical test verifies that you are in good health and can safely operate a commercial motor vehicle.

How Can I Get My DOT Certification?

To begin, you must obtain a Department of Transportation (DOT) number, which is used in identifying a truck and its owner. This aids the FMCSA in gathering information on the company and the driver's safety. New applicants are to register for a DOT number online using the Unified Registration System in order . You will be required to complete an application and then pay a certain fee. After your application has been approved, you will receive your DOT number.

Secondly, you must take and pass a Department of Transportation medical exam. This test verifies that you are physically competent to operate a CMV safely. Furthermore, it demonstrates that you have no medical issues that would preclude you from operating a commercial motor vehicle. A certified DOT medical examiner must complete this exam.

To check whether there are any underlying medical conditions, the DOT examiner will test your hearing, eyesight, blood, and urine. Passing this exam entitles you to a DOT medical card.

Finally, your vehicle must pass a Department of Transportation inspection. A certified DOT inspector must complete this inspection and they will ensure that it is safe and that all parts and accessories are in functioning order. In addition, the inspector will inspect your truck to ensure if your DOT number is correctly displayed.

You'll be held to a higher level of accountability and experience than a regular driver as soon as you're qualified. Note that to keep your DOT certification valid, you must meet all DOT standards.

What Is a DOT Medical Card?

To operate a CMV, every CDL driver must have a DOT medical card. This medical card shows that you are physically able to operate a CMV safely and that you do not have any health conditions that could endanger other drivers.

Anyone driving any of the following vehicles must get a DOT physical and a DOT medical card:

Vehicles with a gross vehicle weight rating (GVWR) of more than 10,001 pounds

When direct remuneration is involved, vehicles built to transport more than 15 people or 8 passengers

Hazardous material transport vehicles

To keep your CDL valid, you must also have a valid DOT medical card. Your DOT medical card can only be issued from a physician on the National Registry of the Federal Motor Carrier Safety Administration, which often includes medical doctors, osteopathic doctors, experienced practice nurses, chiropractic doctors, and assistants of physicians.

The physical screening of this exam will review your medical history, along with your present health status. If there are no health issues, your DOT card will be issued to you. Although the medical card has a validity period of up to 24 months, you will need to do a DOT screening more frequently if you have a health issue that requires monitoring.

What Is a DOT Number?

Every truck driver who satisfies certain requirements will be given a DOT number, which is a unique identifier.

This number enables for easy vehicle entry and surveillance, ensuring that transportation companies adhere to safety rules.

To see if you need a DOT number, confirm if the vehicle you're driving weighs more than 10,000 pounds, if you're transporting hazardous materials, if you're transporting more than 15 passengers, and if you'll be engaging in interstate commerce.

Your local DMV can provide you with further information about your state's DOT number requirements.

How Do I Apply for My DOT Number?

To apply for your DOT number, you will need to provide operation and cargo classification, number and type of vehicles to be operated, ownership status of the vehicles, employer identification, social security, or tax number; operation purpose, names and titles of company officials; and a HAZMAT classification if you intend to transport any.

Once you have all the needed information, you can fill out an application on the unified registration website. On your application, you'll be requested to give the information listed above. Normally, it takes about one and a half hours to fill the application and you do not have to pay any fee to register for the DOT number. After completing the application, simply mail it in or submit the form online.

Your application will then be processed by the FMCSA for some days, after which you will get your USDOT number if approved. This number is valid for up to 24 months and must be renewed if you want to continue driving.

What If I Fail My DOT Drug Test?

Failure to pass a DOT drug test results in immediate suspension from performing safety-sensitive functions, such as driving a commercial motor vehicle. In serious circumstances, your CDL license may be suspended, terminated, or revoked. It could also rule you out as a new-hire candidate. Refusing to take a DOT drug test is the same as failing.

Before you may get your CDL, you must pass a drug test administered by the Department of Transportation. Depending on your company, a failed DOT drug test during CDL training may cause your certification to be delayed or denied.

Testing positive for drugs including cocaine, opiates, marijuana, phencyclidine, amphetamines, and other similar substances might result in a failed pre-employment DOT drug test or a failed random DOT drug test. If your blood alcohol level is up to or above 0.04, it will prevent you from passing your drug test.

A failed DOT drug test will require you to complete a return-to-duty procedure. Although every company will have its own procedure, you must fulfill all of the prerequisites to get your license back.

The majority of companies will refer you to a drug addiction professional, or SAP, who will assess your situation and offer available treatment options. The entire therapy course as well as the return-to-duty process must be completed if you wish to keep driving. Note that you will be responsible for any treatment costs.

You'll be required to undergo another drug test after you've completed treatment. You will be able to return to work if you pass the returning drug test. In the next 12 months, you will be tested at least six times, with the testing requirement possibly lasting up to 60 months to make sure you remain clean.

If you fail the returning drug test, you will have to start the return-to-duty process all over again.

Can I Get My CDL with a DUI?

Yes, you can get a CDL if you have a DUI on your record. However, if your license is currently suspended due to a DUI, you will be unable to obtain a CDL. Getting a CDL with a DUI is usually not the issue; getting work afterward is. It is important that you disclose your DUI past during driving school since it will be revealed as they review your driving record.

Some employers have tight requirements about driving records. For instance, Walmart compensates its employees generously and hires only those with a good track record. The period when the DUI occurred can also have an impact on your job prospects.

The penalties of a CDL DUI are far more severe. If you're driving while inebriated, you're breaking the law and you could be looking at a CDL suspension for up to 1 year. If you get convicted a second time, you may have your CDL revoked.

How Often Can I Expect to Come Home as a Truck Driver?

The average truck driver returns home every 2-3 weeks. The truck driver lifestyle is influenced by a number of factors, including the company you work for, the type of trucker you are (local or over-the-road., your years of experience, area of residence, and so on.

Different firms operate under different routes and schedules. UPS Freight, for example, adheres to union regulations and allows their drivers to work on a more consistent schedule. These are the kinds of trucking businesses that allow their employees to come home during weekends.

More point-to-point (PTP) routes are offered by local companies. The truckers on such routes exchange cargo between two or three locations. These sites are either in the city or in surrounding large cities. The job's home time varies when following PTP routes, ranging from jobs where you'll return home each night to those where you'll return home weekly.

However, the majority of truck driving positions are over-the-road (OTR) which means that drivers are on the road for around 2-3 weeks at a time, with a few days off before returning to work.

Senior employees often get the first pick of their routes, depending on the employer. Because newer drivers are left with more distant routes and isolated locales, this impacts how long truck drivers are away from home. When drivers have routes that are further out, they are less likely to make it home.

Your home's location can also influence how much time you spend at home. If you're from a remote place, you're less likely to be near your home while traveling. Some businesses also require their drivers to park at terminals instead of their houses. You may end up spending more time traveling back home if there is no terminal around your current location.

How Many Hours Can I Drive as a CDL Driver?

A CDL driver is allowed to drive 11 hours in one day under the regulations. The driver is not allowed to resume driving until he or she has taken a 10-hour break after completing the 11-hour shift. The maximum driving time for drivers transporting people is 10 hours, followed by an 8-hour break. It is important for drivers to get some rest and move around so that they can stay awake while driving. As a CDL driver, it's critical to adhere to the Federal Motor Carrier Safety Administration's (FMCSA) regulations on the number of hours a CDL driver can drive when you're at the wheel.

What Is a Truck Driver's Schedule Like?

Many different factors such as the trucking company, weather, vehicle breakdowns, traffic, cargo, appointments, and delays with loading/unloading may affect a truck driver's schedule. However, a typical schedule would likely be something like this:

Morning: Most truckers get up between 4 and 6 a.m. to start their day. They'll start their pre-trip inspection or fill up driving logs after having breakfast and possibly taking a brief shower. Before hitting the road, many truckers check the weather and driving conditions, schedule stops, and locate weighing stations. Drivers will begin driving after everything has been checked and planned.

Afternoon: While the time spent driving varies by trucking firm and haul, many drivers will spend about 11 hours on the road after a 10-hour break. Many trucking laws and regulations prohibit truckers from driving for longer than 14 hours. Violations of this provision might result in exorbitant fines. Most of the afternoons are spent on the road, with a few pauses in between. Loading and unloading a cargo is also usually done in the afternoon.

Evening: Most truckers will stop at a truck stop for the night after hitting the 11-hour limit. They'll park their truck, do a post-trip inspection, and complete any paperwork or workflow that's required. They'll then have some free time to do things like eat, watch TV, read, or check in with their relatives. The majority of truckers go to bed early in order to get enough rest before their early start the next day.

What Truck Driving Jobs Pay the Highest?

The highest-paying truck driving professions are ones that involve a lot of risk and demand certain skills and training. When the long hours and time away from home become too much, you'll need a purpose to keep going.

Setting objectives and finding a career that allows you to grow are also important. The world's highest-paid truck drivers earn almost $80,000 per year. Specialty drivers get more money because of the training and abilities required for the position. When traveling over frozen lakes in the middle of nowhere, ice road truckers face significant dangers. They must be able to repair their own trucks and think fast when something goes wrong. Another specialty driver's load could even contain dangerous items. Truckers who travel more, such as over-the-road truckers, earn more than those who do not.

When compared to being employed by national companies, belonging to a union increases your prospects of greater compensation. A CDL driver's annual salary ranges from $50,000 to $85,000, or $21.00 to $41.00 per hour on average. The driver's annual income is determined by who employs them, their training, the sort of cargo they transport, driving circumstances, and their experience.

Is Truck Driving a Good Career?

If you enjoy being on the road and going to different places, truck driving is an excellent career choice. The trucker lifestyle is appealing to many people, but it is not for everyone. Truck drivers are expected to work long hours, sometimes up to 70 per week. Because you may not be home for weeks at a time depending on the type of trucking you do, many companies allow individuals with seniority to choose the routes they want first. It is critical that you are in good health before considering truck driving as a career. To acquire a DOT medical card, drivers must sit for long periods of time and pass a physical examination.

Take some time to read about the various truck driving occupations if you decide to pursue a career as a truck driver. Driving a truck can range from local to Over-the-Road (OTR) driving. There are also many types of OTR truck drivers. Some drivers have received specific training to navigate over frozen bodies of water, others drive to and fro between two locations while there are some who transport hazardous materials. Different truck driving jobs have varying skill sets, home time and pay. You'll want to identify the best trucking businesses to work for before you start working. It is important for you to decide which matters more to you: the best firm to work for or the one that pays the most.

How Much Does It Cost to Attend Driving School?

The cost of driving school ranges from $3,000 to $10,000. The fee depends on the school you attend, the sort of license you wish to get, and the level of training you want.

Tuition for CDL school can be quite expensive if you choose to pay all at once. It can, however, be considerably less expensive than getting a Bachelor's degree. There are several options for paying for truck driving school. When drivers are hired onto their team, some businesses may pay them for their CDL training costs, which can be up to $7,000. Larger trucking businesses may even have their own CDL schools where new drivers can be trained.

Private CDL schools can help you in getting the best job opportunity, allowing you to potentially earn more money. You may not have to pay money up front with paid CDL training programs, but your starting pay may be much lower, and you will be unable to switch employment offers after you have signed the contract. It's important to carefully consider your options and determine how much money you'll save in the long run between sponsored CDL schooling, paid CDL schooling, and private CDL schooling.

Can I Get My CDL without Going to Truck Driving School?

You don't have to go to trucking school to get your CDL. However, without the formal training and experience provided by a school, you may have difficulty getting work. Some states only need you to take and pass the CDL exam as well as pay the necessary fees. Many companies across the country, however, demand at least 160 hours of formal classroom time.

Trucking businesses want to see proof that you went to and graduated from a CDL driving school. Employers also want to know if you've studied tractor-trailer systems, road operations, and FMCSA procedures.

A CDL driving school can teach you skills that will help you better prepare for the CDL exam and driving test. In the classroom, you'll learn all you need to know to pass the CDL exam, as well as acquire the hands-on driving experience you'll need to take the skills test. The skills you receive in school will help you prepare for a long and prosperous career.

Bear in mind that sometimes, it can be more expensive to get your CDL without going to trucking school than it is to attend trucking school. It's possible that you'll have to take an online course to gain the information you need. Aside from that, you may need to pay for practice driving time when preparing for the driving test. If you're worried about costs, you can try getting a government loan to cover your tuition, or preferably get in touch with trucking companies that own and manage their training programs.

CHAPTER - 16

GLOSSARY

AFV – Alternative Fueled Vehicle. This is a vehicle that runs on any other fuel source than something like gasoline or diesel fuel.

Air Ride Suspension - The suspension of the vehicle is the system that allows the vehicle to bear its load and move in sync for a smooth ride. The Air Ride Suspension uses air instead of traditional springs to do so.

Anchor It - This phrase is used when talking about making an emergency stop.

APU (Auxiliary Power Unit) - This unit allows the driver to continue to use things like the heat or air conditioning or the lights in the cab without using the truck's engine or battery. This allows for comfort in the cab without killing the battery or draining the gas.

AVI (Automatic Vehicle Identification) - an on-board system that automatically identifies the vehicle which combines a transponder and receiver that can manage electronic toll payment, detection of stolen vehicles, and more.

Average Length of Haul - A company that travels frequently between certain points will often calculate the average time it should take and the average distance between those points. This allows them to give an estimate of pick-up and delivery times.

Baffle - A baffle is a large separator inside of a tanker that limits the motion of the liquid inside, thus mitigating the effect of many gallons of sloshing liquid on the motion and control of the vehicle.

Berth – This is the compartment in the back of or behind the cab where the driver can sleep and rest between driving shifts.

Bill of Lading – The Bill of Lading is an itemised list that details all the goods in each shipment.

Blind Spot - A blind spot is any spot on the exterior vehicle that cannot be observed by the driver using either the windows or the mirrors from the driver's seat.

Bobtail – A bobtail is a tractor that is not pulling any cargo or a trailer. See also, Deadhead.

Bridge Formula – This is a formula that can be used by local and federal governments to determine and adjudicate how much of a load can be hauled on each axle of a vehicle, and how far apart those axles need to be for maximum safety.

Bunk – This is the compartment in the back of or behind the cab where the driver can sleep and rest between driving shifts.

Cabover or Cab-Over-Engine (COE) - A truck whose design places the cab above the engine.

Cargo Weight – The full combined weight of the gear, loads, and supplies on a vehicle.

Cartage Company – This is a company that provides the service of local cargo pickup and delivery.

CAT Scale - This is a network of certified, reliable scales across all of North America (United States and Canada.. that allows drivers to weigh their vehicles and ensure that the weight of their loads are exactly as they should be.

CB (Citizens Band Radio) - This is a Push-To-Talk two-way radio system that is used by commercial motor vehicle drivers to communicate with one another regarding special situations, traffic conditions, weather conditions, and even conversation.

CDL (commercial driver's license) - This is the official licensure that allows a driver to transport cargo in support of a business and operate a vehicle that weighs more than 26,001 pounds.

CDLIS - The commercial driver's license Information System allows states to cross-reference information about CDL holders.

CDL Restrictions - Restrictions placed on a CDL that either prevent a driver from operating certain types of vehicles or require a driver to comply with certain requirements while driving.

CFR (Code of Federal Regulations) - This is a sweeping codification of federal regulations in place in the United States. These regulations are written by many different agencies and are organized under 50 subsections that each represent their own broad areas.

Chassis Weight – This is the total weight of the empty vehicle

e before additions and cargo. This is also known as Curb Weight or Tare Weight.

CLP (Commercial Learner's Permit) - This allows a driver to practice the operation of a commercial motor vehicle after passing the written knowledge tests. Just like with a personal vehicle, you can obtain your permit and are given guidelines for gaining familiarity with your vehicle and its operation.

COFC (Container On Flat Car) - This combination freight shipping method requires a flat bed and a shipping container mounted securely onto it.

Combination Vehicle - A combination vehicle is a tractor unit that has been connected to one or more trailers; this is commonly referred to as a semi. These trailers are connected with a fifth wheel and/or a converter dolly.

Common Carrier – A common carrier is a company or individual (public or private) that will transport cargo for a fee to the general public and public companies, unlike private or contract carriers which will only transport for specific customers.

Company Sponsored Training - Companies may choose to foot the bill for their employees to study for and pass their commercial driver's license exams. Typically, companies will offer to allow the employee to pay back the costs with portions from their paychecks until the fees are paid.

Compressed Gas - A substance that is a gas at typical room temperature and pressure which has been subjected to much pressure to contain it in a cylinder for dispensing and later use.

Compression Brake - A compression release that allows the vehicle to slow its traveling speed. See also Decompression Brake, Jake Brake, or Retarder.

Container Chassis – A chassis or trailer that is designed for the purpose of carrying containers.

Contract Carrier – A freight company that only offers its services to a select few customers on a contract basis.

Converter Dolly - This is a mechanical component that allows a tractor to hook up to and carry a trailer. It is an auxiliary axle that contains a coupling device.

Covered Wagon - A flatbed truck which has side plates with no metal on the top. Typically a large tarp is pulled over the bed of the truck to contain the load.

CPM (Cents per Mile) - This is the rate per mile at which commercial drivers are paid for their services.

CSA (Compliance, Safety, and Accountability) - This is an enforcement and compliance program held by the Federal Motor Carrier Safety Administration (FMCsa: that enables them to hold professional drivers accountable for the things they should be doing to ensure safety on the roads.

Curb Weight - This is the total weight of the empty vehicle before additions and cargo. This is also known as Chassis Weight or Tare Weight.

Day Cab - This is a cab (tractor) that has no area inside of it for the driver to lie down or sleep.

Deadhead – A commercial motor vehicle that is in motion without any attached cargo.

Decompression Brake - A compression release that allows the vehicle to slow its traveling speed. See also, Compression Brake, Jake Brake, or Retarder.

Dedicated Route - A route that is routinely followed by a carrier in order to service a regular client or customer.

Dispatcher - The point of contact at the carrier company which serves as a communication point for the driver at all times with regard to the schedule, changes, loads, and important messages they may need while on the road.

DMV (Department of Motor Vehicles) - In some states this is also known as the BMV or Bureau of Motor Vehicles. This is the entity responsible for the testing and licensure of drivers, both professional and individual.

Dolly - A mechanical vehicle component that is designed for the connection to a tractor, truck, or high-traction vehicle.

DOT (Department of Transportation) - This is the government department that sees to the regulation of transportation and travel on the road, air, and railroads.

Double Clutch - The action of depressing the clutch twice while changing gears in a manual transmission vehicle that has no synchronizer.

Doubles – A tractor that has two attached trailers.

Drayage – The transportation of cargo over a relatively short distance. This is usually conducted as a part of a much longer haul, assisted by other carriers over the other portions of the journey.

Drop and Hook - The practice of dropping off a connected trailer and cargo, only to connect up to another at the same location to haul it elsewhere.

Drop Yard - The area where trucks may park their trucks and their trailers.

Dry Freight - Any freight or cargo that is not liquid.

Dry Van - A commercial motor vehicle that has no refrigeration or any other special features and requirements.

DVIR (Driver Vehicle Inspection Report) - This is an official report made by the driver at the conclusion of an inspection of their vehicle. This report should include any notes about what was checked and what was found, if anything. This is a safety measure that ensures that the driver is checking everything on the truck that must be in prime working condition to ensure prime working condition and safe travel.

EDI (Electronic Document Interchange) - A system that allows for the immediate exchange of digital documents that are related to the transportation of cargo, such as Bills of Lading.

Endorsements - CDL Endorsements are needed by commercial drivers in order to operate vehicles that contain or are certified to haul different types of cargo and freight.

EOBR (Electric On-Board Recorder) - This is a recording device that logs information pertaining to the trip made by a commercial motor vehicle.

E-Log – This is a digital system which drivers can use to log the specifics of their distance and services offered. This system is accessible to the driver and the dispatcher at a moment's notice, which allows each party to have optimum control over schedules and to properly coordinate. It is advised by the federal government to use these digital logs over the use of the paper, hand-written logs that were once used.

FHWA (Federal Highway Administration) - This is a division of the US Department of Transportation (see DOT) that specializes in the regulation of highway travel and transportation.

Flatbed – A type of trailer that has no sides or top that allows the carrying of construction materials and of other cargo that is of unique sizes and shapes that are not fit for typical trailers.

Forced Dispatch – When a driver is unable or unwilling to transport cargo from one place to another, yet the company and the dispatcher assigns the load which must be delivered or consequences may be suffered.

For-Hire Carrier - A for-hire carrier is a company or individual (public or private) that will transport cargo for a fee to the general public and public companies, unlike private or contract carriers which will only transport for specific customers.

GAWR (Gross Axle Weight Rating) - This is a rating—a specification—provided by the manufacturer which specifies the amount of weight that an axle may carry.

Grade – This is the number that shows how steep a particular slope or hill is. A 5% grade is a hill that rises five feet per 100 feet traveled.

Gross Mass - This is the total weight of a package or freight including the container and its contents.

Gross Weight - This is the total weight of a package or freight including the container and its contents.

HOS (Hours of Service) – The maximum number of hours a driver may be on duty transporting cargo according to the FMCSA safety regulations.

IFTA (International Fuel Tax Agreement) - The IFTA is an agreement between the lower 48 states of the United States and the Canadian provinces, to simplify the reporting of fuel use by motor carriers that operate in more than one jurisdiction.

Intermodal Transportation - The transportation of cargo that calls for more than one type of transportation to get it from the point of origin to its intended recipient.

Interstate - 1. Between more than 1 state i.e. Across state lines. 2. A highway that runs between and over state lines.

Interstate Commerce - Money earned and business conducted across state lines. This type of commerce is regulated by the federal government.

Intrastate - Within one single state.

Intrastate Commerce - Money earned and business conducted within state lines in the state in which you are properly licensed. Depending on the state in which you are licensed, the regulations for this type of commerce may be regulated differently, so be sure to look up your local regulations.

Jackknife – When the trailer and the tractor are positioned at a sharp angle to one another.

Jake Brake - A compression release that allows the vehicle to slow its traveling speed. See also, Compression Brake, Decompression Brake, or Retarder.

JIT (Just-In-Time) - This is getting the cargo or freight right to the recipient with little to no time to spare. Doing so allows the sellers to keep their costs low by reducing their inventory.

Landing Gear – Large supports or stilts that can be lowered at the front of a trailer to give it support when it stands on its own without an attached tractor.

LCV (Long Combination Vehicle) - Any vehicle that is greater in length than a double trailer. For instance, a triple or larger.

Lessee – An individual or company that has paid for the temporary usage of someone else's equipment or space.

Lessor – An individual or company that has been paid for the temporary usage of their equipment or space by someone else.

Lift Axle – A movable axle that can be latched into position and used for a load that is heavier than the engaged axles can handle. This is done so that vehicles can adapt to larger loads and still adhere to the local and federal weight standards for their vehicles.

Linehaul - This is the hauling of cargo from one terminal to another, where Drayage drivers will take over to make their local deliveries.

Loaded Miles - The number of miles driven in a commercial motor vehicle that has been loaded with freight.

Local Driver - A commercial driver that delivers cargo on a regular, local route. Also referred to as P&D (Pickup & Delivery)

Logbook – This is a written log that contains the miles traveled and activities completed within a 24-hour period.

Logistics – The practice (art and science, if you will) of getting people or things where they need to be on a specific schedule that works for all parties involved.

Long-haul – A trip that covers a long distance.

Lowboy – A lowboy is a flatbed trailer that has a low deck and which is used for carrying materials and cargo that is taller.

LTL (Less-Than-Trucklod) - This distinction is used for trucks that are transporting anything less than one full truckload. This often ranges from one single package to one half load.

LTL Carrier – A shipping company that specializes in the transport of goods in smaller shipments; many of these companies will run these smaller shipments concurrently, as with a parcel delivery route.

MCP (Motor Carrier Permit) - This is a permit that allows a licensed driver to operate a commercial motor vehicle and transport passengers or goods for a fee. This permit is evidence of registration with the California Department of Motor Vehicles.

MVR (Motor Vehicle Report) - This is something that is typically used by trucking companies that allows them to determine the driving record and overall eligibility for potential new employees. These driving records allow a potential employer to see any potential issues the driver may have in the future, based on their past experience.

NHTSA (National Highway Traffic Safety Administration) - A federal agency that is a portion of the Department of Transportation whose mission is to increase safety, reduce injury, and to minimize the possibility of vehicle crashes within the United States.

NTSB (National Transportation Safety Board. - An independent agency that investigates civil transportation and accident matters for the federal government.

Owner-Operator – A truck driver who has ownership of or holds the lease for their own truck(s) rather than needing them from the company.

OTR (Over the Road. - Long-distance or long-haul truck driving and freight movement, as opposed to local deliveries or regional routes.

OTR Driver (Over the Road.. - An Over the Road driver is one that is dedicated to driving long distances and delivering freight. Many Over the Road drivers are away from their homes for several weeks at a time to complete these deliveries and sleep in the cabs of their trucks, showering at truck stops that have them.

Outage - The amount of allowance for a liquid to expand.

Out of Service - This status is imposed on a driver and restricts them from continuing to drive or operate; this is typically done following some kind of infraction.

P&D (Pickup & Delivery) - A commercial driver that delivers cargo on a regular, local route. Also referred to as Local Driver

Payload – The total weight of a load being carried by a commercial driver.

Peddle Run - A route for a loaded commercial motor vehicle that has numerous scheduled stops.

Pintle Hook – A hook used to connect double and triple trailers to tractors.

Pre-Hire - A pre-hire is a person who is still undergoing the training for their trucking career—a student or a trainee—who has been conditionally hired with a guarantee that the student will meet basic hiring requirements. Upon graduation, the company may provide an orientation phase to complete any training or requirements the company has for new hires before the process is considered complete.

PrePass - PrePass is the commercial equivalent of EZpass. This allows commercial motor vehicles to bypass the weigh stations on their route using the Automatic Vehicle Identification (AVI) system which recognizes each vehicle. This service does require pre-certification.

Pre-Trip Inspection - An inspection conducted by the driver before each trip to ensure that the vehicle is in good, working order and that there are no dangerous conditions on the vehicle or its components.

Private Carrier – A freight company that only offers its services to a select few customers on a contract basis.

PTDI (Professional Truck Driver Institute) - This is the institution that is responsible for accrediting and certifying programs for the CDL testing and training. This organization does not provide their own educational classes or training.

Qualcomm – This is a communication system that allows drivers to wirelessly converse and coordinate with one another. This system combines elements of GPS, text messaging, and email to allow the company to keep tabs on each truck and driver, and allows the drivers to know the status of upcoming jobs and weather that might interfere with their route.

Relay – This is a maneuver that allows two drivers to depart from different points of origin, meet in the middle, exchange their loads, and then drive them back home to the destination for each load.

Reefer – A colloquial term for a trailer that has refrigeration, a cooling unit, and insulated walls. These are typically used for the transport of perishable food items.

Retarder - A compression release that allows the vehicle to slow its traveling speed. See also, Compression Brake, Decompression Brake, or Jake Brake.

Road Railer – A versatile trailer that is made to be able to travel on the road as well as on the railroad.

Route - This is the series of directions a trucker may follow to deliver goods to a specific location.

Runaway Ramp – These are often placed on steep grades. They are wide, dirt areas onto which a truck may pull if they have lost power in their brakes. It slopes upward to allow the truck to come to a stop safely.

Semitrailer - A trailer with rear wheels connected to a truck by a fifth wheel or dolly.

Shipping Weight – This is the weight of the whole vehicle, excluding the weight for fluids like coolant and fuel.

Sleeper – A bunk in the back of a trailer's cab so the driver can sleep on their route.

Sleeper Team – A team of two drivers that make deliveries together so that one driver can sleep while the other one drives, allowing the freight to make it to its destination that much more quickly without breaking the federal Hours of Service regulations.

Sliding Fifth Wheel – A fifth wheel that can be positioned differently among axles to change the weight distribution to increase safety and balance.

Step Deck - A flatbed trailer with one portion of the bed at a lower height to accommodate taller or oddly-shaped freight.

Straight Truck – A truck that has its cargo area permanently connected to the cab, as opposed to a tractor trailer that can be hooked and unhooked at will.

Tank Vehicle - A commercial motor vehicle with a tank to carry liquid or gas cargo.

Tare Weight - This is the total weight of the empty vehicle before additions and cargo. This is also known as Chassis Weight or Curb Weight.

Team – Two drivers that make deliveries together so that one driver can sleep while the other one drives, allowing the freight to make it to its destination that much more quickly without breaking the federal Hours of Service regulations.

Terminal - A junction at which the trucks for carrier companies may gather and be sent; a hub facility.

TL (Truckload) - One full trailer's worth of cargo.

TL Carrier – A trucking company that carries a single shipper's freight on one truckload.

Tractor – A truck that is designed for the purpose of pulling a trailer.

Tractor Trailer – A truck with a connected trailer for the purpose of carrying and transporting a load.

Transfer Company – A company which specializes in conducting cross-border transactions.

TSA (Transportation Security Administration) - An agency of the federal government in the Department of Homeland Security whose jurisdiction includes the overseeing of and the security of traveling public in the United States.

Upper Coupler – Part of the connection between the tractor and trailer, it carries weight from the trailer, and houses the kingpin, which connects to the fifth wheel of the tractor.

VIN (Vehicle Identification Number) - A unique number on each vehicle that is connected with the name of the person who owns and operates it, as well as manufacturer information and registration information.

WIM (Weigh-In-Motion) - A way to measure the weight of a vehicle as it rolls through a station, instead of making it come to a complete stop.

Yard Tractor – A tractor that stays at the company headquarters for the express purpose of moving trailers around the warehouse or distribution center; these are not taken on drives to deliver loads.

INTRODUCTION

In order to operate any commercial motor vehicle such as dump trucks, tractor trailers, passenger buses, and the likes, you will first need to get a commercial driver's license. Taking your CDL test is the basic step to starting your professional truck driving career and you will need to study a comprehensive handbook before doing so. Although this book contains only practice tests and multiple-choice answers, you can check out the "CDL Study Guide - Theroy Course" in this bundle for detailed information about acquiring your commercial driver's license.

In the pages below are a total of 354 questions which cover all the topics you need to know to pass your CDL tests. Included are practice tests on Hazardous materials, School Buses, Doubles/Triples, Pre-trip inspections, Tanker vehicles, Air Brakes, and Combination vehicles which will help you prepare for your tests adequately. Get started now and obtain your Class A, B or C CDL license in no time!

GENERAL KNOWLEDGE PRACTICE TEST

This full-length CDL General Knowledge practice test contains 40 questions. This test contains more CDL General Knowledge practice questions than you'll probably need to pass the General Knowledge endorsement, but why take any chances? Answering 40 practice questions will prepare you better than answering a mere 10 questions!

1. Which of the following statements about an escape ramp is false?

- ☐ A. It turns uphill
- ☐ B. It has no use when one is traveling fast
- ☐ C. It is made of soft gravel
- ☐ D. It is located a few miles from the top of a downgrade

2. How many tie downs should you use for a 20-foot load?

- ☐ A. 1
- ☐ B. 2
- ☐ C. 4
- ☐ D. 3

3. What is the best way to calculate one's following distance in seconds?

- ☐ A. Send a text to a friend and tell them to text you back in ten seconds in order to discover how far you have traveled
- ☐ B. Let a vehicle pass a landmark and count the seconds till you get there
- ☐ C. Make use of the stopwatch on your cellphone to know how long to reach a mile marker after the car in front has passed it
- ☐ D. Get ¼ close to the car in front of you and then back off again

4. How can one start moving without rolling back?

- ☐ A. Put on the parking brake
- ☐ B. Use the trailer brake hand valve
- ☐ C. Engage the clutch before removing your feet from the brake
- ☐ D. All of the above

5. In a pre-trip test with your instructor while examining hoses, what will you have to look out for?

- ☐ A. The location of a dipstick
- ☐ B. Frays in the water pump
- ☐ C. Puddles on the ground
- ☐ D. Windshield water fluid level

6. The starter key should be in your pocket key while performing the pre-trip test inspection because...

- ☐ A. So no one can move the vehicle
- ☐ B. The truck could get stolen
- ☐ C. Someone might start the truck
- ☐ D. Any and all of the above could happen

7. One would lose their CDL driving privileges if they are convicted of a second DUI offense in a private or commercial vehicle for how long?

- ☐ A. For life
- ☐ B. At least a year
- ☐ C. 10 years
- ☐ D. 1 year

8. One should not use a B:C fire extinguisher on which type of fire?

- ☐ A. Gasoline
- ☐ B. Wood
- ☐ C. Electrical
- ☐ D. Grease

9. The following tasks are involved in the checking and inspecting of a cab except...

- [ ] A. Starting the engine and putting it in neutral
- [ ] B. Checking on the air pressure gauge
- [ ] C. Transmission control check
- [ ] D. Listening for unusual noise

10. A normal tractor-trailer takes how many seconds to clear a double track?

- [ ] A. More than 15
- [ ] B. More than 30
- [ ] C. 14
- [ ] D. 15

11. What is black ice?

- [ ] A. A thin layer of clear ice
- [ ] B. A mixture of rain and snow
- [ ] C. Dirty snow
- [ ] D. Ice with dark substances in it

12. How can one prevent another accident from happening in a place where an accident has already occurred?

- [ ] A. Drink in order to calm your nerves
- [ ] B. Get to the higher ground
- [ ] C. Stay in your vehicle and wait for help to come
- [ ] D. Put warning devices so as to make sure that other vehicles are aware

13. How many hours of sleep does the average person need per night?

- [ ] A. 7-8 hours
- [ ] B. 8-9 hours
- [ ] C. 6- 8 hours
- [ ] D. 6-7 hours

14. Is it absolutely safe to remove a radio cap if the vehicle engine is not overheated?

- ☐ A. Yes
- ☐ B. Yes, as long as there is no overflow
- ☐ C. As long as the radiator is not damaged, yes
- ☐ D. No

15. What will help a driver get sober?

- ☐ A. Fresh air
- ☐ B. Time
- ☐ C. Coffee
- ☐ D. A glass of water

16. Which will get stuck at a railroad crossing?

- ☐ A. A car carrier
- ☐ B. A moving van
- ☐ C. The lowboy
- ☐ D. All of the above

17. When driving on a wet road, one should reduce their speed by...

- ☐ A. One-third
- ☐ B. 60 percent
- ☐ C. One-quarter
- ☐ D. One-half

18. In what situation should one totally downshift?

- ☐ A. When starting up a hill and finishing a curve
- ☐ B. When starting down a hill and entering a curve
- ☐ C. When starting down a hill and finishing a curve
- ☐ D. When starting up a hill and entering a curve

19. Which of the following is not a benefit of making plans when you spot a hazard?

- [ ] A. To avoid having to perform an action like sudden braking that is much more likely to cause an accident
- [ ] B. Improving the safety of other drivers on the road as well as your own by being prepared
- [ ] C. Gives you more time to hang up your phone call or finish something you might have been eating or drinking
- [ ] D. Gives you more time to do something

20. Where should you be looking ahead of your vehicle while driving?

- [ ] A. Straightforward at all times
- [ ] B. Foward the left side of the roadway
- [ ] C. Toward the right side of the roadway
- [ ] D. Both far and near, then back and forth

21. What is the greatest amount of play that should be in your steering wheel?

- [ ] A. 1 inch / 10 degrees
- [ ] B. 5 inches / 5 degrees
- [ ] C. 2 inches / 10 degrees
- [ ] D. All of the above

22. What is the major difference between road rage and aggressive driving?

- [ ] A. Intent to do harm or physically assault
- [ ] B. Level of anger
- [ ] C. Outcome of the situation
- [ ] D. All of the above

23. What action should be taken when your vehicle begins to hydroplane?

- [ ] A. Accelerate very slightly
- [ ] B. Brake gently to start slowing your vehicle
- [ ] C. Release the accelerator
- [ ] D. Let go of the wheel so it can correct itself again

24. Why is it a good idea for drivers to carry out the pre-trip inspection exactly the same way every time?

- ☐ A. Most companies require you to do so
- ☐ B. You will be less likely to forget something
- ☐ C. You should not do it the same way every time as doing so may make you too comfortable in your inspection
- ☐ D. The law requires you to do it the same way every time

25. What is the most important and obvious reason to always conduct a pre-trip inspection of your commercial motor vehicle?

- ☐ A. For safety reasons
- ☐ B. To make sure your paint is not chipped
- ☐ C. Employer liability
- ☐ D. To see if your vehicle needs a wash

26. Which of the following are correct methods for knowing when you should shift up?

- ☐ A. The road speed and engine speed
- ☐ B. Wind speed and shift indicator light
- ☐ C. Every 3 to 5 seconds and road speed
- ☐ D. None of the above

27. When stopped on a hill, what is the proper procedure to start moving without rolling back?

- ☐ A. Engage the clutch before you take your right foot off the brake
- ☐ B. Put blocks behind the tires
- ☐ C. Increase engine rpm and let the clutch out quickly
- ☐ D. Leave the trailer brakes on and drag the tires, releasing the brake after moving forward

28. When it comes to driving safely, what does it mean for drivers to communicate?

- ☐ A. Making use of hand signals
- ☐ B. Getting a helper before backing up a vehicle
- ☐ C. B radio to talk to others
- ☐ D. Making use of the vehicle's 4-way flashers, turn signals, horn, and headlights

29. If you have to stop your vehicle to load passengers or cargo, you should...

- [ ] A. Flash the vehicle's brake lights to serve as a warning for drivers behind you
- [ ] B. Slow down the vehicle but do not bring it to a complete halt
- [ ] C. Swerve slowly from side to side to warn other drivers
- [ ] D. Brake suddenly to get the attention of drivers behind you

30. Where can the maximum weight loading for a set tire pressure be found?

- [ ] A. Under the seat
- [ ] B. On the side of each tire
- [ ] C. On the vehicle's dashboard
- [ ] D. On your manifest

31. While driving, you should always look up ahead for two main things. They are...

- [ ] A. Tunnels and overpasses
- [ ] B. Detours and law enforcement officers
- [ ] C. Gas stations and truck stops
- [ ] D. Traffic signs and other vehicles

32. What should be done as soon as the trailer starts going off the right path while backing?

- [ ] A. The top of the steering wheel should be turned in the drift's direction
- [ ] B. The top of the steering wheel should be turned in the opposite direction of the drift
- [ ] C. The steering wheel should be released and the vehicle's brakes engaged
- [ ] D. The steering wheel should be held tighter

33. When starting down a long downgrade, which of the factors below should not influence the driver's speed?

- [ ] A. Weather and road conditions
- [ ] B. The driver's schedule
- [ ] C. How steep the downgrade is
- [ ] D. The vehicle's total weight including its cargo

34. During nighttime driving, you should...

- ☐ A. Always have the vehicle's high beams on
- ☐ B. Keep your windows rolled down to allow the fresh air keep you alert
- ☐ C. Have some coffee or any other caffeinated products so that you can remain awake
- ☐ D. Ensure your speed is slow enough to enable you stop within the headlights' range if there is an emergency

35. What should be done as a driver approaches a work crew on a highway?

- ☐ A. They should slow down
- ☐ B. They should sound the horn repeatedly
- ☐ C. They should rev the engine
- ☐ D. They should flash the vehicle lights

36. In a 55 mph zone where traffic is moving at 35 mph, what is an ideal driving speed?

- ☐ A. 45 mph
- ☐ B. 50 mph
- ☐ C. 35 mph
- ☐ D. 55 mph

37. One of the statements below about a vehicle's spare tire is false

- ☐ A. It must have the same manufacturer as the main tires
- ☐ B. It must be the right size
- ☐ C. It must be free from any damages
- ☐ D. It must be correctly inflated

38. All of these are signs of a tire blowout apart from...

- ☐ A. A smoky odor
- ☐ B. A loud noise
- ☐ C. The vehicle vibrating
- ☐ D. A thumping noise

39. Which of the substances below can impair a driver's ability to drive safely?

- ☐ A. Certain prescription medicines
- ☐ B. Alcoholic drinks
- ☐ C. Certain cold medicines
- ☐ D. All of the above

40. Which of the statements below about a GPS device is true?

- ☐ A. Its screen should be more than 4 inches in size
- ☐ B. It should be equipped with both visual and audible warnings
- ☐ C. It should be manufactured in the USA
- ☐ D. It should be specially made for truck navigation

ANSWERS

1. B
2. B
3. B
4. D
5. C
6. D
7. A
8. B
9. A
10. A
11. A
12. D
13. A
14. D
15. B
16. D
17. A
18. B
19. C
20. D
21. C
22. A
23. C
24. B
25. A
26. A
27. A
28. D
29. A
30. B
31. D
32. A
33. B
34. D
35. A
36. C
37. A
38. A
39. D
40. D

PRE-TRIP INSPECTION PRACTICE TEST

This full-length CDL Pre-Trip Inspection practice test contains 44 questions. This test contains more CDL Pre-Trip Inspection practice questions than you'll probably need to pass the Pre-Trip Inspection endorsement, but why take any chances? Answering 44 practice questions will prepare you better than answering a mere 10 questions!

1. The engine compartment should not have more than...

- [ ] A. ½ inch play at the center of the belt
- [ ] B. ¾ inch play at the center of the belt
- [ ] C. ¾ inch play at the middle of the belt
- [ ] D. 2/4 inch play at the end of the belt

2. In order to check the power steering fluid, one should...

- [ ] A. Remove the oil fill cap and check the level
- [ ] B. Check the reservoir sight glass
- [ ] C. Check the power steering fluid dipstick
- [ ] D. All of the above

3. During the inspection of the dipstick to ensure that the lubrication level is above the refill mark, one is checking the...

- [ ] A. Power steering fluid level
- [ ] B. The coolant level
- [ ] C. A and B
- [ ] D. The engine system

4. Puddles on the ground or dripping fluids on the underside of the engine and transmission indicates...

- [ ] A. A leaking hose
- [ ] B. A water pump problem

- [ ] C. An engine problem
- [ ] D. None of the above

5. In step three of the pre-trip inspection (starting of the engine and cab inspection), what is to be done first?

- [ ] A. Get into the car and start the engine
- [ ] B. Put gear shift into neutrality
- [ ] C. Get into the car and make sure the parking brakes are on
- [ ] D. None of the above

6. The normal oil temperature range of engine oil is...

- [ ] A. 20 - 35 psi
- [ ] B. 30 - 70 psi
- [ ] C. 10 - 20 psi
- [ ] D. 60 - 90 psi

7. Which part of the gauge has a governor cut?

- [ ] A. The air
- [ ] B. The oil pressure
- [ ] C. The voltmeter
- [ ] D. The nuts

8. Which one of these should be cleaned and adjusted from the inside?

- [ ] A. The mirrors
- [ ] B. The nuts
- [ ] C. The windshield
- [ ] D. None of the above

9. When the pedal is pumped thrice and held down for five seconds making sure that the pedal does not move, what is being inspected?

- [ ] A. The air brakes
- [ ] B. The hydraulic brake
- [ ] C. The parking brake
- [ ] D. None of the above

10. What belt should one make sure is securely mounted and adjusted and is not ripped off or frayed?

- [ ] A. The safety belt
- [ ] B. The air compressor
- [ ] C. The power steering
- [ ] D. None of the above

11. _____ gauge should come up to normal within seconds after the engine is started

- [ ] A. Oil pressure
- [ ] B. Air pressure
- [ ] C. Coolant pressure
- [ ] D. All of the above

12. _____ gauge pressure should build from 50 - 90 psi within 3 minutes

- [ ] A. Air pressure
- [ ] B. Oil pressure
- [ ] C. Coolant pressure
- [ ] D. None of the above

13. When checking for damage to the longitudinal numbers, cross members, what are you inspecting?

- [ ] A. Frame
- [ ] B. Fuel tank
- [ ] C. Exhaust system
- [ ] D. None of the above

14. What transforms steering column action into wheel action?

- [ ] A. Steering box and hoses
- [ ] B. Suspension
- [ ] C. Steering link
- [ ] D. None of the above

15. What is the best way to check the coolant level?

- ☐ A. Check the sight glass
- ☐ B. Check the dipstick
- ☐ C. Check the temperature gauge
- ☐ D. All of the above

16. Make sure the ______ are not cut, chaffed, or worn out and not dragged against tractor parts

- ☐ A. Locking jaws
- ☐ B. Door ties and lift
- ☐ C. Air lines and electrical lines
- ☐ D. All of the above

17 One of these keeps your vehicle from rolling when parked

- ☐ A. The parking brake
- ☐ B. The locking pin
- ☐ C. The service brake
- ☐ D. The gear system

18. What carries air to the wheel brake assembly?

- ☐ A. Slack adjusters
- ☐ B. Brake hoses and lines
- ☐ C. Brake chambers
- ☐ D. None of the above

19. One of these converts air pressure to mechanical force to operate the brake at the wheels

- ☐ A. Brake chambers
- ☐ B. Drum brake
- ☐ C. Brake hoses
- ☐ D. All of the above

20. A driver can easily check that the vehicle's oil level is adequate if there is a sight glass on the wheel. Otherwise, they should look for leaks around the...

- [ ] A. Battery
- [ ] B. Hub oil seals and axle seals
- [ ] C. Hydraulic brakes
- [ ] D. All of the above

21. Which external lights should one check?

- [ ] A. Brake lights
- [ ] B. Turn signals
- [ ] C. All of the above
- [ ] D. None of the above

22. What is responsible for the transmission to the drive axle?

- [ ] A. The steering play
- [ ] B. The driveshaft
- [ ] C. The air compressor belt
- [ ] D. None of the above

23. What is responsible for the heating of the cab and prevents frosting from forming on the windshield?

- [ ] A. The header board
- [ ] B. The heater / the defroster
- [ ] C. The air compressor
- [ ] D. All of the above

24. What do you inspect to make sure all are present and show no signs of looseness such as rust trails?

- [ ] A. Rims
- [ ] B. Lug nuts
- [ ] C. Dodger
- [ ] D. None of the above

25. What should one make sure is tightly secured and the taps are tight?

- ☐ A. Air compressor
- ☐ B. Fuel tanks
- ☐ C. Water pump
- ☐ D. The steering gear

26. What structure supporting the fifth wheel skid plate should be checked for cracks and breaks?

- ☐ A. Platform
- ☐ B. Kingpin
- ☐ C. Apron
- ☐ D. The gear shift

27. Which of the following can disengage the engine from the drive train?

- ☐ A. The driveshaft
- ☐ B. The parking brake
- ☐ C. The gearshift and clutch
- ☐ D. The gear pin

28. Which gauge helps you prevent engine failure, seizure, or breakdown?

- ☐ A. The oil pressure
- ☐ B. The ammeter
- ☐ C. The power steering
- ☐ D. None of the above

29. Which of the following is not part of inspecting a vehicle's coupling?

- ☐ A. Checking that the fifth wheel jaw has closed on the correct part of the king pin
- ☐ B. Driving a few feet to test if it is connected correctly
- ☐ C. All of the above
- ☐ D. None of the above

30. What is responsible for maintaining air pressure in the air brake system?

- ☐ A. The alternator
- ☐ B. The water pump
- ☐ C. The air compressor
- ☐ D. All of the above

31. If you cannot make a right turn without swinging into another lane, what should be done?

- ☐ A. Turn wide as you complete the turn
- ☐ B. Turn wide before starting the turn
- ☐ C. Find some other location to turn
- ☐ D. None of the above

32. Which of the following is not true about an Antilock Braking System?

- ☐ A. It only activates when the wheels are in danger of locking up
- ☐ B. It increases the vehicle's normal braking ability
- ☐ C. It is found on all tractors manufactured after the year 1998
- ☐ D. All of the above

33. What helps in releasing the fifth wheel locking jaw so that the trailer can be coupled?

- ☐ A. The release arm
- ☐ B. The locking pin
- ☐ C. The draw bar
- ☐ D. The brake system

34. What is the sliding mechanism for tandem axles on trailers?

- ☐ A. The locking pins
- ☐ B. The landing gear
- ☐ C. The suspension system
- ☐ D. All of the above

35. Which of a vehicle's tires should have a minimum tread depth of 4/32 inches?

- [ ] A. The spare tires
- [ ] B. The non-drive axle tires
- [ ] C. The steering axle tires
- [ ] D. None of the above

36. What should be clean with no dirt, illegal sticker, or any form of obstruction?

- [ ] A. The headlights
- [ ] B. The windshield and mirrors
- [ ] C. The light indicators
- [ ] D. All of the above

37. What is to be checked that it is free from damages and securely bolted to the tractor frame?

- [ ] A. The catwalk
- [ ] B. The kingpin
- [ ] C. The apron
- [ ] D. None of the above

38. What is responsible for the carrying of hydraulic fluid to the wheel brake assembly?

- [ ] A. The slack adjuster
- [ ] B. The brake linings
- [ ] C. The brake chambers
- [ ] D. The brake hoses and lines

39. ______ are the brackets, bolts, or bushings that are used to attach the spring to the axle or vehicle frame

- [ ] A. The torque
- [ ] B. The spring mounts
- [ ] C. The mounting bolts
- [ ] D. The tongue

40. One of the following may happen if you try to couple a trailer when it is too high

- ☐ A. It may not couple correctly
- ☐ B. The trailer nose could get damaged
- ☐ C. The tractor might strike and damage the tractor
- ☐ D. All of the above

41. When doing the pre-trip inspection, you should tell the examiner each item you are checking and two or three reasons why you're checking them. True or false?

- ☐ A. True
- ☐ B. False
- ☐ C. Maybe
- ☐ D. Only if asked

42. Should an overview of your vehicle be done as you approach it (including looking for leaks, leaning, or excessive damage)?

- ☐ A. Yes
- ☐ B. No
- ☐ C. Maybe
- ☐ D. Only if the vehicle had mechanical issues during the last trip

43. When opening the hood, you should check...

- ☐ A. The hinges, catches, and springs
- ☐ B. Nothing
- ☐ C. For damage
- ☐ D. Both A and C

44. When checking the mirrors on the outside of the vehicle, you should ensure that...

- ☐ A. They are properly mounted
- ☐ B. There are no cracks
- ☐ C. They are clean
- ☐ D. All the above

ANSWERS

1. B
2. C
3. C
4. A
5. C
6. B
7. A
8. A
9. B
10. A
11. A
12. A
13. A
14. A
15. A
16. D
17. A
18. B
19. A
20. B
21. C
22. B
23. B
24. B
25. B
26. A
27. C
28. A
29. B
30. C
31. A
32. B
33. A
34. A
35. C
36. B
37. A
38. D
39. B
40. A
41. A
42. A
43. A
44. D

AIR BRAKES PRACTICE TEST

This full-length CDL Air Brakes practice test contains 44 questions. This test contains more CDL Air Brakes practice questions than you'll probably need to pass the Air Brakes endorsement, but why take any chances? Answering 44 practice questions will prepare you better than answering a mere 10 questions!

1. What kind of air is needed in air brakes?

- ☐ A. Heated air
- ☐ B. Decomposed air
- ☐ C. Warm air
- ☐ D. Compressed air

2. What 3 types of brake systems are used in commercial vehicles' brake systems?

- ☐ A. The service brake, the emergency brake, and the parking brake
- ☐ B. The anti-lock brake, the service brake, and the emergency brake
- ☐ C. The hand brake, parking brake, and the emergency brake
- ☐ D. The service brake, the hand brake, and the emergency brake

3. What pumps air into the air storage tank?

- ☐ A. The safety valve
- ☐ B. The air compressor
- ☐ C. The governor
- ☐ D. The evaporator

4. One of the following statements is true about spring brakes

- ☐ A. It will not function if the system loses air pressure

- [ ] B. They are held by mechanical force
- [ ] C. They come on at 60 psi
- [ ] D. They make use of air pressure to stop vehicles

5. At what psi level is the safety relief valve supposed to be set to be safe to open at?

- [ ] A. 125 psi
- [ ] B. 60 psi
- [ ] C. 150 psi
- [ ] D. 100 psi

6. One of the following is the most common type of foundation brake

- [ ] A. Disc brake
- [ ] B. Wedge brake
- [ ] C. The anti-lock brake
- [ ] D. S-Cam drum brake

7. What is the basic function of the alcohol evaporator?

- [ ] A. It is for the purpose of heating the air tank
- [ ] B. It is to put alcohol into the air system
- [ ] C. It is to remove water and oil from the brake system
- [ ] D. It is to keep alcohol out of the vehicle parts

8. One of the following is true about the front wheel braking

- [ ] A. The front wheel braking is good under all conditions
- [ ] B. It is ineffective under slippery conditions
- [ ] C. It will cause skids on ice
- [ ] D. One should put a limiting valve if equipped on the slippery positions in adverse conditions

9. What is the perfect time to drain one's air tanks?

- [ ] A. The end of a trip
- [ ] B. The end of the month
- [ ] C. The end of every working day

- ☐ D. The end of the fiscal quarter

10. On what kind of vehicle is a low-pressure warning signal required to be?

- ☐ A. Buses only
- ☐ B. Vehicles with air brakes
- ☐ C. Straight trucks
- ☐ D. The gear

11. What causes a vehicle's brake to fail?

- ☐ A. The brakes being out of adjustment
- ☐ B. The excessive use of service brakes
- ☐ C. Not relying enough on the engine brake
- ☐ D. All of the above

12. Modern air brake systems are made up of three different systems: the service brakes, parking brakes, and ________ brakes.

- ☐ A. S-Cam
- ☐ B. Emergency
- ☐ C. Foot
- ☐ D. All of the above

13. What is the maximum acceptable leakage rate per minute after the initial drop?

- ☐ A. 5 psi for single vehicles and 6 psi for combination vehicles respectively
- ☐ B. 1 psi for single vehicles and 7 psi for combination vehicles respectively
- ☐ C. 3 psi for single vehicles and 4 psi for combination vehicles respectively
- ☐ D. 5 psi for single vehicles and 10 psi for combination vehicles respectively

14. How are the truck slack adjusters checked?

- ☐ A. Press the brake pedal while listening for any strange noise
- ☐ B. Pull hard on each slack adjuster you can reach
- ☐ C. Accelerate and then brake hard
- ☐ D. Do all of the above

15. In air brake vehicles, parking brakes should be used...

- ☐ A. Whenever the vehicle is left unattended
- ☐ B. As little as possible
- ☐ C. During pre-trip and post-trip inspection
- ☐ D. None of the above

16. What is the function of a supply pressure gauge?

- ☐ A. To show how hot the air in the tank is
- ☐ B. To show how much air is in the tank
- ☐ C. To warn if the air in the tank is too low
- ☐ D. All of the above

17. At what measurement will the safety valve open?

- ☐ A. 100 psi
- ☐ B. 250 psi
- ☐ C. 200 psi
- ☐ D. 150 psi

18. In what manner do brakes work especially on a long steep downgrade?

- ☐ A. They work on the main braking system
- ☐ B. They work as a supplement to the braking of the engine
- ☐ C. They work as the main braking mechanism with the engine braking effect as an emergency backup
- ☐ D. They are not applicable

19. One of the following is not a part of the drum brake

- ☐ A. The return brake
- ☐ B. The safety valve
- ☐ C. The slack adjusters
- ☐ D. The brake drum

20. What will happen if the air tanks are not drained?

- ☐ A. One will drive too quickly

- ☐ B. Brakes may fail cause of water freezing
- ☐ C. Transmission fluid may drain out
- ☐ D. The vehicle's left side brake will cease to operate

21. Vehicles with air brakes have...

- ☐ A. A supply pressure gauge
- ☐ B. An air use gauge
- ☐ C. Backup hydraulic system
- ☐ D. None of the above

22. How should the air leakage rate be tested?

- ☐ A. Turn the engine off and release of the parking brake
- ☐ B. Charge the air system completely and leave the engine running
- ☐ C. Leave the engine running and release the parking brake
- ☐ D. Depress the brake pedal while keeping an eye on the air pressure gauge

23. What should be done before leaving one's vehicle?

- ☐ A. Chock the wheels
- ☐ B. Remove the keys
- ☐ C. Set the parking brakes
- ☐ D. Do all of the above

24. One of the following is not a part of the air brake system

- ☐ A. The emergency air brake system
- ☐ B. The radio signal
- ☐ C. The parking brake system
- ☐ D. The emergency brake system

25. When is the parking brake required to be used?

- ☐ A. Every time you leave your vehicle with few exceptions
- ☐ B. Only if you are away from your vehicle for a selected period of time
- ☐ C. Only in urban areas

☐ D. Only when there are other motorists around

26. What set of vehicles should have low air pressure signals?

☐ A. Vehicles built after the year 2010
☐ B. Vehicles built after the year 2015
☐ C. All vehicles with air brakes that are currently in operation
☐ D. None

27. One of the following is true about a dual air brake system

☐ A. It uses a single set of brake controls
☐ B. One of the systems is called "primary" while the other is called "secondary"
☐ C. One system operates the front axle and the other operates the rear axle
☐ D. All of the above

28. In what conditions are the front wheel brakes good?

☐ A. In good weather
☐ B. In every weather condition
☐ C. Icy conditions only
☐ D. None of the above

29. How best can one check if their vehicle's spring brakes come on automatically?

☐ A. Step on and off the brake pedal until the manufacturer's low psi specification is met, in order for springs to deploy
☐ B. Step on and off the brake pedal until the parking valve pops out
☐ C. On single vehicles, continue to step on and off the brake pedal until the parking valve pops out
☐ D. All of the above

30. What is an Anti-lock braking system?

☐ A. It activates when wheels are about to lock up
☐ B. It increases one's normal braking capability
☐ C. It shortens one's stopping distance
☐ D. It decreases normal braking capability

31. One of the following is true about the brake function when the anti-lock brake system fails

- ☐ A. It will slow the truck to a halt and cause you to pull over
- ☐ B. There will be a lack of brake function and the truck will be out of control
- ☐ C. You will still be able to use your brakes normally, but you will need to have the ABS serviced as soon as possible
- ☐ D. It may cause a huge fire risk

32. Using brakes on a downgrade acts as a supplement to...

- ☐ A. The use of the spring brakes
- ☐ B. The braking effect of the engine
- ☐ C. The use of the front brake limiting valve
- ☐ D. All of the above

33. In a vehicle that has a properly functioning dual air brake system and minimum-sized air tanks, the air pressure would build from 85 - 100 psi within how many seconds?

- ☐ A. 45
- ☐ B. 60
- ☐ C. 20
- ☐ D. 70

34. What will happen if the air pressure warning signal is not working?

- ☐ A. There will be a sudden emergency braking in the single circuit air system
- ☐ B. Air pressure will be lost
- ☐ C. Nothing will happen
- ☐ D. There will be a skid

35. The braking power of the spring brake...

- ☐ A. Increases when the service brakes are hot
- ☐ B. Depends on whether the service brakes are in proper adjustment
- ☐ C. Is unaffected by the condition of the service brakes
- ☐ D. Depends on the gas

36. You would know if your brakes are fading off if...

- ☐ A. You release the brake pedal and the vehicle's speed increases
- ☐ B. You have to press the brake pedal harder than usual to control your speed
- ☐ C. The brake feels spongy when you apply pressure
- ☐ D. All of the above

37. What does the service line in a vehicle well-equipped with air brakes do?

- ☐ A. It carries fuel at the filling station
- ☐ B. It supplies air to the trailer air tanks
- ☐ C. It carries air from the vehicle's foot brake or the trailer hand brake
- ☐ D. None of the above

38. In perfect conditions, the average driver of a vehicle who is equipped with air brakes and traveling at 55mph would need to stop at what distance?

- ☐ A. More than 300 feet
- ☐ B. 150 -250 feet
- ☐ C. 50 - 150 feet.
- ☐ D. All of the above

39. The application of the pressure gauge shows the amount of air pressure...

- ☐ A. In the tanks
- ☐ B. In the modulating control valve
- ☐ C. Being applied to the brakes
- ☐ D. Nothing happens

40. For what reason should one not fan the brake when driving on a long downgrade?

- ☐ A. The brakes won't cool
- ☐ B. Air usage becomes less when fanning
- ☐ C. Brake linings do not get hot when fanning
- ☐ D. None of the above

41. Where is the safety valve situated in a vehicle well-equipped with air brakes?

- ☐ A. The dashboard
- ☐ B. The first tank from which the air compressor pumps out
- ☐ C. Under the brake pedal
- ☐ D. In the second tank from which the air compressor pumps out

42. In a walk-around inspection, check the brake drums to be sure that no cracks are longer than ______ width of the friction area

- ☐ A. One-half
- ☐ B. One-third
- ☐ C. One-quarter
- ☐ D. All of the above

43. In a vehicle that is well equipped with air brakes, what activates the stoplight switch when you brake?

- ☐ A. The air pressure
- ☐ B. The spring pressure
- ☐ C. The mechanical force
- ☐ D. None of the above

44. The brake pads should be _____ for the brakes to be on

- ☐ A. Worn 1/32 of an inch
- ☐ B. Against the drum
- ☐ C. Disconnected from the slack adjusters
- ☐ D. Worn dangerously thin

ANSWERS

1. D
2. A
3. B
4. B
5. C
6. D
7. B
8. A
9. C
10. B
11. D
12. B
13. C
14. B
15. A
16. B
17. D
18. B
19. B
20. B
21. A
22. A
23. D
24. B
25. A
26. C
27. D
28. B
29. D
30. A
31. C
32. B
33. A
34. A
35. B
36. B
37. C
38. A
39. C
40. A
41. B
42. A
43. A
44. B

TANKER VEHICLES PRACTICE TEST

This full-length CDL Tanker Vehicles practice test contains 42 questions. This test contains more CDL Tanker Vehicles practice questions than you'll probably need to pass the Tanker Vehicles endorsement, but why take any chances? Answering 42 practice questions will prepare you better than answering a mere 10 questions!

1. One of the following is true about managing spaces from side to side

- ☐ A. Avoid traveling alongside other vehicles
- ☐ B. Keep your vehicle to the right side of your lane
- ☐ C. Strong winds make it easier to stay in one's lane
- ☐ D. All of the above

2. When is a tank endorsement required?

- ☐ A. They are required for vehicles that transport liquid and gases
- ☐ B. They are required for vehicles that transport passengers
- ☐ C. They are required for hazardous materials transportation
- ☐ D. They are required for air system

3. In what way does a liquid surge affect the handling of a tanker?

- ☐ A. It increases the wind drag of the tank
- ☐ B. The surge allows one to turn corners tighter
- ☐ C. It can move the truck in the direction of the liquid waves move
- ☐ D. All of the above

4. When loading small tanks of a cargo tank equipped with bulkheads, one should check for...

- ☐ A. The distribution of weight
- ☐ B. The water content
- ☐ C. The air-to-fuel ratio
- ☐ D. None of the above

5. One should have the knowledge of the outage needed for the liquids carried because...

- ☐ A. The heaviest liquids do not need any outage
- ☐ B. Tank baffles are not always legal with outage
- ☐ C. Some liquids expand more when they are warm
- ☐ D. All of the above

6. The best way to take a curve in a tanker is to slow to a safe speed before entering the curve and then ______

- ☐ A. Brake lightly
- ☐ B. Speed up slightly
- ☐ C. Downshift twice
- ☐ D. Speed up high

7. How often should one check the tires of a placarded vehicle with dual tires?

- ☐ A. Every 5 hours
- ☐ B. At the beginning of each trip and each time one stops
- ☐ C. Every week
- ☐ D. Every 1 hour

8. One should be very cautious when driving smoothbore tankers, especially when one is...

- ☐ A. Driving against the wind
- ☐ B. Starting or stopping
- ☐ C. Driving uphill or downhill
- ☐ D. Sliding

9. A vehicle carrying hazardous materials must have a placard on how many sides?

- ☐ A. 4
- ☐ B. 3
- ☐ C. 2
- ☐ D. 7

10. A smoothbore hole tank is also referred to as...

- ☐ A. Aluminium tank
- ☐ B. Unbaffled tank
- ☐ C. Baffled tank
- ☐ D. All of the above

11. Tankers that haul liquid require special care due to what reasons?

- ☐ A. The liquid movement
- ☐ B. The high center of gravity
- ☐ C. All of the above
- ☐ D. False, there is no need to be extra careful when transporting liquid cargo

12. When driving on a clear night, a driver must dim their headlights from high to low. They should also adjust their speed so they can stop within...

- ☐ A. The distance they can see ahead
- ☐ B. The length of the vehicle
- ☐ C. The distance to be covered in the next 15 seconds
- ☐ D. None of the above

13. One of these is true about tank vehicles

- ☐ A. The posted speed for a curve will be too fast for a tank vehicle
- ☐ B. The emergency brakes in a tank vehicle can be used to avoid crashes
- ☐ C. Loaded tanks take longer to stop than empty ones
- ☐ D. All of the above

14. The person who is qualified and is watching the offloading and loading of the tank should be...

- ☐ A. Within 30 feet of the tank
- ☐ B. Within 25 feet of the tank
- ☐ C. Within 35 feet of the tank
- ☐ D. None of the above

15. What does an outage mean?

- ☐ A. The allowance for the expansion of liquid
- ☐ B. The liquid weight
- ☐ C. How fast the liquid tanks drain
- ☐ D. All of the above

16. What do you do to steer your tanker quickly in order to avoid a hazard?

- ☐ A. Neutral"
- ☐ B. You should avoid braking as you turn
- ☐ C. You should brake hard and fast
- ☐ D. None of the above

17. What is a baffled tanker?

- ☐ A. They are separate tanks inside a tanker
- ☐ B. They are hollow balls floating in the liquid to slow movement
- ☐ C. They are bulkheads with holes that allow the liquid to flow through
- ☐ D. All of the above

18. What does the amount of liquid allowed to be loaded in a tank depend on?

- ☐ A. The amount of liquid it would expand to in transit
- ☐ B. The legal weight limit
- ☐ C. All of the above
- ☐ D. None of the above

19. One of the statements below about tankers is true

- [ ] A. They can turn over at the speed limit posted for curves
- [ ] B. The load weight is carried high up off the road
- [ ] C. All are true
- [ ] D. None of the above

20. One of these is a true statement about stopping distance and speed

- [ ] A. One needs about twice as much stopping distance at 40mph than at 20mph
- [ ] B. Wet roads double the stopping distance at any speed
- [ ] C. Both options are true
- [ ] D. All of the above

21. A side-to-side surge can cause:

- [ ] A. Over speeding
- [ ] B. A rollover
- [ ] C. Suspension system failure
- [ ] D. None of the above

22. When an emergency forces you to stop your tanker quickly to avoid a crash, what should you do?

- [ ] A. Make use of the emergency brakes
- [ ] B. Make use of controlled or stab braking
- [ ] C. Brake hard until you lock the wheels
- [ ] D. All of the above

23. The effects of a liquid surge is reduced by...

- [ ] A. The hauling of thicker liquids
- [ ] B. Starting, turning, and stopping the vehicle smoothly
- [ ] C. All of the above
- [ ] D. None of the above

24. Which of the following makes a liquid tanker harder to handle?

- [ ] A. The width of the cargo
- [ ] B. The high center of the gravity of the cargo
- [ ] C. The low center of the gravity of the cargo
- [ ] D. All of the above

25. A smoothbore tanker is used in transporting:

- [ ] A. Heavy liquid
- [ ] B. Liquid or milk products
- [ ] C. Acidic liquid
- [ ] D. None of the above

26. When should the escape ramp be used by a driver in the occurrence of him losing his brakes?

- [ ] A. Never
- [ ] B. Always
- [ ] C. If the tank is baffled
- [ ] D. Only if there are other vehicles around

27. If a vehicle is placarded, one must stop how many feet before the nearest rail at a railroad crossing?

- [ ] A. 15 - 50
- [ ] B. 10 - 36
- [ ] C. 5 - 20
- [ ] D. 15 - 65

28. What kind of surge can liquid in a tank with baffles have?

- [ ] A. Front-to-back
- [ ] B. Side-to-side
- [ ] C. Top-to-bottom
- [ ] D. None of the above

29. How do you expect a truck with a cargo tank that has baffles to handle on the road?

- ☐ A. To have lesser forward and backward surge than a tank without baffles
- ☐ B. The truck will seem heavier than it really is
- ☐ C. It will handle the same way as a tanker without baffles
- ☐ D. None of the above

30. Tanker drivers require special skills because...

- ☐ A. Liquid surge occurs in tankers
- ☐ B. Tankers have an increased risk of rollover
- ☐ C. All the above reasons
- ☐ D. False, tanker drivers do not need to have any special skills

31. Which of the following is a potential danger of a side-to-side surge?

- ☐ A. The suspension of the system failure
- ☐ B. Rollover
- ☐ C. Contentment breach
- ☐ D. None of the above

32. How should a tanker truck be driven in a curved place?

- ☐ A. One should accelerate before the curve and then downshift as you go through the curve
- ☐ B. One should use controlled braking as you go through the curve
- ☐ C. One should slow down before the curve and then accelerate as you go through the curve
- ☐ D. None of the above

33. One of the following is a divider between compartments inside of a tank

- ☐ A. Separation walls
- ☐ B. Baffles
- ☐ C. Bulkhead
- ☐ D. None of the above

34. Dividers inside tankers have holes that are in them and are called...

- ☐ A. Barriers
- ☐ B. Baffles
- ☐ C. Separators
- ☐ D. None of the above

35. Manhole covers should be...

- ☐ A. Left partially open to prevent a buildup of fumes
- ☐ B. Opened and reclosed before driving the vehicle
- ☐ C. Closed before driving the vehicle
- ☐ D. All of the above

36. How exactly should a tank vehicle be inspected?

- ☐ A. Do it the same way you inspected other tank vehicles before
- ☐ B. Read the vehicle's manual to learn how to do it
- ☐ C. Ask a fellow driver how to do it
- ☐ D. All of the above

37. Liquid surge is especially dangerous...

- ☐ A. On narrow city streets
- ☐ B. On hills
- ☐ C. On slippery roads
- ☐ D. All of the above

38. Drivers hauling liquids in tankers will need to be extra careful for two main reasons. One of them is the _____ center of gravity that tankers have.

- ☐ A. Flat
- ☐ B. Wide
- ☐ C. High
- ☐ D. None of the above

39. You must have a tank vehicle (N) endorsement to drive a vehicle with...

- [ ] A. Individual tanks over 225 gallons or a total of at least 2,400 gallons
- [ ] B. Individual tanks over 119 gallons or a total of at least 1,000 gallons
- [ ] C. Individual tanks over 65 gallons or a total of at least 500 gallons
- [ ] D. All of the above

40. Which of these is the most important thing to remember about emergency braking?

- [ ] A. If the wheels are skidding, you cannot control the vehicle
- [ ] B. Disconnecting the steering axle brakes will help keep your vehicle in a straight line
- [ ] C. Never engage a vehicle's emergency brakes without downshifting first
- [ ] D. All of the above

41. Which of these equipment needs to function properly if they are present in your vehicle?

- [ ] A. Vapor recovery kit
- [ ] B. Grounding and bonding cables
- [ ] C. Emergency shut-off systems
- [ ] D. All of the above

42. If a hill or curve prevents drivers behind you from seeing the vehicle within 500 feet...

- [ ] A. You should move the rear reflective triangle further down the road to give early adequate warning to other motorists
- [ ] B. You do not need to put out reflective triangles unless If the vehicle will be stopped for less than 30 minutes, there is no need to put out reflective triangles
- [ ] C. The vehicles taillights should be kept on to serve as a warning for other drivers
- [ ] D. None of the above

ANSWERS

1. A
2. A
3. C
4. A
5. C
6. B
7. B
8. B
9. A
10. B
11. C
12. A
13. A
14. B
15. A
16. B
17. C
18. C
19. C
20. B
21. B
22. B
23. C
24. B
25. B
26. B
27. A
28. B
29. A
30. C
31. B
32. C
33. C
34. B
35. C
36. B
37. C
38. C
39. B
40. A
41. D
42. A

HAZARDOUS MATERIALS PRACTICE TEST

This full-length CDL Hazardous Materials practice test contains 48 questions. This test contains more CDL Hazardous Materials practice questions than you'll probably need to pass the Hazardous Materials endorsement, but why take any chances? Answering 48 practice questions will prepare you better than answering a mere 10 questions!

1. When carrying a 100-pound cargo of silver cyanide, what precautions should be taken when given 100 cartons of battery acid to carry at a dock?

- [ ] A. Do not load the battery acid
- [ ] B. Make sure the silver cyanide is loaded on top of the battery acid
- [ ] C. Make sure the battery acid is loaded on top of the silver cyanide
- [ ] D. None of the above

2. For the hazard classes in Placard table 2, one should use them only if they are transporting a total of...

- [ ] A. 501 pounds and more
- [ ] B. 1,001 pounds and more
- [ ] C. 1,501 pounds and more
- [ ] D. None of the above

3. A technical name is...

- [ ] A. The name of a hazardous material used in scientific texts, and it is recognized as its biological name
- [ ] B. The medical name for hazardous materials used by medical personnel
- [ ] C. The name of a hazardous material used in the truck community
- [ ] D. None of the above

4. Placards should be used how many inches away from other markings?

- ☐ A. 3 inches
- ☐ B. 7 inches
- ☐ C. 12 inches
- ☐ D. 20 inches

5. What is necessary for the qualification of non bulk packaging?

- ☐ A. A maximum net mass of 400kg or less and a maximum of 450l or less for a receptacle liquid
- ☐ B. A maximum capacity of 450l or less for a liquid
- ☐ C. Both options above
- ☐ D. None of the above

6. When a truck carrying explosives has collided with another vehicle, you should not pull them apart until...

- ☐ A. You have placed the explosives 200 feet away from the building in the environment
- ☐ B. 30 minutes have passed
- ☐ C. The shipper's foreman is present
- ☐ D. None of the above

7. A vehicle containing 500 pounds each of division 1.1 explosives and division 1.2 explosives must have...

- ☐ A. Blasting agent placards
- ☐ B. Dangerous substances placards
- ☐ C. Explosives placards
- ☐ D. All of the above

8. When can you be allowed to move an improperly placarded vehicle?

- ☐ A. Never
- ☐ B. During an emergency only
- ☐ C. If the load isn't truly hazardous
- ☐ D. Only when the cargo is very important

9. Hazard shipping papers should include the description of the hazardous material and...

- [ ] A. Monetary value
- [ ] B. Contact information of the driver's next of kin
- [ ] C. Emergency response information
- [ ] D. None of the above

10. Other places where the hazardous material identification must appear are...

- [ ] A. On all bulk packaging and the cargo tank
- [ ] B. On the gas tank and the sticker in the glove compartment
- [ ] C. On the temporary license holder and the steering wheel
- [ ] D. None of the above

11. Placarded vehicles should carry a fire extinguisher with a minimum rating of...

- [ ] A. 20 B:C
- [ ] B. 10 B:C
- [ ] C. 5 B:C
- [ ] D. None of the above

12. Smoking and performing of any similar activity are not allowed within 25 inches of...

- [ ] A. Class 4.2 only
- [ ] B. Class 5.2 only
- [ ] C. Class 1,2,3 and 4
- [ ] D. All of the above

13. On receiving a leaking package, the driver should...

- [ ] A. Refuse the package
- [ ] B. Transport it as it is
- [ ] C. Fix the package before transportation
- [ ] D. Hide it

14. In the determination of the use of placards, which of the following is not needed?

- ☐ A. The amount of the substance shipped
- ☐ B. The manufacturing date of the substance
- ☐ C. Amount of all the hazardous material of all classes being shipped
- ☐ D. None of the above

15. What is the function of the Emergency Response Guidebook?

- ☐ A. It is created by the department of transportation and is used nationwide
- ☐ B. It is studied by emergency personnel to keep the public safe
- ☐ C. All of the above
- ☐ D. None of the above

16. One of the following is not an acceptable way of marking for hazardous materials

- ☐ A. Written in italics
- ☐ B. UN marks
- ☐ C. Roman description
- ☐ D. Written boldly

17. Engines run a pump when you are delivering compressed gas. After delivery, when should the engine be turned off?

- ☐ A. Before unhooking
- ☐ B. After unhooking
- ☐ C. Turn it off on arrival: use the power to run the pump
- ☐ D. None of the above

18. If an "X" or "RQ" is in the "HM" column of the shipping paper entry, what does this imply?

- ☐ A. The material is regulated by hazardous material regulations
- ☐ B. The entry only refers to materials that must be top-loaded
- ☐ C. The material listed on the line is the largest part of the shipment
- ☐ D. All of the above

19. One of the following materials is an acceptable floor liner used in moving division 1.1 and 1.2 materials

- ☐ A. Stainless steel
- ☐ B. Carbon steel
- ☐ C. Non-ferrous metal
- ☐ D. None of the above

20. The major difference between a cargo tank and a portable tank is...

- ☐ A. Temporary versus permanent attachment
- ☐ B. Being filled on the vehicle versus being filled off the vehicle
- ☐ C. All of the above
- ☐ D. None of the above

21. What is a safe haven?

- ☐ A. A safe place to dump hazardous materials
- ☐ B. A place that has been approved for parking unattended vehicles carrying explosives
- ☐ C. A slang term for the last stop at the end of one's transporting of hazardous materials
- ☐ D. All of the above

22. In the hazardous materials table, which column provides the hazardous material identification number for each material?

- ☐ A. Column 4
- ☐ B. Column 3
- ☐ C. Column 2
- ☐ D. Column 6

23. What is a placard used for?

- ☐ A. To make other drivers stay away up to a minimum of 20 feet
- ☐ B. To warn those with children to drive in the other lane
- ☐ C. To communicate risk
- ☐ D. For fun purposes

24. What is a cargo tank?

- ☐ A. Bulk packaging attached to a vehicle
- ☐ B. Bulk packaging temporarily attached to a vehicle
- ☐ C. They are filled while they are off your vehicle and attached for transportation
- ☐ D. None of the above

25. What is the purpose of the shipper's certification on packaged materials?

- ☐ A. To make it as light as possible
- ☐ B. To make it easy for identification
- ☐ C. To make opening and closing of the package very easy
- ☐ D. For safety purposes

26. One of the following three hazard classes should not be placed in a temperature-controlled trailer

- ☐ A. Class 2.3 and 6
- ☐ B. Class. 1, 2.1 and 3
- ☐ C. Class 1, 3 and 6
- ☐ D. None of the above

27. Where is the best place to keep shipping documents that describe the hazardous material?

- ☐ A. Hidden in a safe place inside the tractor
- ☐ B. In a holder inside the driver's side door or sitting on the driver's seat
- ☐ C. In a locked glove compartment anytime you are out of the vehicle
- ☐ D. All of the above

28. One of the following hazardous classes uses a transport index to determine how much of it can be loaded on a single vehicle for transportation

- ☐ A. Class 4 (flammable solids)
- ☐ B. Class 3 (flammable liquids)
- ☐ C. Class 7 (radioactive materials)
- ☐ D. Class 2 (inflammable solids)

29. How many feet is one allowed to park from a bridge, tunnel, or building when carrying division 1.2 or. 1.3 materials?

- ☐ A. 300 feet
- ☐ B. 500 feet
- ☐ C. 600 feet
- ☐ D. 800 feet

30. What can be done in a scenario where you discover hazardous material leakage at a rest stop but there's no phone available?

- ☐ A. Send someone for help with all the necessary information
- ☐ B. Drive for help as quickly as possible
- ☐ C. Drive slowly and cautiously until you get to a phone
- ☐ D. None of the above

31. What does it mean if a "W" appears in column one of the hazardous material table?

- ☐ A. It identifies a proper shipping name that is used in international transportation
- ☐ B. It only applies when the material is being transported by water
- ☐ C. It only applies when the material will be exposed to air
- ☐ D. None of the above

32. How is the hazardous material table ordered?

- ☐ A. In numerical order by hazard class
- ☐ B. In alphabetical order by the proper shipping name
- ☐ C. In numerical order by identification number
- ☐ D. Roman numerals

33. You are not allowed to use a hazard class name or ID number to describe...

- ☐ A. A non-hazardous material
- ☐ B. Hazardous waste
- ☐ C. The reportable quantity of hazardous material
- ☐ D. None of the above

34. What kind of materials are classified under hazard class 7?

- ☐ A. Radioactive materials
- ☐ B. Corrosive materials
- ☐ C. Flammable and combustible liquid
- ☐ D. Inflammable materials

35. The letter "G" in the hazardous material column means...

- ☐ A. Ground shipping
- ☐ B. Generic shipping name
- ☐ C. Geographical shipping name
- ☐ D. None of the above

36. A hazardous material's identification is determined by...

- ☐ A. The receiver
- ☐ B. The shipper
- ☐ C. The driver
- ☐ D. All of the above

37. If a shipment contains both hazardous materials, the shipping paper must...

- ☐ A. List the hazardous materials first
- ☐ B. Highlight the hazardous materials in contrasting colors
- ☐ C. All of the above
- ☐ D. None of the above

38. Who is responsible for finding out special routes needed to haul hazardous materials?

- ☐ A. The carrier
- ☐ B. The driver
- ☐ C. The shipper
- ☐ D. All of the above

39. The hazard class 6 includes...

- ☐ A. Poisons
- ☐ B. Infectious substances
- ☐ C. All of the above
- ☐ D. None of the the above

40. Examples of substances under hazard class 1 are...

- ☐ A. Gasoline, methanol
- ☐ B. Dynamite, fireworks
- ☐ C. Food flavorings
- ☐ D. None of the above

41. One of the following does not belong in hazard class 1 through 9

- ☐ A. Medicine, food flavoring
- ☐ B. Dynamite, fireworks
- ☐ C. Gasoline, methanol
- ☐ D. All of the above

42. Most identification numbers are preceded by the letters "UN" or "NA". The proper shipping names that are associated with the letters "NA" are used where?

- ☐ A. Canada
- ☐ B. Internationally
- ☐ C. All of the above
- ☐ D. None of the above

43. Containment rules are rules that _______

- ☐ A. Instruct the driver on how to unload hazardous materials
- ☐ B. Instruct the driver on how to load hazardous materials
- ☐ C. Instruct the driver on how to transport hazardous materials
- ☐ D. All of the listed answers

44. There is a hazard warning label placed by shippers on all packages of hazardous materials. What shape is the hazard warning label on the majority of packages?

- ☐ A. Oval
- ☐ B. Circle
- ☐ C. Diamond
- ☐ D. Rectangle

45. The letters of the shipping name must be, at minimum, how tall on portable tanks with capacities of more than 1,000 gallons?

- ☐ A. One inch
- ☐ B. Three inches
- ☐ C. Five inches
- ☐ D. Two inches

46. Upon discovering a fire while you are transporting hazardous materials and the trailer doors feel hot, you should ______

- ☐ A. Try to fight the fire regardless of whether the cargo is already on fire
- ☐ B. Not open the doors
- ☐ C. Fan the fire
- ☐ D. Open the doors

47. Bulk packaging is...

- ☐ A. A single container with a capacity of 50 gallons
- ☐ B. Triple containers with each not exceeding a capacity of 25 gallons
- ☐ C. A single container with a capacity of 119 gallons or more of hazardous materials
- ☐ D. Double containers with a capacity of 100 gallons

48 When transporting hazardous waste, you need to ______

- ☐ A. Carry a Uniform Hazardous Waste Manifest in the truck
- ☐ B. Have the word "WASTE" before the name of the material on the bills
- ☐ C. Sign a uniform Hazardous Waste Manifest
- ☐ D. All of the answers above

ANSWERS

1. A
2. B
3. A
4. A
5. C
6. A
7. C
8. B
9. C
10. A
11. B
12. C
13. A
14. B
15. C
16. A
17. A
18. A
19. C
20. C
21. B
22. A
23. C
24. A
25. B
26. B
27. B
28. C
29. A
30. A
31. B
32. B
33. A
34. A
35. B
36. B
37. C
38. B
39. C
40. B
41. A
42. A
43. D
44. C
45. D
46. B
47. C
48. D

DOUBLE/TRIPLE TRAILERS PRACTICE TEST

This full-length CDL Double/Triple Trailers practice test contains 43 questions. This test contains more CDL Double/ Triple Trailers practice questions than you'll probably need to pass the Double/Triple Trailers endorsement, but why take any chances? Answering 43 practice questions will prepare you better than answering a mere 10 questions!

1. Whenever you're pulling more than one trailer, which should be behind the tractor?

- ☐ A. The heaviest trailer
- ☐ B. The shortest trailer
- ☐ C. The lightest trailer
- ☐ D. None of the above

2. One of the following is true about quick steering movement and double/triple vehicles

- ☐ A. They flip over from quick steering movement more easily than other vehicles
- ☐ B. Counter steering is easier in double/triple vehicles than in other vehicles
- ☐ C. Applying the brakes at the same time will let you perform the quick steering movement
- ☐ D. None of the above

3. How can one make sure to apply air to the second trailer?

- ☐ A. Watch each trailer air gauge for a drop of 30 psi
- ☐ B. Go to the rear of the second trailer and open the emergency line shut off valve
- ☐ C. Apply the hand valve at 10mph and stop at the same distance as a truck with the trailer at 5mph
- ☐ D. None of the above

4. Some trucks have convex or spot mirrors. What are they used for?

- ☐ A. They make things look smaller and farther than they really are
- ☐ B. They need not be checked as often as flat mirrors
- ☐ C. They make things look larger and closer than they really are
- ☐ D. All of the above

5. Driving a trailer or truck with a double or triple trailer requires the driver to...

- ☐ A. Allow for more following distance than with smaller vehicles
- ☐ B. Take care in special conditions
- ☐ C. All of the above
- ☐ D. None of the above

6. One of the following statements about steering is true

- ☐ A. You should apply brakes while turning
- ☐ B. It is not necessary to put both hands on the steering wheel
- ☐ C. The sharper you turn, the more likely the vehicle will skid or rollover
- ☐ D. None of the above is true

7. What will happen if the pintle hook is unlocked while the dolly is still under the second trailer?

- ☐ A. The dolly tow bar may fly up
- ☐ B. The air lines will rupture
- ☐ C. Nothing will happen
- ☐ D. None of the above

8. To check if the converter dolly is coupled to the rear trailer, one should...

- ☐ A. Pull against the pin of the second trailer
- ☐ B. Release spring brake and check the movements
- ☐ C. Pull forward and do a visual check of the coupling
- ☐ D. None of the above

9. One of the following statements about driving through a curve is false

- ☐ A. Slow down before entering the curve

- ☐ B. Brake and downshift in the curve
- ☐ C. Speed up as soon as you are out of the curve
- ☐ D. None of the above

10. One of the following is true about handling doubles and triples

- ☐ A. Triple bottom rigs can stop quicker than a 5-axle tractor semi-trailer due to off tracking
- ☐ B. Sudden movements with the steering wheel can result in a tipped-over rear trailer
- ☐ C. All of them is true
- ☐ D. None of them is true

11. When you want to hook your combination vehicle to a second trailer that has no spring brakes and wheel chocks, you should...

- ☐ A. Supply air to the trailer air system with the tractor and disconnect the emergency line
- ☐ B. Make sure the trailer will roll freely when coupling
- ☐ C. Hook the trailer electric cord to a portable generator for braking power
- ☐ D. All of the above

12. One of these statements is true

- ☐ A. Empty rigs are more likely to turn over than fully loaded rigs
- ☐ B. When driving a straight truck, you should look further ahead than when you are pulling doubles
- ☐ C. You should drive a double or triple very smoothly to avoid a rollover
- ☐ D. All are true

13. When driving a 100-feet twin trailer combination at 50mph and the road is dry with good visibility, you should leave at least ___ seconds of space ahead of you

- ☐ A. 11
- ☐ B. 9
- ☐ C. 10
- ☐ D. 7

14. What is a converter dolly?

- ☐ A. It is an electronic device that connects the electric power from a semi-trailer to the rear of the tractor-trailer
- ☐ B. It is a coupling device that connects a semi-trailer to the rear of a tractor-trailer

- [ ] C. All of the above
- [ ] D. None of the above

15. When pulling a trailer at under 40mph, how much following distance should you maintain behind the vehicle in front of you?

- [ ] A. 3 seconds
- [ ] B. 1 second
- [ ] C. 2 seconds
- [ ] D. 5 seconds

16. With the hand valve on, a driver should test the trailer brakes by opening the service line valve at the rear of the rig. When this is done, what will be heard?

- [ ] A. The emergency line valve open
- [ ] B. Air escape from the open valve
- [ ] C. Service brake slowly move into the fully applied position
- [ ] D. None of the above

17. When doing the walk-around inspection of a vehicle, you should check landing gear to be sure that....

- [ ] A. It is fully raised
- [ ] B. It isn't damaged
- [ ] C. All of the above
- [ ] D. None of the above

18. Drivers should make sure that the converter dolly air tank drains are ____ and the pintle hook is _____

- [ ] A. Closed : latched
- [ ] B. Open : free
- [ ] C. Open : latched
- [ ] D. Closed: open

19. In a vehicle that loads twin semi-trailers, one should lower its landing gear until _____ while uncoupling the rear semi-trailer

- [ ] A. It touches the ground
- [ ] B. It is enough to take the weight off the dolly

☐ C. It lifts the trailer off the dolly

☐ D. None of the above

20. For coupled doubles and triples, what is the correct position for the converter dolly air tanks petcocks?

☐ A. Closed

☐ B. Open

☐ C. Open, except for the dolly connected to the last trailer

☐ D. Free

21. When driving double trailers and you have to use your brakes to avoid a crash, you should _____ for emergency brakes:

☐ A. Use controlled or stab braking

☐ B. Use trailer brakes only

☐ C. Push the brake pedal as hard and hold it there

☐ D. Steering wheel

22. When pulling doubles and a set of trailer wheels go into a skid, which of the following is likely to happen?

☐ A. The rig will continue to move in a straight line no matter how the steering wheel is turned

☐ B. The rig will stay in a straight line

☐ C. The rig may jackknife

☐ D. None of the above

23 ______ are gas or hydraulic devices that cushion the vehicle ride and stabilize the vehicle

☐ A. Springs

☐ B. Brakes

☐ C. Shock absorbers

☐ D. Water pump

24. Part of the vehicle inspection test especially if you have a cargo lift is to...

☐ A. Check for leaks and damages

☐ B. Explain the process of checking it for correct operation

☐ C. All of the above

☐ D. None of the abov

25. Which of the gauges indicates that the alternator or generator is charging?

- ☐ A. Temperature
- ☐ B. Voltmeter
- ☐ C. Oil pressure
- ☐ D. Spring brakes

26. In order to improve vision during stormy weather, what must be secure, undamaged, and operating smoothly?

- ☐ A. The lightning indicators
- ☐ B. Windshield wipers and washers
- ☐ C. The emergency equipment
- ☐ D. None of the above

27. In the case that the coolant overflow is not part of the pressurized system, check the coolant level by...

- ☐ A. Removing the container cap and checking the visible
- ☐ B. Inspecting the reservoir
- ☐ C. Doing either A or B
- ☐ D. None of the above

28. What is a shipper's certification?

- ☐ A. A shipper's statement that the product is not safe to inhale
- ☐ B. The shipper's certification that the shipment has been prepared according to applicable rules
- ☐ C. ID number, and the packing group
- ☐ D. All of the above

29. How much space should be between the upper and fifth lower wheel, especially during the inspection of the coupling of a converter dolly to the rear trailer

- ☐ A. None
- ☐ B. ½ and ¾ inch space
- ☐ C. It depends on the load
- ☐ D. All of the above

30. When transporting class 1.1, 1.2, or 1.3 materials, you should use a placard if they exceed...

- ☐ A. 440 pounds
- ☐ B. The reportable quantity amount
- ☐ C. Any amount
- ☐ D. There is no need to use a placard for such materials

31. In the case that someone is attending to a placarded vehicle that is parked, that person should...

- ☐ A. Be able to move the vehicle if necessary
- ☐ B. Either be in the vehicle, awake, or within 100 feet of the vehicle
- ☐ C. Both A and B
- ☐ D. None of the above

32. One must stop at a railroad crossing if their vehicle:

- ☐ A. Has an empty hazardous material cargo tank
- ☐ B. Is carrying less than 1000 pounds of chlorine
- ☐ C. All of the above
- ☐ D. None of the above

33. Before connecting a converter dolly to the second or third trailer, you should check the height of the trailer. The trailer height is right if...

- ☐ A. The kingpin is resting on the fifth wheel
- ☐ B. The trailer will be raised slightly when the converter dolly is backed under it
- ☐ C. The center of the king pin lines up with the locking jaws
- ☐ D. None of the above

34. When transporting materials from hazard table one, which rule applies?

- ☐ A. A placard is required for any amount
- ☐ B. A placard is required if the total amount transported is up to 1,001 pounds or more
- ☐ C. You may use dangerous placards if you have 1,0001 pounds or more of two different classes
- ☐ D. None of the above

35. The official CDL manual section on double and triple trailers usually describes how to couple and uncouple...

- [ ] A. Every type of combination
- [ ] B. Only the more common types of combination
- [ ] C. Only doubles
- [ ] D. None of the above

36. Parking brakes should be used whenever you park excluding what situation?

- [ ] A. The brakes are very hot
- [ ] B. All of the listed answers
- [ ] C. You have just come down a steep grade
- [ ] D. The brakes are wet in freezing temperatures

37. A typical low air pressure warning signal is in what color?

- [ ] A. Purple
- [ ] B. Blue
- [ ] C. Yellow
- [ ] D. Red

38. Vehicles with ABS have malfunction lamps that are what color?

- [ ] A. Yellow
- [ ] B. White
- [ ] C. Green
- [ ] D. Blue

39. What should be done first to test the trailer emergency brakes?

- [ ] A. Push in the trailer air supply control
- [ ] B. Pull harshly on the trailer
- [ ] C. Pull gently on the trailer with the tractor
- [ ] D. Charge the trailer air brake system

40. Why should the use of automatic transmission when going into a lower gear at high speed be avoided?

☐ A. None of the listed answers

☐ B. It will always completely destroy the transmission

☐ C. It could damage the transmission and lead to a loss of the engine's braking effect

☐ D. You should force an automatic transmission into a lower gear while you are driving at a high speed as doing so will help you maintain control of the vehicle.

41. What differentiates a wedge brake from other types of brakes?

☐ A. None of the listed answers

☐ B. It stops the vehicle completely

☐ C. Activated by Air Pressure

☐ D. The brake chamber push rod pushes a wedge directly between the ends of two brake shoes

42. Why do doubles and triples require more space in comparison to other types of commercial vehicles?

☐ A. They have more height and length than tractors

☐ B. They have more length and swing from side to side as a result

☐ C. They have more length and cannot be stopped or turned abruptly

☐ D. It is a requirement by the law

43. Why do doubles and triples have a higher probability of skidding in slippery conditions, bad weather, and during mountain driving?

☐ A. There may not be any brakes on the front wheels

☐ B. There is greater length and more dead axles to be pulled

☐ C. The brakes are more prone to failure

☐ D. The drive wheels only secure the pulling unit

ANSWERS

1. A
2. A
3. B
4. A
5. C
6. C
7. A
8. A
9. B
10. B
11. A
12. C
13. A
14. B
15. D
16. B
17. C
18. A
19. B
20. A
21. A
22. C
23. C
24. C
25. B
26. B
27. C
28. B
29. A
30. C
31. C
32. C
33. B
34. A
35. B
36. B
37. D
38. A
39. D
40. C
41. D
42. C
43. B

COMBINATION VEHICLES PRACTICE TEST

This full-length CDL Combination Vehicles practice test contains 44 questions. This test contains more CDL Combination Vehicles practice questions than you'll probably need to pass the Combination Vehicles endorsement, but why take any chances? Answering 44 practice questions will prepare you better than answering a mere 10 questions!

1. What is the best way to tell if your trailer has started to skid?

- ☐ A. Seeing it in the mirror
- ☐ B. Feeling for pulling in the cab
- ☐ C. Hearing the wheels skidding

2. When inspecting the landing gear after uncoupling the trailer, where should the tractor be?

- ☐ A. Completely clear of the trailer
- ☐ B. With the tractor frame under the trailer
- ☐ C. The fifth wheel directly under the kingpin

3. There are two things the driver can do to prevent a roll-over- keeping the cargo as close to the ground as possible and...

- ☐ A. Going slowly around turns
- ☐ B. Making sure the vehicle brakes are properly adjusted
- ☐ C. Keeping the fifth wheel free play as tight as possible

4. After locking the king pin into the fifth wheel, how can you check the connection?

- ☐ A. Pull the tractor ahead gently with the trailer brake locked
- ☐ B. Pull forward 50 feet, then turn right and left
- ☐ C. Pull the tractor ahead sharply to release the trailer brake

5. If you have a semi-trailer, where should you put the front trailer that supports it before driving away?

- ☐ A. Raised halfway with the crack handle secured in its bracket
- ☐ B. Fully raised with the crack handle secured in its bracket
- ☐ C. None of the above

6. The safest way to turn right from a two-way road is...

- ☐ A. Turning wide as you complete the turn
- ☐ B. Turning wide before starting the turn
- ☐ C. Backing up if there are vehicles in that lane if you have to cross to the opposing lane

7. While uncoupling, you should disconnect the electrical cable and...

- ☐ A. Coil it to keep it out of the way
- ☐ B. Hang it with the plug down
- ☐ C. Hang it with the plug up

8. More than half of truck drivers' deaths is as a result of...

- ☐ A. Speed
- ☐ B. Following too closely
- ☐ C. Roll-overs

9. Low-slung vehicles can be risky at railroad crossings because...

- ☐ A. They may take longer to stop
- ☐ B. They are more likely to get stuck on a railroad crossing
- ☐ C. They are more likely to jackknife on the uneven ground

10. Which of the following is true regarding the use of drugs when it comes to driving?

- ☐ A. Prescription or non-prescription drugs are not allowed for any reason
- ☐ B. Prescription drugs are allowed as long as the doctor says it will not affect your driving ability
- ☐ C. Speed is allowed as long as you are taking drugs to stay awake

11. One of the following statements is true about tires in hot weather

- [ ] A. You should inspect your tires every two hours or every 100 miles when driving in very hot weather
- [ ] B. You should check tire mounting and air pressure before driving
- [ ] C. You should bleed a small amount of air to keep tire pressure steady

12. Some suspension system defects are...

- [ ] A. Leaking shock absorbers
- [ ] B. Broken leaves in a leaf spring and a cracked spring hanger
- [ ] C. All of the above

13. If the trailer has an Antilock Braking System but the tractor doesn't, what is likely to happen?

- [ ] A. The trailer is likely to swing out
- [ ] B. The trailer is still less likely to swing out
- [ ] C. None of the above

14. When you are pulling doubles or triples, the shut-off valves should always be...

- [ ] A. Open, except for those on the last trailer
- [ ] B. Open
- [ ] C. Open, except for those on the first trailer

15. After connecting the air lines but before backing under the trailer, one should...

- [ ] A. Make sure that the trailer brakes are off
- [ ] B. Supply air to the trailer system and then pull out the air supply knob
- [ ] C. Walk around the rig to make sure that it is clear

16. What is a crack-the-whip effect according to one of these statements?

- [ ] A. The rearmost trailer will swing out the most and will be more likely to roll over
- [ ] B. If a sudden movement is made from your steering wheel, the tractor will tend to rock and sway
- [ ] C. When your trailer is half full and loaded in the front of the trailer, sudden movement of your steering wheel will cause your cargo to slide

17. If your vehicle gets stuck on a railroad track, you should...

☐ A. Get away from your vehicle and call 911

☐ B. Radio in for assistance

☐ C. Honk the horn loudly and call 911

18. Before uncoupling, you should...

☐ A. Call in for any special requests

☐ B. Make sure your vehicle is parked on a level surface, the ground is solid and can support the weight of the trailer

☐ C. Make sure the trailer has enough air supply for the brakes to hold

19. Combination vehicles take longer to stop when they are empty because...

☐ A. There is less traction

☐ B. You are likely to brake as hard

☐ C. The center of gravity is lower

20. If you must drive on slippery roads, what is a good thing to do in such situations?

☐ A. Slow down gradually

☐ B. Use smaller following distance

☐ C. Apply brakes during turns

☐ D. None of the above

21. One can confirm if air is going to all brakes in the trailer by...

☐ A. Opening the emergency line shut off-valves at the rear of the last trailer and listening for air escaping

☐ B. Opening the emergency line shut-off valves and the service line valve at the rear of the last trailer and listening for air escaping each time

☐ C. Confirming that the air pressure is at a normal level

22. To prevent a roll-over, cargo should be...

☐ A. Spread evenly across the rig as low as possible

☐ B. Stacked closest to the door

☐ C. Stacked as close to the front of the rig as possible.

23. When testing only the trailer service brakes, which of the options below about the air valves is correct?

- [ ] A. Service Brake: off; Parking Brake: off; Trailer air supply: in / open; Trolley: applied
- [ ] B. Service Brake: off; Parking Brake: off; Trailer air supply: in / open; Trolley: released
- [ ] C. Service Brake: off; Parking Brake: off; Trailer air supply: out / closed; Trolley: applied

24. How should you test the tractor-trailer connection for security?

- [ ] A. Pull gently forward in low gear against the locked trailer brakes, then inspect the coupling
- [ ] B. Rock the trailer back and forth with the trailer brakes locked
- [ ] C. Put the tractor in gear and pull ahead with a sharp jerk

25. You should not use the trailer hand valve while driving because...

- [ ] A. You should only use the parking brake
- [ ] B. Of the danger of making the trailer skid
- [ ] C. It won't work as well as the foot brake

26. The air leakage rate for a combination vehicle (engine off, brakes on) should not be more than ____ psi per minute

- [ ] A. 2
- [ ] B. 3
- [ ] C. 4

27. Why should you lock the tractor gladhands to each other or to the storage bracket when you are not towing a trailer?

- [ ] A. Because the connected brake circuit becomes a backup air tank
- [ ] B. Because it will keep dirt and water out of the lines
- [ ] C. Because if you do not, you can never build system pressure

28. The hand valve should be used...

- [ ] A. Only with the foot brake
- [ ] B. To test the trailer brakes
- [ ] C. Only when the trailer is fully loaded

29. If the brakes do not release when you push the trailer air supply valve, you should...

- ☐ A. Check the electrical cables
- ☐ B. Cross the air lines
- ☐ C. Check the air line connections

30. In general, the higher your truck's center of gravity, the...

- ☐ A. Easier it is to turn over
- ☐ B. Easier it is to turn around corners
- ☐ C. More stable it is when turning

31. When you test the tractor protection valve, the red air supply control knob should go into the ________ position

- ☐ A. Emergency
- ☐ B. Normal
- ☐ C. Neutral

32. When the front trailer supports are raised, and the trailer is resting on the tractor, you should make sure that...

- ☐ A. There is enough clearance between the tops of the tractor tires and the nose of the trailer
- ☐ B. There is enough clearance between the tractor frame and the landing gear
- ☐ C. Both answers are correct

33. To test the tractor protection valve, charge the trailer air brake system, turn off the engine, and...

- ☐ A. Keep pressing the brake pedal firmly
- ☐ B. Flash your high-beam headlights on and off several times
- ☐ C. Step on and off the brake pedal several times

34. One of these vehicles off-tracks the most

- ☐ A. A 5-axle tractor towing a 45-foot trailer
- ☐ B. A 5-axle tractor towing a 42-foot trailer
- ☐ C. A 5-axle tractor towing a 52-foot trailer

35. Describe what the trailer air supply control does

- ☐ A. It is a device used to keep the trailer behind the tractor
- ☐ B. It is a six-sided yellow knob used to control the tractor protection valve
- ☐ C. It is used to supply the trailer with air, shut the air off, and apply the trailer emergency brakes

36. Why should you connect the glad hands to the dummy couplers if your vehicle is equipped with them?

- ☐ A. It will keep dirt and water out of the lines
- ☐ B. If you don't, you will never build system pressure
- ☐ C. The connected brake circuit becomes a backup air tank

37. In what position should the tractor protection valve control be placed in order to test the trailer air brakes when coupling a tractor-semitrailer?

- ☐ A. Up
- ☐ B. Down
- ☐ C. Normal

38. Trucks roll over more easily when fully loaded and are...

- ☐ A. Five times more likely to roll over during a crash than empty rigs
- ☐ B. Two times more likely to roll over during a crash than empty rigs
- ☐ C. Ten times more likely to roll over during a crash than empty rigs

39. If the driver crosses the air lines when hooking up to an old trailer, what will happen?

- ☐ A. You can drive away if the trailer has no spring brakes, but you will not have trailer brakes
- ☐ B. Instead of the trailer brakes, the hand valve will apply the tractor brakes
- ☐ C. Instead of the air brakes, the brake pedal will work the trailer spring brakes

40. Why should you be sure that the fifth wheel plate is greased as required?

- ☐ A. To ensure good electrical connections
- ☐ B. To prevent steering problems
- ☐ C. To reduce heat and noise

41. What is a tractor jackknife?

- [ ] A. When the drive tires on the tractor get locked up and the tractor spins out sideways as the trailer continues pushing forward
- [ ] B. When the drive tires on the trailer get locked up and the trailer spins out sideways as the tractor continues pushing forward
- [ ] C. Neither of the above

42. After you have uncoupled the trailer and are inspecting the trailer supports, in what gear should the tractor engine be?

- [ ] A. Neutral
- [ ] B. High reverse
- [ ] C. Low reverse

43. You should line up ____ as you get ready to back under the semi-trailer

- [ ] A. About 15 degrees away from the line of the trailer
- [ ] B. So that the king pin engages the driver's side locking jaw first
- [ ] C. Directly in front of the trailer

44. During uncoupling, you should disengage the electrical cable and...

- [ ] A. Coil it to keep it out of the way
- [ ] B. Hang it with the plug down
- [ ] C. Hang it with the plug

ANSWERS

1. A
2. B
3. A
4. A
5. B
6. A
7. B
8. C
9. B
10. B
11. B
12. C
13. B
14. A
15. B
16. A
17. A
18. B
19. A
20. A
21. B
22. A
23. B
24. A
25. B
26. C
27. B
28. B
29. C
30. A
31. A
32. C
33. C
34. C
35. C
36. A
37. C
38. C
39. A
40. B
41. A
42. A
43. C
44. B

SCHOOL BUS PRACTICE TEST

This full-length CDL School Bus practice test contains 49 questions. This test contains more CDL School Bus practice questions than you'll probably need to pass the School Bus endorsement, but why take any chances? Answering 49 practice questions will prepare you better than answering a mere 10 questions!

1. In a school bus, what do drivers use the overhead inside rearview mirror for?

- ☐ A. To monitor the passengers actively inside the bus
- ☐ B. To monitor traffic that approaches
- ☐ C. To see the blind spot immediately behind the bus
- ☐ D. All of the above

2. When loading students and you cannot account for a student, what should be done?

- ☐ A. Look in your mirror for the student
- ☐ B. Secure the bus, take the key and check around for the student
- ☐ C. Ask other students if they saw that particular student
- ☐ D. None of the above

3. The blind spot behind the school bus may extend up to...

- ☐ A. 200 feet
- ☐ B. 400 feet
- ☐ C. 100 feet
- ☐ D. 500 feet

4. What is a passive railroad crossing?

- ☐ A. A railroad crossing that doesn't have a crossbuck sign
- ☐ B. A railroad crossing that doesn't have any type of traffic control design
- ☐ C. A railroad crossing at which one is not required to stop
- ☐ D. All of the above

5. During a pre-trip vehicle inspection, drivers should make sure that...

- ☐ A. Emergency exit signs are working
- ☐ B. Emergency exit is closely secure from the inside
- ☐ C. Both of the above are correct
- ☐ D. None of the above

6. If your bus has a manual transmission, you should never _______

- ☐ A. Accelerate
- ☐ B. Honk your horn
- ☐ C. Change gears while crossing railroad tracks
- ☐ D. Slow down your vehicle before approaching a railroad crossing

7. As a bus driver, you need to avoid...

- ☐ A. Inspecting your bus before you drive
- ☐ B. Fueling the bus in a closed building while there are passengers on board
- ☐ C. Maintaining the speed limit
- ☐ D. All of the listed answers

8. If an object is dropped by a student in front of the bus, what should you tell the students to do as the bus driver?

- ☐ A. To attempt to grab your attention to retrieve the object
- ☐ B. All of the listed answers
- ☐ C. To leave any dropped object behind
- ☐ D. To move to a point of safety out of the danger zones

9. What should you tell your students to prevent dangerous situations during their loading and unloading?

- ☐ A. Tell students to leave behind any dropped object, step out of the danger zones, and call your attention so that the object can be retrieved
- ☐ B. Tell students that any dropped objects can be picked as long as they are not under the bus
- ☐ C. Tell students not to use the handrail when exiting the bus because they could be caught doing so
- ☐ D. None of the above

10. What is the best way to control student safety during an emergency (e.g. the bus engine failing)?

- ☐ A. Having the students evacuate the bus
- ☐ B. Ignoring the students
- ☐ C. Accelerating and driving as quickly as possible to a safe destination
- ☐ D. Keeping the students on the bus if possible

11. The recommended safe distance to stop before a drawbridge is _______

- ☐ A. 100 feet
- ☐ B. 50 feet
- ☐ C. 150 feet
- ☐ D. 200 feet

12. When refueling your bus, it is extremely important that you remember to never _________

- ☐ A. Pay for gas
- ☐ B. Refuel your bus in a closed building with passengers on board
- ☐ C. Be polite
- ☐ D. None of the listed answers

13. Which of the following parts of your bus needs to be in safe working condition before driving?

- ☐ A. Each handhold and railing
- ☐ B. Emergency exit handles
- ☐ C. Signaling devices
- ☐ D. All of the above

14. In the case of a fire outbreak on the bus, where should you lead students?

- ☐ A. Upwind of the bus
- ☐ B. To the left of the bus
- ☐ C. To the right of the bus
- ☐ D. Downwind of the bus

15. Remember, as a school bus driver, you should ___________ before entering traffic flow

- ☐ A. All of the listed answers
- ☐ B. Allow congested traffic to disperse
- ☐ C. Call the parents and tell them when their children will arrive
- ☐ D. Open the bus doors

16. Students may drop an object near the bus during loading and unloading, you should _______

- ☐ A. All of the listed answers
- ☐ B. Watch carefully as they enter and exit the bus
- ☐ C. Ignore them
- ☐ D. Leave the students behind

17. The bus' alternating flashing amber warning lights must be activated in accordance with state laws or at least _____ before the school bus stop

- ☐ A. 100 feet
- ☐ B. 25 feet
- ☐ C. 200 feet
- ☐ D. 50 feet

18. The driver must evacuate the bus when __________

- ☐ A. The bus is on fire
- ☐ B. All of the listed answers
- ☐ C. The bus is stalled on a railroad-highway crossing
- ☐ D. There is an imminent danger of collision

19. If the bus is so equipped, how many seconds before reaching a stop do school bus drivers need to switch on their alternating flashing amber warning lights?

- ☐ A. 5-10 seconds
- ☐ B. 60 seconds
- ☐ C. 15-20 seconds
- ☐ D. 6-9 seconds

20. Who should you reach out to if you are having difficulty driving in high winds?

- ☐ A. No one
- ☐ B. The students' parents
- ☐ C. Your dispatcher
- ☐ D. Your loved ones

21. How many versions of the Class A Pre-trip Inspection test are there?

- ☐ A. Two
- ☐ B. Eight
- ☐ C. Three
- ☐ D. Four

22. After you have finished the route, you should __________

- ☐ A. None of the listed answers
- ☐ B. Conduct a post-trip inspection
- ☐ C. Call your loved ones
- ☐ D. Fill your gas tank

23. It's important for bus drivers to understand...

- ☐ A. What students do when crossing the street in front of the bus
- ☐ B. What students do when exiting the school bus
- ☐ C. Students might not always do what they are supposed to do
- ☐ D. All of the above

24. What should you do if there is no police officer and you believe the signal at an active railroad crossing is malfunctioning?

- ☐ A. Call your dispatcher
- ☐ B. Contact the school officials first
- ☐ C. Turn around and find another route
- ☐ D. Avoid the intersection

25. School bus drivers need to concentrate while they are driving and while the students are loading and unloading the bus. If a student exhibits a behavior problem that distracts you from this task, what should you do?

- ☐ A. Ignore the problem as much as you can and report the distracting child later on
- ☐ B. None of the listed answers
- ☐ C. Hold on until the students unloading get off the bus safely and move away or pull over to resolve the problem
- ☐ D. Then you should drop off the other students and then deal with the student after you have finished your route

26. Without _______ from the appropriate school district official, you should never change the location of a bus stop

- ☐ A. None of the listed answers
- ☐ B. A signed paycheck
- ☐ C. Written approval
- ☐ D. Verbal agreement

27. In preparing for your CDL Skills test, which of the following parts should you be able to identify?

- ☐ A. Emergency equipment
- ☐ B. Air brakes
- ☐ C. Exhaust system
- ☐ D. All of the listed answers

28. To perform a proper inspection of suspension mounts, you need to ______

- ☐ A. Inspect the mounts at each point where they are secured to the vehicle frame and axle(s)
- ☐ B. Look for cracked spring hangers
- ☐ C. Check for missing bolts
- ☐ D. All of the above

29. Which of the following is a reason why it is so important for the bus driver to inspect the bus' interior at the end of their shift?

- ☐ A. To collect and catalog all items left behind on their bus
- ☐ B. To find loose change that will help them pay for it
- ☐ C. To make sure they can report necessary repairs to a mechanic before they drive the bus again
- ☐ D. None of the above

30. What is the standee line in a bus?

- ☐ A. A two-inch line on the floor (or some other marking) that indicates where passengers cannot stand
- ☐ B. The number of standing spots you have on your bus
- ☐ C. The line of passengers standing at the bus stop
- ☐ D. Anywhere passengers are standing

31. During an emergency, remember that you can possibly evacuate through _______

- ☐ A. The window
- ☐ B. The rear door
- ☐ C. The side door
- ☐ D. All of the above

32. The _______ establishes the official routes and official school bus stops

- ☐ A. The school district
- ☐ B. States
- ☐ C. Each school bus driver determines their routes and stops
- ☐ D. The parents of the children riding on the school bus

33. The Department of Transportation requires that ABS be on ________

- ☐ A. All of the listed answers
- ☐ B. March 1, 1997
- ☐ C. March 1, 1998
- ☐ D. March 1, 1999

34. Which of the following would be an emergency situation that a school bus driver may encounter?

- ☐ A. A crash
- ☐ B. A student's medical emergency
- ☐ C. All of the listed answers
- ☐ D. An electrical fire in the engine compartment of a school bus

35. Before leaving the unloading area, be certain...

- ☐ A. The students are standing
- ☐ B. No students are returning to the bus
- ☐ C. The doors are open
- ☐ D. You have a tank full of gas

36. If you need to back up a bus without a lookout, you should...

- ☐ A. Use your mirrors and back up quickly
- ☐ B. Back up quickly and pray
- ☐ C. Set the parking brake, turn off the motor, take the keys with you and walk to the rear of the bus to determine whether the way is clear
- ☐ D. None of the above

37. If your fifth wheel plate is not well lubricated, this could cause...

- ☐ A. Nothing
- ☐ B. Steering problems
- ☐ C. None of the listed answers
- ☐ D. Less air to reach the emergency line

38. For school bus drivers, the danger zone is...

- ☐ A. A blind corner
- ☐ B. A forbidden street
- ☐ C. The front of a police station
- ☐ D. The area on all sides of a school bus

39. When trying to decide if the school bus should be evacuated during an emergency, which of these questions do you not need you ask yourself?

- ☐ A. Is there a chance the bus could be hit by other vehicles?
- ☐ B. Is there a fire?
- ☐ C. Is there a smell of leaking fuel?
- ☐ D. All of the above

40. When securing the bus during an evacuation, remember to...

- ☐ A. Placing transmission in Park
- ☐ B. Set parking brakes
- ☐ C. Activate hazard-warning lights
- ☐ D. All of the above

41. When the red flashing lights on an eight-light system bus are activated, what does it signify to other drivers?

- ☐ A. That the school bus is stopped for a red light
- ☐ B. That the school bus is stopped for a train crossing
- ☐ C. That the school bus is stopped because it has broken down
- ☐ D. That the school bus is stopped to pick up or discharge pupils

42. If you're operating a bus on a divided highway or a highway that has up to or above four lanes, which of the following statements below describes the procedure for the proper pick-up and discharge of students?

- ☐ A. The students can only be picked up or dropped off on the resident side of the road
- ☐ B. The students can be dropped off or picked up on either side of the highway
- ☐ C. The students must be picked up and dropped off in the center of the road
- ☐ D. No answers are correct

43. The "golden rule" for school buses when they approach or cross railroad tracks is...

- ☐ A. Stop, go, and stop
- ☐ B. Stop, look, and listen
- ☐ C. Stop, look, and turn on the emergency flashers
- ☐ D. None of the above

44. When under the age of 21 years old, a driver will be considered intoxicated at... ("Tolerance levels vary depending on the state one lives in, so it's important to check and refer to the regulations of one's state")

- ☐ A. Zero tolerance
- ☐ B. More than .02 but less than .10 BAC
- ☐ C. 10 BAC like any other driver
- ☐ D. None of the above

45. You should maintain your position _________ of the rightmost lane when you approach a bus stop on a multilane roadway

- ☐ A. Toward the right edge
- ☐ B. Toward the left edge
- ☐ C. In the center
- ☐ D. All of the above

46. Is the bus driver allowed to crack or open the service door prior to stopping to pick up a student?

- ☐ A. Yes
- ☐ B. No
- ☐ C. Maybe
- ☐ D. It depends on the situation

47. Which of the people listed below have the authority to remove or suspend a student from riding the bus?

- ☐ A. The school bus driver
- ☐ B. The school principal
- ☐ C. The school principal, superintendent, or the superintendent's designee
- ☐ D. The student's teacher

48. When are substances like alcohol, tobacco, and non-prescription drugs allowed to be used on the school bus?

- ☐ A. At any time
- ☐ B. Never
- ☐ C. Only when the bus driver says it is okay
- ☐ D. No answers are correct

49. The driver's seat should have a seat belt except when ______

- [ ] A. The driver has assumed responsibility for the risk
- [ ] B. It's very hot outside
- [ ] C. The driver's seat always needs to have a seat belt
- [ ] D. The bus was created before 1980

ANSWERS

1. A
2. B
3. B
4. B
5. C
6. C
7. B
8. B
9. A
10. D
11. B
12. B
13. D
14. A
15. B
16. B
17. C
18. B
19. A
20. C
21. D
22. B
23. D
24. A
25. C
26. C
27. B
28. D
29. C
30. A
31. D
32. A
33. A
34. C
35. B
36. C
37. B
38. D
39. D
40. D
41. D
42. A
43. B
44. A
45. C
46. B
47. C
48. B
49. C

CONCLUSION

Thank you so much for purchasing *"CDL Study Guide: Exam Prep Book With 425+ Questions and Explained Answers to Pass the Commercial Driver's License Exam on Your First Attempt (Full Length Exams for All Classes)"*!

There are so many resources on the market today for test prep and study materials, so we are proud that you have chosen us to help you through to the next part of your career phase.

This book was written with the utmost care for correct, complete, and factual information that can help you to pass your commercial driver's license exam the first time you take it.

Driving professionally is a wonderful career path that has the potential to take you all around the highways and routes of North America. Traveling on this nation's roads and seeing those areas of the country allows you to see the real beauty that this country has to offer!

It is our hope that the information in this book has enlightened you on the regulations, standards, and precedents in the automotive and transportation industries. These regulations were painstakingly created and put in place by those who did the research to find us the safest and most efficient means of regulating travel on this nation's highways.

For more information on these topics that is right from the source, please check the websites for the federal agencies listed in this book such as the TSA, the PDTI, the DOT, and more.

Thank you once again for reading and best of luck to you in your examinations and your new career as a commercial driver!

If you enjoyed it, please scan the QR CODE below and write a brief review.

Your feedback is important to me and will help other readers decide whether to read the book too.

Made in the USA
Middletown, DE
05 October 2023

40314285R00166